Tradition and Authenticity
in the Search for Ecumenic Wisdom

Tradition and Authenticity in the Search for Ecumenic Wisdom

Thomas Langan

University of Missouri Press
Columbia and London

Library of Congress Cataloging-in-Publication Data

Langan, Thomas.
    Tradition and authenticity in the search for ecumenic wisdom /
Thomas Langan.
      p.   cm.
    Includes index.
    ISBN 0–8262–0800–2 (alk. paper)
    1. Methodology.   2. Authenticity (Philosophy)   3. History—
Philosophy.   4. Tradition (Philosophy)   5. Civilization,
Modern—20th century.   6. Wisdom.   I. Title.
B53.L333   1991
140—dc20   91–32300
                                              CIP

Designer: Rhonda Gibson
Typesetter: Connell Zeko Type & Graphics
Printer: Thomson-Shore, Inc.
Binder: Thomson-Shore, Inc.
Typeface: Bem

To four thinkers who have offered friendly encouragement along the way,
In Memoriam:

Etienne Gilson
Martin Heidegger
Eric Voegelin
Hans Urs von Balthasar

 # Contents

Acknowledgments

Five thoughtful critics have, at one time or another, raised issues and suggested improvements in this volume: Professor Janine Langan, my wife; Dr. Michel Vaillant, retired director of the Paris Research Laboratories of Pechiney-St. Gobain and distinguished chemist and philosopher of science, who took special pains with the sections on truth, especially what I said about the methods of science; and my assistants, Mr. Hugh Miller, Miss Christina Banman, and Mr. Bruce Stewart, all of whom have inspired sections of the book. Mr. Stewart's insights are woven into the entire text, and he is helping to complete subsequent volumes of my project. Several excellent pages about the foundation of the state were drafted by Mr. Miller. Almost a generation of students in my Philosophy of History class at the University of Toronto have suffered through various stages of the development of this project. Thanks to all for their help, encouragement, and insight.

Tradition and Authenticity
in the Search for Ecumenic Wisdom

Introduction

Around us we see a highly technological urban society, obscuring nature and disorienting the hurrying inhabitants of the metropolitan canyons. Here we find the image of a "liberated person," especially the self-made, self-directing, instantaneous success. "Therapeutic man," as Phillip Rieff calls the denizen of this latest mode of life, is fascinated with self-development. This he understands as some kind of psychic recipe for success, or failing that, at least a means of lessening the pain of loneliness. Is this not the inevitable lot of those supermen whose destiny it is to forge for themselves the sense of existence? "Save yourself by giving yourself grace," exhorted Nietzsche.[1] Curious that somehow the therapist, of all people, gets mixed up in this heroic process of pulling oneself up by the bootstraps.

Well, here comes another book about development. But what follows is decidedly not trendy. For I shall emphasize and explore our debt to the past, the grace of what is given. No one would deny that to know where we should head, we need the direction offered by the past. Yet the past is not "in" just now. Everyone knows that the past can affect us as a complex, a drag keeping us from adjusting to new conditions; our inherited vocabulary steers us, and hence limits our vision. At the same time, we should not forget that traditions hand us concrete possibility. Our inherited vocabulary may be limited, but it is a gift, a vast fund of possible expressions. The wisdoms of the past, all kinds, distill experience, insight, and reflection. All genuine creativity, all worthwhile opening of the future, even in physics, is rooted in the best the past has to offer, even when the new corrects the old.

In this book we shall explore fresh ways of interrogating history, not out of antiquarian interest, but as a vital part of finding our way. Truth comes as much from making use of the discoveries of our ancestors as it does from present experience. We are obliged to start by using the symbol systems—the linguistic, mathematical, and musical systems—that they have handed down to us. Social order is not just the product of

1. Friedrich Nietzche, *Daybreak* (*Morgenrote*), trans. R. J. Hollingdale (Cambridge: Cambridge University Press, 1982), 48.

1

present action, but is structured by institutions which have been slowly matured over centuries and into which present action must be fitted.

Everyone admits this. Yet affirmations of indebtedness to the past frighten many contemporaries because they have suffered ideological constraints imposed by others, the religious, moral, and political dogma that violate freedom in the name of tradition. At the same time, they recognize that the search for truth requires innovation, experimentation, and adaptation to changed circumstances. While granting the problems involved, I shall show, in opposition to popular therapy rages and any existentialist tendency to overplay creation by the will out of nothing, that genuine self-development involves a dimension other than voluntarist bootstrap-tugging. To gain the perspective accorded by the past, we must know how truth can be transmitted from antiquity. We must see how it is taken up and recreated. But this creation is not completely free of content. Truths taken up are reformed and renewed by being projected into the future as intelligible possibility through a creative act.

Fitting oneself to that type of creative act is a work of self-development. In the manner of our Greek forebears I call this *authenticity*, after the Greek word for "self," *autos*. We are all inheritors of the past, for our individual selves have, as Gabriel Marcel says, "a certain thickness."[2] We each have a biogenetic inheritance, experienced as temperament, as well as that which Aristotle called our "second nature": systems of signs and symbols into which we have been acculturated. Above all, these are found in the common language and in institutional roles, which are governed by the traditions passed on by social groups in their concrete demands upon us. If I am to develop myself in a genuine manner, these must be understood; it is simply a matter of honoring my actual reality if "I am to become what I am."

For Heidegger the condition for the self's authentically becoming as fully itself as possible is critical appropriation of: (1) the possibilities handed to us by nature, (2) the meaning in the symbols handed on by the traditions, and (3) the sense of the role-possibilities demanded by institutions in the situation into which we are thrown. For all of Heidegger's conditions, I shall borrow the existentialist term *appropriation*, but modify its meaning somewhat. By appropriation I mean the lifelong critical process through which I take as full conscious possession as possible of what is properly mine, that is, of the relevant needs and possibilities

2. Gabriel Marcel, *The Mystery of Being* (Chicago: Regnery, 1960), 1:55.

which make me up and constitute my situation. I achieve this both by becoming increasingly aware of the significance of these needs and possibilities and by undertaking to act on them with integrity, developing the necessary character, the set of virtues, required to act in consequence. Appropriation is growth in *response-ability*. It is the same as maturation.

A keen and necessary balance in this version of appropriation is kept between the intellectual and the moral, and between the theoretical and the practical. Truth is not just theoretical formulation, it is something one pursues and then puts into action by living out the vision that the truth offers. The exercise of certain virtues is the precondition for the possibility of pursuing truth, and knowledge of the reality of the full situation in which one finds oneself is necessary for the development of character. Aristotle, meet Heidegger!

Of course, my own reflection owes a debt to all three of these thinkers—Marcel, Aristotle, and Heidegger—for their having alerted a generation to issues of the self in situation. One should not assume, however, just because the term *authenticity* takes center stage here, that I want to take in more of their thought than is actually the case. However, I do not want to interrupt the development of this work to go into an elaborate analysis of the divergences of my thought from Heidegger's. (As far as that goes, I must admit that I find less in Marcel's thought to cause me to hesitate than in Heidegger's, but I should also confess that I have a way of interpreting Heidegger, much like Otto Pöggeler's, which makes him much more compatible with Marcel than many would accept.)

The process of appropriation may sound rather unbelievably awake and aware, but much of our acculturation is in fact implicit. It occurs largely through imitation, constituting a body language, a spoken and written language, and a set of roles in the various institutions, starting with the family, all of which is scarcely reflective and critical. Indeed, we are more appropriated than appropriating.

As most of these impacts of tradition are taken for granted (one unthinkingly perceives one's language, for instance, as completely natural), critical appropriation demands an immense effort for one to acquire some distance. How does this happen? First there is the question of motivation: the grace of a will to truth, which is really an affair of love. Then, too, one does not start with the implicit—it is too hard even to see. Rather, one begins by confronting the explicit truth claims the traditions hold out to us, critically measuring them against one's full experience and striving to harmonize conflicting claims both within one tradition and between competing ones, seeking to integrate them into a coherent wisdom. As this proceeds, one will begin to perceive the aura of implicit issues surrounding the explicit discourse, and so start to engage the most difficult task: bringing up to explicit awareness as much as possible the implicit claims about the world that are embedded in one's natural faith and have such influence, much of it partly hidden to view, on one's action. Such a progress of reason is of course an ideal, never-ending process, with the full illumination of the implicit never achieved and the integration of what has been made explicit wisdom never fully realized.

One is helped in such a pursuit of wisdom by the explicit traditions that have formed one because they give a kind of ready-made perspective and distance from some of these harder-to-spot, built-in themes of the actual situation. In an explicit tradition, the institution which has been spawned as custodian of that tradition has, for whatever reason, taken the pains over the years, centuries, perhaps millennia, to express what the tradition wants handed on as truth. The government of a nation, for instance, spells out its laws. These explicit prescriptions and even truth claims can sometimes, by the enormity of what they claim, shock us into taking some distance from our implicitly acculturated selves. Think of the effect of the Copernican revolution, which denied that the earth was the center of the universe. Christians speak of *metanoia,* or *conversio,* a turning about. That is certainly what happened in the Copernican revolution; the phenomenon of paradigm shift is not limited to the physical sciences.

The long history of the development of critical distance, beginning with the discovery of a historical sense at Sinai, continuing with the Greeks' discovery of *psyche,* through the subjectivist and transcendental turns of the seventeenth and eighteenth centuries, down to the development of the social sciences and modern theories of interpretation (hermeneutics) is no simple affair. Central to it is the progress of the explicit in illumining what had been only implicit, but nonetheless effective, in ruling action.

It is this unfolding project of obtaining critical distance through explicit tradition and its implications for self-development that the present volume will explore, with particular attention to the maturing (and ever more complex) question of truth in an ecumenic situation. Inquiry into the effect of the larger situation on the pursuit of truth brings out the connection between larger issues of social and economic development and the authenticity question at the heart of personal development. My central concern here is to explore the proper role of the great explicit traditions, transmitters of vast "treasure-houses of symbol," as Eric Voegelin termed them, in guiding us towards truth. But this pays unexpected dividends in the form of hints for a more adequate strategy of worldwide social and economic development, in which the pursuit of authenticity by the individual has a role to play.

Critical appropriation of the needs and possibilities handed down by traditions, both implicit and explicit, takes place on four levels corresponding to different foci, all important for self-knowledge and the pursuit of truth. The first is that of my personal situation, formed in part by a unique intersection in me of different traditions mediated through my own experience, and in part by the influence of my natural, genetic inheritance, my health and temperament. The second is the local situation I share with others: we participate in communities and institutions (familial, local, regional, and national) formed by particular traditions interacting in a complex local chemistry, civic and ethnic. The third is the civilizational situation, in our case industrialized, urban, high-technology culture, which permeates every individual and local situation in the "developed" world. Finally, there is the planetary epochal situation which we share with our contemporaries, virtually all of whom have now been gathered into an emerging world system through the global spread of occidental technology, causing development problems with world-shattering implications. The meeting of disparate traditions in the tightening planetary situation has heightened Western society's awareness of the ecumenic dimensions of the truth question. This planetary encounter has been made possible by the achievement of a certain level of economic and social development, beginning in the West.

The second part of the present volume will outline the problem of getting a responsible hold on the present situation of mankind, which in growing planetary has become overwhelmingly complex. I do not take for granted, of course, that every individual, as part of his personal effort to guide his own life wisely, must wrestle with understanding what is going on in the whole world. Part of our dilemma, however, is just that: how much of the planetary context must we know if we are to prosper as individuals? Even to begin to answer this quite practical question about the pursuit of wisdom, some survey of the present planetary situation is necessary. Part 2 of this volume is a start in that direction. Entitled "The Place of Traditions in the Emerging World System," it traces the interacting web of international institutions and symbol systems through which traditions operate and explores the implications for the methodic pursuit of truth. It attempts to put some order into the dense network of relations between traditions, institutions, symbol systems, and ongoing processes of change, with a view to guiding research into the intertwining truth claims as mankind seeks ecumenic wisdom.

In the last chapter, we return to what the quest for authenticity is all about—the truth question as such and our efforts to orient ourselves in truth. A balancing act is outlined there, as I try to combine the strategic overview, which in a time of planetary awareness we can scarcely do without, with the pressing exigencies of personal living. The truth question in a time of ecumenic awareness can be formulated thus: How and from what standpoint can one adjudicate reasonably, in the light of one's natural faith, between clashing truth claims advanced by disparate traditions with distinctive objects of interest and relevance to them, and how ought we to synthesize truths of different orders of experience into a genuine and authentic ecumenic wisdom?

It is the purpose of this volume to convince the reader that confronting this daunting question is a necessary task. It can only be avoided by living inauthentically, by a personal and collective, indeed massive, sticking of heads deep in the sand. There is no lack of narcotics, including the most effective, workaholism, to help us. These preliminary studies of the present planetary situation and the clash of traditions provide criteria for discerning which are the most relevant traditions confronting us, those most urgently requiring critical study. My aim in this volume is to outline a method for sharpening our focus on these traditions as a part of the task of making a better use of history to enrich our wisdom and guide our action. The exploration of epistemological and ontological implications of what emerges from this preliminary consideration and the examination of major traditions I have reserved for future (nearly complete) volumes.

The painter Paul Gauguin inscribed upon one of his greatest paintings, "Where Do We Come From? What Are We? Where Are We Going?" We, too, place these questions at the center of our search. Unlike Gauguin, however, who sought the answers to them in the primitive, the unconscious, the lush tropic of the ahistorical, we seek them in that very history and tradition from which he fled. Reason demands that we raise the question of our own being in terms of the traditions which have formed us and determine what in those formative powers is still defensible and liveable, what they still offer us that is true, and how we root out what should no longer be allowed to influence us.

Everyone engages in some appropriation of tradition, most of it un-methodical, its critical aspect not always very sharp-sighted. This book seeks to offer guidance in increasing the scope and rendering more effective this central aspect of the quest for wisdom. It presupposes no prior philosophical training (though I encourage the reader to make use of the Glossary in Appendix A, as well as the tabular displays of traditions in the other two appendixes). It requires no particular faith, beyond commitment to the search for truth, which implies a belief that some progress in finding meaning is possible. While I do not take for granted any particular religious commitments, I shall not pause here to argue against skeptics who have despaired altogether of the project of reason. I shall, however, try to make clear what I believe to be a basic reasonableness.

I.

Explicit Tradition in the
Pursuit of Authenticity

1.

On Finding the Way

Responding to the Reality of the Situation

The Project of Authenticity

At the center of our consideration stands the individual agent, the lonely self struggling for self-realization—to grow up. Maturity is growth in responsibility. Responsibility entails enhanced freedom through better direction of one's development, both through increased understanding of one's needs and possibilities, and through the strengthening of one's virtue, that is, the good habits which permit, among other things, self-control and generosity.

Authenticity here means achieving the fullest possible self-understanding and self-control so as to be able to respond to the needs and possibilities of the situation. What is involved in such self-understanding? The essence of a self is certainly not self-evident. Selfhood is neither the ontological given-ness of the person, nor is it personality. At least this much is clear from the start: by a self we always mean something like the aware center of initiative in the person.

The self as center of conscious action is in some complex way necessarily and dialectically related to the non-self, the Other. Some of that otherness is part of me as a person and only becomes self when it swims into awareness. The boundaries fuzzily separating the center of awareness from the not-so-aware provide that sense of the "thickness of the self" described by Gabriel Marcel. So a certain ambiguity surrounds those unconscious aspects of my person; they form a resistance to the center of awareness. The development of the self is a process somehow essentially related to that otherness within my person and in the situation, as I am caught up to some degree in the alien world. Yet, through awareness and creative will, I am also able in some degree to transcend it and therefore consciously to affect it.

The reality of the self includes both needs and possibilities:

11

1. Needs may be thought of, first of all, as conditions limiting us, so to speak, from below, givens of our nature which place demands on us and at the same time limit what we can do. If not met, they can sometimes wreak disaster. But there are also culturally induced needs, conditions of what Aristotle called "second nature," acculturated habits which mold our drives in the form of induced desires or control of desires. These represent results of the cultural situation lodged deep within our being. From the past, they steer our search for the future.

2. Possibilities are openings from beyond what we already are, or from above, rooted in that "already having been" reality (as Aristotle termed the essential), without which they would not be relevant, would not be real possibilities for me, the already-having-been essentials permitting us to reach out to new Being. Needs and possibilities are both, at once, limited and future-opening, with a difference in accent: the need is more imperious, the possibility more stretching. Authenticity is the process of becoming aware of this self-transcending reality of the self, both need and possibility—what Marcel terms "this superior reality in the depths of myself, which is more me than I am myself."[1]

Answering the old command of Apollo, "Know thyself!" is then more than just understanding the unique interaction in me of cultural experience, temperament given by nature, and institutional roles handed me by traditions. It is also grasping all this "in situation," understanding the interaction of the natural and traditional forces operating in me and in the world of our decisions.[2]

That is why authenticity is the opposite of the narcissistic. It demands that we lovingly open ourselves to the claims about how it stands with Being. The sciences and cultural and religious traditions confront us with their different claims. Bringing our action into harmony with that critically purified reality in all its various dimensions—as the truth emerges from our efforts to harmonize the sometimes conflicting visions offered by the various traditions—is the challenge each of us faces. It necessitates growth in the ability to cope with the demands of pursuing truth, in-

1. Gabriel Marcel, *The Mystery of Being* (Chicago: Regnery, 1960), 1:65.
2. Many years ago I raised these problems and reviewed the dimensions of the issue in "The Problem of the Self," *The Review of Metaphysics* 15 (September 1961): 19–33. Paul Vitz has recently shown the limits of egocentric theses of self in *Psychology as Religion: The Cult of Self-Worship* (Grand Rapids: Eerdmans, 1977). See also Philip Rieff, *The Triumph of the Therapeutic* (New York: Harper and Row, 1966).

cluding the essential ability to find a strategic and prudential balance between the requirements of daily living and the long-range goals of the search for wisdom. It demands that we sacrifice the comfort of the familiar, for the challenge of the true.

Authenticity depends on our being able to obtain and maintain a certain distance from ourselves while remaining able to face up to what we are. At times, we must somehow pull out of the hurly-burly of everyday living. Crisis in our daily affairs can cause a break, pushing us to seek a larger perspective. The grace of coming to realize that we need to search for sense in our lives can cause us to want to create a space for such a search.

Does it happen to everyone? Is it even possible outside a particular social environment, where a certain education is offered and a kind of leisure is possible? Unfortunately, many in our highly developed society do not appear to confront the challenge very seriously. But if an individual does become convinced of the need to pursue truth, where can he find such a perspective, transcending immediate concerns, aiding him to maintain a time-space for wisdom?

Such a place is offered essentially through the ideals which are held up to us by institutions, especially those of philosophy, science, and religion, which were created within the great traditions to pass on the vision that gave them birth. Such claims about the "sense of it all" not only inform our personal ways of responding to the daily challenges of life, they also provide the refuge of great visions into which we can withdraw when seeking a broader perspective on the crises of daily life. But there is also the nature of our concrete daily experiences, including the not always happy experiences provided by the institutions of one or another great tradition, experiences of Church, government, industry, or the academy, which may turn us away from searching in these visions.

Neither the distance offered by a traditional vision nor experience as ground for criticisms of tradition guarantees that our critical judgments will in fact be genuine, that is, in keeping with all that we are able to know about the facts.[3] Even the call to authenticity and the decision to pursue it does not guarantee genuineness. We are much driven by our needs and immediate desires. Faults of character and plain mistakes, especially those growing out of the complexity of interpreting the sym-

---

3. I employ *genuine* in Heidegger's sense of *echt*. For a fuller discussion, see the next chapter.

bols through which we hold onto many aspects of reality, can cloud our interpretations of them.

Maintaining a space for critical evaluation of our concrete personal experience is a severe challenge. A set of moral and psychological capabilities is required, much the same as those needed for people to communicate: one must be both willing to listen and to open up. That demands the right kind of personal security. Communication, you may have noticed, is in short supply. Here is a vicious circle: the condition for developing an ability to cope is our having already in some way coped. This is what makes the road to freedom, as progress towards authenticity may justifiably be called, so difficult for everyone, but seemingly impossible for those who lack psychological security.

We are all, to some degree, without grace in this way. It is the challenge posed by human freedom. The Catholic tradition, for instance, recognizes this difficulty in its understanding of God's difficulty in dealing with free men and in its understanding of God's grace as a gift of "coping power" with which to start toward even greater freedom and one's ideal human state.[4] The ideal—the vision of an ultimate reality, for the attaining of which steps must yet be created—can seem remote when struggling against any intense, immediate pain or passion. Paradoxically, however, only the ideal sustains us through the trial; whether the ideal is that of scientific quest, of the well-being of the family or nation, or of probing the source of ultimate reality, it is supported by the community of authentic individuals it motivates.

There is another unsettling fact about such explicit reflection: the very possibility of it grows out of a recent development in the Western tradition—a peculiar kind of philosophical-religious self-awareness. Founded in the Greek discovery of "interiority" and the sweep of Hebraic and Christian revelation, it is nonetheless in its fullness the result of the subjectivist turn taken in the seventeenth century by Western thought. This shift led to the present (Enlightenment) consciousness of ourselves as sharing a responsibility for our destiny, which remains to this moment a predominately occidental phenomenon. With the growth of a sense of responsibility for our own self-directing, it has become both possible and

---

4. Saint John Chrysostom claimed that God finds it easier to create another heaven and earth than to get a free man to change his mind; Teilhard de Chardin showed God bound, by his own decision to create, to a struggle against evil and to a cooperation with human freedom.

necessary for us to inquire into the sense of the entire situation. Only with that awareness does the concept of development (including the exaggerations of progressivism and voluntaristic existentialism) see the light of day.

Yet the "Enlightenment" viewpoint is not wholly new. St. Paul was aware of man's essential role in building the Kingdom, and St. Augustine knew that this required an understanding of the dynamics of sacred history. What gets developed (and a Christian would judge sometimes exaggerated) after the seventeenth century is the properly creative role of free human subjectivity in this building of a kingdom—a kingdom which after Feuerbach and Marx, is considered uniquely of this world.[5]

The project of authenticity has to be maintained somehow between the extremes of historical determinism and historical relativism, between fatalism and voluntarism. Were we unable to do anything at all about the ultimate unfolding of destiny, we would fall back into lethargy. If, on the other hand, the only sense to be found among the shifting sand dunes of historical information is that projected by human will, the study of history would yield no signposts leading us beyond ourselves toward something that might save us from our self-constructed follies.

The great philosophies of history from the last century were not shy in their espousals of a sense of history, most of them either rather deterministic or, like Nietzsche's, so voluntaristic as to leave little real guidance for future action. Because of these over-inflated philosophies of history, anyone now looking for sense in history must at once explain that he means by *sense* something much more modest than claimed by Comte, Hegel, Marx, Spencer, and Spengler.[6] For this reason, I want to make it clear that I am not proposing a new search for a single, global meaning to the whole of human history, as though history were somehow already complete enough to permit an intuition of its essence. So before explaining how a certain way of searching in history for *sense* can serve the project of

5. In a future work I intend to argue against such a reductionist, immanentist notion of self-redemption (to borrow the terminology of Eric Voegelin; see *The New Science of Politics* [Chicago: University of Chicago Press, 1952]).

6. This is less so of Marx's own work than of the line from Engels through Lenin to Stalin; some would argue that Marx himself would not have been sympathetic to extreme forms of dialectical materialism. See George Lichtheim, *Marxism* (London: Routledge and Kegan Paul, 1967), 47, 234. More evolved forms of Marxism, such as that proposed by Jean-Paul Sartre in his *Critique de la raison dialectique,* avoid determinism.

authenticity, the worst of these misunderstandings about sense in history should be allayed.

Born of Christian theology, philosophy of history had as its starting point the conviction that human history marches toward a preordained end, an eschatological fulfillment decreed by the Creator. To search for sense in history, then, would be to read events as clues to the eternal plan, as signs confirming the sense of history hinted at in revelation. Etienne Gilson's little book *Les métamorphoses de la cité de Dieu* economically traces the secularization of this notion. The process of secularization—leading us from Augustine to Hegel and finally to Marx—brought about the sort of philosophy of history which lost credibility for the notion of sense in history.

Eric Voegelin, in his five-volume magnum opus on this subject, *Order and History,* has said most clearly what I am trying to get at here. In his *The New Science of Politics,* he explains that "the course of history as a whole is not object of experience; history has no *telos* because the course of history extends into the unknown future. The meaning of history, thus, is an illusion; and this illusionary *telos* is created by treating a symbol of faith as if it were a proposition concerning an object of immanent experience." [7]

Is There a Unity to History?

I shall not in this volume enter into the question of whether history has either a divine plan of cosmic proportion crowned by an educated and united humanity or has certain inevitable natural tendencies leading to a state of being for mankind that is clearly superior—or, if you follow Spengler's arguments for decline, inferior—to present conditions. For my part, I do not believe that the Christian faith imposes (though many have thought that it encourages) the view that mankind in this earthly city is bound to achieve collective success. If everyone were freely to cooperate with the abundance of grace held out by God, one could envision a society developing on earth that would constitute a veritable foretaste of heaven. The sober study of history furnishes no compelling empirical evidence for any such trend. I do not deny the beauty, for instance, of the Teilhardian synthesis. It expresses a faith of great attractiveness against which pessimistic arguments drawn from evidence of

7. Voegelin, *The New Science of Politics,* 120.

dehumanization and brutalization shatter. But anyone not animated by the good father's confidence in the inevitability of the triumph of the divine plan in evolution will want to remain more open to at least the possibility of ultimate failure of the earthly city that God's gift of freedom seems to allow.

The eagle-eyed reader may note here that Spengler's pessimism is also associated with a different development in the philosophy of history—that of multiple, independent, unitary structures *in* history, such as his culture-civilizations—rather than the singular structure of that philosophical tradition of historical analysis credited originally to St. Augustine. Whether our occidental tradition of philosophizing in this manner is either appropriate to the study of non-Western peoples or "translatable" in terms of their experiences are subjects I will turn to in subsequent chapters. But the sense of history I put forward here must be one presupposed by my claim that, as both persons and societies develop, we should inquire into how traditions, by holding forth ideals to direct further development, inform the situation in which we make our way. For our quest for sense to begin, we need presuppose nothing more than the temporal unity of intentionality—that conscious events are to be understood through the grasp of their conditions and of the projects motivating them. The understanding of the fact of development demands only the kind of unity which is to be found in a single continuous line of intentionality, another way of saying a "tradition."

By having a history, a person or institution in some way takes up possibilities handed on from the past and carries them forward through action. To the extent that agents are consciously aware of and express this (for instance, by enunciating the rules of an institution), the tradition is explicit. When they are either not consciously and critically aware of their roots in the past or are not called upon to express any such awareness in order to act, then the tradition comes across to us as implicit. In that case, the sense of what is going on has to be interpreted from what is observed happening—the task of the social sciences.

A Minimal Sense of Sense

If I here avoid absolutist sources of sense in history, such as that found in Hegelianism or Marxism, it is to clear the way for the very modest meaning of *sense* required for the present study. To prove the existence in history of some sense worth searching for, one has only to show that some development is discoverable among the facts of history and that rational action requires an analytical understanding of the vectors of development. Development does not of course have to be positive. All perceived process need not be progress. Some developments might better be termed degeneration, decay or decline. A process may also be shown to be cyclical, or even to progress and retrogress irregularly. Finally, judgments which affirm some direction may or may not involve a "value judgment" depending on the process and the criterion in question. It is easy when assessing progress to mistake a later point of view for a more valid one, when in truth it may only be different. The positivists held mythological thinking to be inferior because it appeared more obscure to them than a mathematically inspired kind of rational analysis. Today many critics recognize the richness and subtlety of the mythic imagination, which has created sophisticated and long-lived categorical systems.[8]

As regards the Enlightenment sort of supposition that the nature of things will inevitably bring mankind's progress to a condition ensuring universal justice, many have yet to be convinced by the analyses of the data brought forward by both Hegelians and Marxists. Not that every claim of fundamental progress is to be rejected. The Hegelian notion of a growing self-awareness of spirit contains a number of elements which may be defended through an analysis of the Western philosophical and scientific tradition. In the notion presupposed by the present study—that of *une prise de conscience,* a becoming aware of the traditional influences that have formed us—there is an echo of the Hegelian idea, but as I hope will be evident, it is not at all absolutized. There is indeed something irreversible about finally having understood something: once we have seen, there is no going back, at least not for those who have themselves understood.

But where no Absolute Idea guarantees necessary progress, there is always the very real possibility that poor education and preoccupation with other concerns will cause later generations to forget something of what the earlier ones more or less clearly saw. Moreover, the terrible gift of freedom includes the possibility of a spasm of destruction at any moment, though virtue—a set of habits built slowly and fairly consis-

8. See Eric Voegelin's comparison of "differentiated" symbol systems and "compact" mythologies in *Order and History* (Baton Rouge: Louisiana State University Press, 1956–1985), 2:12–13.

tently over long periods of decision making and reinforced by reasonable institutional structures—fortunately works against such spasms. These spasms need not be as violent as we, from our twentieth-century nuclear perspective, fear: Toynbee's "time of troubles" and Spengler's transition from *Kultur* to *Zivilization* point to more likely kinds, as indeed does the Protestant revolt (to a Catholic). Developments may be considered both progressive and regressive, depending on the natural faith of the seeker after truth. A balanced and advanced view will often find elements of good and evil in immensely complex events.

It can be difficult, as we can now see, to make explicit the criteria for appreciating the sense of developments. Judgments of progress or decline are often subtly interwoven in the analysis of the process itself. In the early stages of inquiry when one is merely trying to discern the order and structure of events, it is not yet crucial to decide their worth. But implicit judgments about the significance of what has happened will determine our judgments as to what is relevant and will subtly influence our construction of the events. As we grow in awareness of our assumptions and implicit judgments and begin to criticize and clarify them, this enhanced awareness of our presuppositions should improve the objectivity of our grasp on what is really happening. Such, anyway, is the presumption of reason.

It is a long way from the micro-level of everyday experience to an encompassing sense of processes, from our knowledge of the consistency of a person's character and our counting on familiar processes in our natural and cultural surroundings, to the macro-level of our efforts to grasp the sense inherent in vast traditions, perhaps reaching back millennia. Let us begin modestly by first understanding the importance of the minimal level of intelligibility.

The Importance of Understanding Direction

Daily Concerns

As children become self-aware, they discover themselves having always existed in a concrete, dynamic situation, in the midst of processes confronting them incessantly with the need to decide courses of action *in medias res*. Such decisions require constantly revised estimates of the situation, which necessarily include judgments as to the directions the dynamic developments are likely to take. These judgments are made by extrapolation and therefore essentially depend on some kind of (modest) historical knowledge.

Some extrapolations are merely anticipations of regularities with which we have become familiar: we expect the sun to come up each morning, and we expect the subway trains to show every two minutes or so at our station. Others require the imaginary prolonging of a direction which has already established itself: Toronto has been attracting immigrants and people from the small towns for years. Some of the processes we must take into account are of hoary origin and of great sweep. Industrialization, for instance, begun in the eighteenth century, is now spreading to every corner of the globe.

Note that a proper appreciation of the significance of a process demands consideration on an appropriate scale. The Great Depression, viewed from a perspective that reaches only from 1920 to 1940, appears monstrous, trend-reversing, and interminable. But if one graphs all the economic ups and downs since the middle of the nineteenth century, it appears to have been the steepest among a series of quite regular declines, a number of which in the later part of the last century were very serious. The appropriateness of the scale is determined by what we are after in studying a given process. The appropriateness of the question is in turn determined by needs inherent in one's situation. Another "hermeneutic circle"? Yes, one cannot judge the appropriateness of questions without assessing the totality of needs, and needs cannot be adequately judged without asking appropriate questions. More on this later.

In dealing with individuals on the everyday level, we are required to extrapolate trends based on our reading of the sense of something rather like a built-in implicit tradition—what we have learned of their character. If I know a person to be choleric, I shall likely approach him with caution, choosing every word carefully. Here my judgment presupposes a constant: habits (recall Aristotle again) constitute a "second nature." But if I have noticed that recently this person is more often in the best of humor, I might wonder if he is not mellowing. Such an analysis presupposes a knowledge of personal history, in which a pattern of behavior is revealed. It is in the diachronic dimension, rather than synchronically, that we implicitly extrapolate the sense. A value judgment is woven right into the term "mellowing."

We search in history and in our immediate experience incessantly and inevitably for sense in this modest use of the term—the understanding and evaluation of the vector of a development. To say, for instance, that the world population is in progression is to affirm a proposition based on an arithmetic criterion. From different points of view, this development may be further judged either as progress or as a decline. A rising population is progressive, for instance, insofar as it marks fertility and decreased mortality thanks to improved nutrition and sanitary conditions; it is regressive from the standpoint of the capacity of a limited ecosystem.

Tradition as a Unit of Research

Quite the contrary to assuming that some sense unites all developments, all human traditions, in a single adventure, I believe critical philosophy of history should investigate from the ground up the processes underlying the formation and perpetuation of particular developments, especially traditions which have had great impact on human affairs and which continue to influence us and our situation, molding institutions and transmitting the treasures of symbols rich in meaning. Interpreting the symbols and the institutional structures in which traditions are expressed and incarnated, philosophers should search for the basic features in the traditions with a view to the properly philosophical question posed by each tradition: the critical evaluation of the truth of what is transmitted as the ground for deliberately embracing and carrying on its heritage. This is the work of development properly understood.

There has been much discussion, especially growing out of the philosophies of history proposed by Toynbee and Voegelin, about the proper unit or object of study. Is it, as Toynbee was convinced, the civilization, so that comparative study of how civilizations arise, flourish, languish, and die provides the proper structure to the science of history? Or is it, as Voegelin came to believe, the study of the great symbolizations through which we differentiate our fundamental experience of ourselves, our relations with others, with nature, and with God?

In the midst of this debate, I now seem to be suggesting a new and much more varied kind of unit or object of study, the tradition, with central focus, as we shall see, on those traditions whose institutions explain their visions, the explicit traditions. In fact, what I shall propose is not quite so simple. As I shall explain briefly in a moment and more fully in Part 2, given that for action we need to understand the situation in which we act, the question becomes what constitutes the situation. For every person, as self-directing agent, the situation is an inevitable object of study: we always require the best possible grasp of the needs and possibilities of ourselves personally, our intimates, and of the institutions upon which we depend.

The situation is complex. We can focus on our situation, so to speak, in different ranges, reaching from the narrow circle of immediately personal concerns out to the planetary situation in which man now finds himself. In each of these ranges, the various forces at work are to some degree controlled and channelled by the concerted activity of institutions. These institutions function because of the inculcation of attitudes and habits conformed to traditional visions handed down by the institution.

The condition for the possibility of a responsible, in-depth understanding of this kind of institutionalized structuring of the situation requires that one get beyond mere sociological description of how people act in their role-playing, to address the question of why these roles have been formed as they are in the first place. That requires knowledge of the sense of what is being passed on traditionally and ultimately of the truth claims on which this sense is founded. Consequently, we are led from an analysis of the processes—on-going change consistent enough to be noticeable—found in any situation to inquiry into the sense of the development of those processes, as the struggle between conflicting goals of self-interest within the bureaucracies and the ideal of the tradition goes on. The ideal itself must ultimately be confronted as a set of truth claims. Institutional structures provide a handy frame. Symbols used in expressing the evolving traditional vision provide access to the history of the tradition. Together, these help the student see and understand the sense of the processes of change and of the direction-changing events which keep the situation fluid.

The situation as object of study includes and requires the correct relating of processes, symbol systems, institutions, traditions, and events. The truth of the situation is in all these and in their often tense interrelations. In Part 2 I will show how, in considering the present planetary situation, these elements of the emerging world system can be analyzed and related.

In all this, traditions are vital because they are store-houses of accomplishment and transmitters of vision. Traditions and the symbol systems they produce and the institutions they motivate can span many eras and, for those such as Christianity, Buddhism, Islam, or Marxism, even particular cultures and civilizations. Through acculturation into the vision of a great tradition, one is lifted to some extent beyond the narrow limits of a particular national culture and even of modern technological civilization. Traditions that drive such spans of human history become inevitable units of study, perhaps of more lasting significance than Toynbee's civilizations and perhaps more coherent—with an emphasis on institution as well as symbol—than Voegelin's symbolic differentiation of experience.

Study of particular civilizations and comparisons of civilizations remain worthwhile endeavors. So, too, is the civilization-spanning development of a growing "treasure-house of symbol," its differentiation and contraction.[9] But, in honoring both and more, I wish to make a positive point: the exigencies of life demand of the responsible agent study of the traditions operative through his institutions and through the diffuse effect of symbols on himself and other agents. All of this will become clearer when we shall have examined how traditions function and how the different kinds affect our lives through the distinctive sorts of truths they transmit.

Grounding the Quest for Sense

This effort to get around the widespread suspicion of ideology by introducing a modest meaning of *sense* cannot disguise the fact that we are all, however we might like to avoid it, confronted with a large question of sense, the meaning of human existence. This is inevitable in at least the context of another question: To what ought we to devote our long-range action? Any thinking person, no matter how resolute, who sets out to understand the sense of human existence as an integral part of the quest for authenticity must, like everyone else, start from a position of natural faith. He believes there is good reason for undertaking a methodical investigation of what we can know about ourselves and our origins; where we, as individuals, as a society, and as a species, are tending; what may be desirable as goals—personal, natural, cultural, artistic, human; and what the possibilities are, really and concretely, of influencing our personal and collective destiny, despite the evident conflict of ideals visible in the world.[10]

9. Eric Voegelin, *The Philosophy of Order*, ed. P. Opitz and G. Sebba (Stuttgart: Klett und Cotta, 1981), 456.

10. The question of scale applies even to the whole of human history. Compared to the known existence of the planet, to that of life on earth, to the million years human life has existed, the mere hundred generations covered by written tradition are as nothing. As Karl Jaspers has observed, "In terms of time, history is like the first minute of a new happening. It has just begun" (*Vom Ursprung und Ziel der*

I call this starting point "natural" in the root sense, not in opposition to cultural or artificial, but calling attention to the given-ness of the situation. It is not given to some to share this faith. Rather they are led by their overall examination of their experience to the opposite conclusion, to the belief that there is no point whatever in trying to understand where we are headed. Some believe we cannot sufficiently discern the trends or know what is ultimately desirable; others think we can do nothing about it in any event—better to enjoy the immediate pleasures of life. People with such convictions will not blossom into philosophers, not in the sense of someone engaged in the project of authenticity. In fact, they are likely to be critics of the philosophers. By blasting holes in our overly ambitious and overly optimistic constructions, they render a negative service to the philosophical enterprise. Such skeptics may for some reason develop into logicians and methodologists; they cannot, without a conversion of attitude, be lovers of wisdom.

Fed up with dogmatism of all kinds, many contemporaries have seen the skeptics as existentialist heroes, the only ones with the courage to face the reality that there is no sense to human existence, that we do not know where we are going because, neither as individuals nor as a society, even less as mankind, have we any ultimate goal that is fixed and defensible. So the existentialist tries to wring from daily life a little peace and some modest enjoyment—despite the inevitability of death and the final decay of every civilization. From the perspective of this negative natural faith, the resolute pursuit of a way to appropriate the traditions that formed us looks like nothing so much as wishful thinking or an escape.

To the extent that our inheritance of a tradition remains uncritical and we blindly engage in our role-playing, our inspiration by its ideals, our taking consolation from the rich garment of symbols and exercises it weaves around us, it has indeed the potential for dogmatism, for gnostic escapism, an unwillingness to face hard reality. The ideologue, Marcel reminds us, has "mortified" a part of himself, and because of the resulting complex, inevitably tends to tyrannize those he can in no way hope to convince. No one is exempt from the steering effect of his natural faith, whatever it may be. Everyone, even the most resolutely skeptical, has such a starting point, and all such faiths include half-conscious, ill-thought-through assumptions.

Geschichte [Frankfurt: Fischer, 1955], 40). In Chapter 4, we shall return to the question of scale.

To what degree can one achieve some sort of rationally defensible personal development despite the temptation to close-mindedness which comes from a defensiveness about the unexamined aspects of our faith and despite the debacles which are always going on in every epoch and on all sides, tending to push us to such defensiveness? We depend on society for the transmission of concepts of goals and of traditional possibilities and challenging cultural needs; we in turn contribute to society by working in the service of its institutions, including opposing them when they pursue evil, provided we can get free enough to recognize the evil for what it is. But how can we personally judge those possibilities, and make out of them something of our own? How do we achieve enough distance from the massive influences on the very questions we ask, to begin a searching inquiry into the sense of our existence?

Appropriation of Our Own Traditions

I believe that the quest for the sense of our existence most profitably begins with serious appropriation of the sense of the particular traditions which have in fact formed us. In support of this crucial assumption, first let us recognize the nervousness this should raise. The notion of a sense of history—a pretention of the metaphysical philosophies of history—could easily, almost without notice, slip into our reflection. From any number of analyses of senses of particular developments, however, one cannot and ought not proceed to any consideration of *the* sense of history until one shows that there is evidence of a unity of some sort—over and beyond a general sense of human nature—to history itself.

Second, the search must focus on our own experience of the traditions which have formed us. For this, I propose three considerations, which, I admit, are less than compelling:

1. I am of course not just what the traditions—Catholic, American, capitalist, middle-class—have made me; I am also nature and the result of experiences unique to me. But, I argue, each of us is formed (to some undetermined, but, I believe, considerable extent) by acculturation into the various roles he plays in the institutions fashioned to pass on the traditions, by the mind sets he has taken on, often through imitative symbiosis with a milieu that is itself shot through with traditional influences, and by the ideal vision of what is expected out of life and to which he may have been privileged through an explicit

education.[11] Without some degree of critical appropriation of these most influential traditions, we obviously do not know ourselves.

2. Such self knowledge is indispensable for the proper conduct of our affairs.

3. Only the person secure in the knowledge of himself can afford the risk of letting the other be other.

4. Our posing the question of whether we have a destiny in common, the other and I, depends on our first coming to know ourselves and the other, as we grow in mutual understanding by working and searching together.

One Tradition Becomes Planetary

The Age of Faith, when European society was united in a common vision of our earthly mission, is over and so is the Age of Reason, when most searchers shared a common understanding of the criteria of scientific judgment. What we share now is a sense of pluralism, of a world of clashing traditions, of powerful forces which man has unleashed and which we may eventually be able to control, but which for the moment seem to grow willy-nilly, threatening the very survival of our civilization if not human life itself.[12]

At the same time, we are aware of having come into a planetary vision of mankind, a concrete understanding of the variety of cultures and traditions, each with its own vision from which there is something to learn and most of which are now interacting in the emerging world system. There is a growing awareness that one among the many cultures has spawned an insatiable monster: our Western technology and industrialization in both its "capitalist" and "socialist" forms, which is threatening to absorb all the other cultures, levelling them to serve its demands and spawning planetary institutions which may yet create a unified history through force.

Various cultures, even different classes and sexes within the same

11. The philosopher who accepts as part of his natural faith the claims of either a tradition of revelation or of some philosophy professing insight into the inevitable and universal destiny of mankind must, in undertaking appropriation, be prepared to examine critically the experiential grounds for these claims, including a critical look at them in the context of competing claims in the world system.

12. For a perceptive catalogue of these tensions, see the encyclical of Pope John XXIII, *Pacem in Terris*.

culture, are characterized by different rhythms of development, from the almost imperceptible change of those "traditional" societies whose consciousness does not rise above the mythological, to the bewildering explosion of change threatening to tear our own highly technological civilization apart. We have come to understand something of the existential processes by which societies in equilibrium maintain themselves. Now we see the need to understand better how our own has become so wildly dynamic, as we seek ways to manage that development by helping poor societies to produce wealth without creating intolerable strains, and how to make our own growth process sustainable. Within such a bearable process, the individual then must seek his own fullest personal development, in his particular community.

Societies in the Western technological tradition are so different from the nonindustrialized that our dynamic culture has created strained relations between developed and less-developed peoples. We are not just possessors of the great wealth-producing machine and the saviors of mankind, but a terrible menace for every culture that commits the crime of simply being different. There is the problem, not just of the material threat of Western civilization to the rest of the world's cultures, but also of a cultural threat: we believe we belong to the final culture, the culture which can come to an understanding of all other cultures through a science of culture.

But if this sense of ourselves is based on an erroneous view of history and science and we are ourselves members of a situated (not a universal, ahistorical, free-floating) culture, then the attempt to put into practice a science of culture amounts to the most sophisticated form of ideological imperialism yet attempted. Any culture with which we come in contact is ruined by being infected with the germ of our pluralism and objectification of self. Surely one of the things the developing world must hate most is our robbing them of immediacy. Within our industrialized civilization, rapid, radical change and alienation threaten to deprive the individual of all sense of identity. All this, including the imperialism and the alienation, imposes on us the need to understand ourselves in our situation in a much more fundamental way. Fortunately, that same tradition, as we have seen, now gives us the possibility of doing so.[13]

13. Even the long-lived Chinese civilization seems to owe its present phase of self-examination to contact with the West. Such is the opinion of Roger Alain Peyrefitte in his recent study of Mao's China, *Quand la Chine s'éveillera, le monde*

In searching for our own roots, we shall be looking not only for the ground that sustains this phenomenal growth, but also for our attachment to what is solid and lasting in the tradition. If we are to learn to manage development—personal and societal—we shall have to understand what its life-giving forces are and how they can be sustained, directed, prudently cultivated, and transformed where necessary to prevent them from becoming destructive to the peoples of the world.

The first task is one of self-appropriation through appreciation, not of the whole civilization at once, but of one's own particular traditions, which for Westerners are also sub-traditions of the West. We start there because these sub-traditions—Christianity, philosophy, the many elements of modernity, including everything which has pushed us toward world conquest—provide whatever cognitive tools we possess for trying to answer this pressing need for self-understanding.

So our inquiry should not lose this existential focus: a method for studying history that yields results for responsible self-direction through appropriation of the most relevant traditions. This would seem, at first glance, to remove any problem about using a method that is so obviously Western in origin and spirit, since it is our own occidental traditions that raise the question and that we are seeking to appropriate with its help. But there does remain a problem. In the next chapter, we shall see that our situation, in its epochal dimensions, brings us into intimate contact with thoroughly foreign traditions. Can we legitimately hope to understand Muslim, Indian, or Chinese traditions, with which we must now deal, through an existential, structural, situational analysis, derived from and motivated by characteristically Western preoccupations? We must face this problem.

---

tremblera (Paris: Fayard, 1974). Voegelin likewise points out that all philosophy of history is Western philosophy of history (*Order and History* 2:23).

2.

A Space for Authenticity

Can Western Methods Be Used?

The Origin of the Consciousness of Authenticity

Only the possibility of nuclear conflict makes my students more nervous than the thought of truth being imposed by one group on another. "How dare one person tell another what he ought to do?" was the extreme formulation of an outraged twenty-five-year-old commenting to me on her perception of the "fascism of Catholic sexual morality." This attitude evokes extreme resistance to anything from Western culture that is exported and imposed as superior on other civilizations. The whole way of perceiving things in terms of authenticity—the notion that mankind has a destiny, that we are called to take up the truth transmitted by the traditions which have formed us, to criticize it in the light of all we are able to know about reality, and to exercise the best possibilities for the fulfillment of our potential—is a most Western way of looking at things. It is indeed very Christian, or at least secularized post-Christian.

We shall say more about the origin and development of this way of thinking about our responsibilities. Today, as a vast social phenomenon, this mode of thought, this critical sense, is clearly the fruit of a certain level and kind of development. Such thinking is sustained by a hypereducated class enjoying the benefits of their society's legacy of large social capital investments in the infrastructure necessary to make authenticity possible, and at a personal level, the wealth generated by the application of some of these attitudes. These conditions, however, are necessary but not sufficient for concerted critical reflection on an institutional scale.

By itself social capital can never cause the grace of creative intuition or revelation; nor, on the other hand, does it exclude their possibility as phenomena happening to individuals. But without it, the results of past discoveries in all their richness and complexity will not be transmitted to the society at large. Without it there will be no advanced institutions fostering research and dissemination (but also a banalizing) of revelational, philosophic, and scientific truth. The medieval university, for instance, would have been impossible without the revival of commerce and the growth of cities in the twelfth century. The classical Marxists had half the story right: the superstructures do depend on the substructures producing wealth.[1] But I hold the converse as well: the superstructures of ideas and their attendant institutions are, in their turn, vital for creating the wealth-producing machine itself. The relationship of superstructure and substructure is, it turns out, dialectical.

As though this occidentalism were not bad enough, I think we can fairly add a charge of modernism. As I suggested before, prior to very recent times no one could have been authentic. While it seems not to trouble anyone that it was impossible to engage in psychoanalysis before the middle of the last century or that there existed no sense of development before the industrial revolution, it still seems shocking that authenticity before Kierkegaard and Nietzsche was impossible and that only with the publication of Heidegger's *Sein und Zeit* was understanding of its essential historicity achieved.[2]

But the shock is due to a misunderstanding. If one mistakenly thinks of authenticity as a general synonym for moral goodness, then the suggestion that authenticity is a recently discovered possibility would of course be nonsense. The project of authenticity is obviously not just the will to be good. It is the conscious, critical undertaking to achieve the greatest possible self-responsibility. It presupposes a certain notion of goodness related to a particular understanding of how we are in the world.

In the tradition out of which the project of authenticity has grown, we are understood to be in the world as our situation, that is, as a set of needs and possibilities which can and should be taken in hand knowingly as we respond to the demands of the situation in opening the future, and hence

1. Most Marxists would now admit the opposite claim: things of the spirit produce the material modes of production as well.
2. Every epochal turn taken by Being not only opens radical possibilities for man, but also reveals deadly traps. The deadly counterpart of authenticity is the subjectivism of selfish existentialist psychologies of self-development, described and criticized, for instance, by Paul Vitz in *Psychology as Religion: The Cult of Self-Worship* (Grand Rapids, Mich.: Eerdmans, 1977). In the essays contained in his *Nietzsche* (Pfullingen: Neske, 1961), Heidegger has probed especially successfully the way Being dissimulates itself in revealing itself.

consciously seek personal and societal development. Operating here is a whole tapestry of notions of temporality, of how history unfolds, of existential action, a concept of being that emphasizes concrete possibility and truth as unveiled and obscured over time.

Obviously, before any such sense of self, temporality, history, or development was evolved, there must have been as many good, responsible persons as now. Goodness combines integrity with genuineness. The genuine person strives to keep himself open to all of the facts. Integrity, a question of virtue, results from living consistently according to one's best lights, respecting the full range of reality so far as one knows it. The striving to be integral ought, ideally, to be accompanied by the openness of mind which leads to enhanced genuineness. These are existential ways of expressing the ideal of lived truth.

The term genuine (*echt*) comes from Heidegger.[3] A genuine tradition hands down a discovery of Being that in some way expresses an aspect of what is or of what can legitimately come to be without destroying needlessly what already is. The term authentic (*eigentlich*) must not be confused with it. Authenticity refers to my taking responsibility for what I am, thereby becoming fully a self (*autos*). The relationship between genuineness and authenticity is complex, as we shall see in Chapter 4.

Let me quickly give an example, for *genuine* and *authentic* have acquired other meanings over the past three decades. If I take responsibility for an aspect of what the tradition has handed on to me in the way of a formative influence and that aspect is not genuine (in other words, illusory—expressing something that has no hold on reality) or inadequate (ignoring other aspects of reality that have subsequently been discovered), my move toward authenticity is on shaky grounds. The Nazi who is true to himself by living the movement to the hilt comes to destruction because everyone else in the situation, courageous or desperate enough to do so, rises up against him. I shall be returning to these questions repeatedly in later chapters.

All that authenticity adds to this is a certain enhanced degree of awareness of how such responsibility is to be exercised and its relationship to interpretation, as a projective response to what is given in a situation. Individuals manifest different degrees of integrity, ranging from that of

---

3. The term is adopted from Heidegger's *Sein und Zeit* (Tübingen: Niemeyer, 1953), ¶30, where it is introduced with very little elaboration despite its importance.

well-adjusted individuals to the dynamic unity of saints and heroes. Well-adjusted people live comfortably within the accepted community horizons of interpretation, playing loyally the roles assigned, going along unquestioningly with the ruling mythology and staying within the accepted thresholds of illusion. The degree of genuineness required by the everyday world is not too demanding: one must respect the obvious facts, in the way and to the extent that everyone else does, as interpreted by the ruling mythology ("common sense"), a mixture of securely possessed fact and wide-sweeping supposition.

Saints and heroes, on the other hand, in every age disturb the precarious equilibrium of myth and reality with which the mass is comfortable.[4] Unrelenting in their integrity and persistent in seeking an ever more ample genuineness, saints and heroes live their vision to the hilt, which inevitably puts the implications of that vision to the test. But does not the fanatic, too, live his obsession "to the hilt?" His refusal to compromise is also revealing, in a negative way. The world learned from the Nazis more than from the comfortable mediocrities of common sense—but at a severe price in destruction. The fanatic's perverse integrity is made destructive by his pathological closure to parts of reality; he is flagrantly not genuine and certainly not authentic.

Genuineness, then, *is* the issue—not what I or others think is the case, but what really is. What we must realize is that the society at any one moment accepts a tacitly agreed-upon state of the question, which includes muddling through with the help of a mythology. The integrity of the saint and his devotion to Being challenge the collective view, which of course results in his treatment by the mass as a madman or an eccentric until general recognition that Being is manifesting itself through him begins to dawn on everyone. At first, when Francis stripped off all of his clothes before the bishop on the square in Assisi, everyone was certain he was crazy. Eventually, however, they came to admire and approve his unusual behavior, unleashing a "Franciscan" incarnation of Christ that is still alive today.

It is because the genuine hero and saint live the most ample truth available that, however unsettling to the *status quo,* what they bring to

---

4. According to R. D. Laing, "True sanity lies . . . in the negation of the psychotic negation of the false original premise. I am not what they say I am, nor what I say I am" (*Self and Others* [London: Penguin, 1969], 97). I am not sure that Laing has here thought the matter through entirely, as my comments on genuineness show.

the community is constructive possibility, an ampler light on the situation, and a further articulation of the traditional vision that in its openness strives to retain all that has before proven fruitful. So in seeking the essence of the possibilities handed down, they open themselves and through them the society to a new revelation of Being by striving to recuperate the soul of what has already been.

Authenticity is not sainthood achieved, but more an attitude and comportment (*verhalten*) rooted in awareness of all that is involved in the integrity, openness, and interpretative scope of real holiness. A saint today must strive for authenticity as well, if his situation permits, for with the development in awareness it has become a necessary but not sufficient condition for wholeness on the part of those with the education to achieve it. Peasant sanctity remains as viable as ever, but not for bishops or university professors.

I am revealing here the foundation of my conviction that genuine tradition is vital. The genuine radical is always a true conservative. He plumbs the depths of what the past offers as possibility for the future, in the full light of present experience, and seeks in realizing that possibility to justify what is good in what has been—to show how much sense the full treasury of the past still makes as "light of Being." In the saint and hero of any epoch, such generous goodness exhibits a strong selfhood, before the development of full awareness of the self as situated and of being responsible for what happens in the co-creative way, a discovery only made in the era of historicity.[5]

Anyone whose own natural faith is rooted more in disillusion with the past will probably find Polyannish my optimism about drawing on it in the light of the fullest present knowledge to secure the best future. Neither the sense of the past as more a dead weight upon us, nor the sense of the past as source of inexhaustible wisdom and possibility can be demonstrated. Partly to establish the credibility of this optimistic natural

5. But clearly the term *authenticity* is here extended back anachronistically. Some, such as Bernard Lonergan might want to argue that we are wrong to reserve the term for the pursuit of selfhood that begins only with the development of a consciousness of situatedness, historicity, and the kind of responsibility and sense of development they entail (see Lonergan's *Insight* [London: Longmans Green, 1958] and *Method in Theology* [New York: Herder, 1972]). But without these essential dimensions, the self remains less than fully developed. In common with the philosophers in the existentialist tradition, I shall reserve the term for the project of the fullest possible self-realization.

faith by showing what indeed can be drawn from the rich treasure houses of life-giving meaning, I intend in subsequent studies to undertake detailed appropriation of two traditions, one that has helped form me, the Catholic, and one foreign to me, the Muslim. For now I can only point out that the pursuit of authenticity is open for all who learn of it. Although recent and still the affair of an elite, there is nothing inherent in the project of authenticity to exclude a pursuit of the project by every adult, if the society were to develop to the point that it could provide the education and the leisure required and if individuals will at least try to explore appropriatively some rich tradition that holds out challenging truth claims. Neither the learning nor the time for methodic appropriation is beyond the reach of most people working hard for a living in our developed societies. This is due to the immense social capital that has already been invested in their education and the ready accessibility of excellent sources and critical studies. The only problem is that the will to pursue truth would have to be strong enough in the individual to withstand seductive distractions and to overcome pathological blocks to openness. Pascal considered *divertissement* the greatest danger facing man. Manipulating corporate and political power is most *dis-tracting*—we are pulled this way and that in the very opposite of integrity. At the same time, insecurity and fear block communication.

The present study is intended to show a way to read history that would be practical ultimately for everyone who enjoys the necessary health, intelligence, and commitment to pursue truth in the mode of authenticity. Such a demonstration is essential if the project of authenticity is to be acknowledged as a response to a genuine need of our present world situation. Of course, it could be that the situation has developed needs which cannot be met. (We certainly need, in some sense, peace between the great powers, but will we continue to meet that need? We need better management of governmental affairs in many lands, but will the need be met?) But to motivate the pursuit of methodic appropriation in the face of what I hope to show is a real need of the situation, it will be better if the feasibility of our endeavor becomes apparent.

The power concentrated by Western technological development brings with it the need for a heightened sense of responsibility for the world. The same developments which have placed unimaginable power in the hands of a few have given rise to a new need for many to understand our situation in a broader perspective. Do the times then call for heroic efforts from every educated person in developed society? If they do require those efforts, as I believe, then those who glimpse this need but fail to rise to the challenge would not be genuine in their inauthenticity. In other words, the claim (yet to be established) would be this: the times call for authenticity as the appropriate kind of goodness for those in whose hands is concentrated such power and who have been handed such possibilities for awareness—the historical knowledge, sciences, and self-understanding. To fail to see this need, really inherent in the facts of the situation, for a new level of responsibility would be to proceed by ignoring the facts of the situation—that is, it would not be genuine. In the developed world now, it is not genuine to seek goodness without striving for authenticity.

Is This Cultural Imperialism?

If our challenge is to rise to the requirements of personal authenticity in the interests of our social needs, one can say the development of critical self-awareness has destroyed in our Western society the equilibrium of good adjustment that characterizes some societies whose development was not primarily influenced by occidental traditions. The most isolated of these societies can still maintain a slow pace of change within a mythological structure that itself only evolves very slowly (though they continue to pay a price in narrow horizons, authoritarian governing structures, short life expectancy, and miserable income). We in the developed societies have created for ourselves, on the other hand, a drastic need for conscious orientation, the need of which a large portion of the society seems unaware.

It is because of this cultural need that we have had to develop methods for critical appropriation of our traditions, ways of getting economically at their essence, of bringing out and critically confronting their central truth claims. That such ways of reflection should be suited for understanding the very traditions which have given rise to them is natural enough. But that brings us back to our question of cultural imperialism: can they be applied to non-Western traditions without distorting them to fit its needs? Is appropriation of non-Western traditions even an appropriate concept?

A distinction renders the paradox less paralyzing. What we need to know of other cultures divides into two tasks, only one of which actually confronts us with this problem of the translatability of the vision of one culture into another. There are two distinct truth questions confronting the appropriator as he approaches a tradition: (1) the question of the pragmatic truth about the practical impact a tradition has on the world through its institutions and its inspiring or guiding effect on many individuals, and (2) the question of the ontologic or ultimate truth of its vision, that is, what it claims about Being, both explicitly in overt symbol systems and implicitly through what the institutions it spawns inspires people to do, as interpreted and integrated into one's overall wisdom. To a point, both the pragmatic and the ontologic truth of a tradition may be appreciated without the other. Yet either sort profits from an understanding of the other: the sense of an ideal vision is revealed in the struggle to realize it, and every course of practical action begins to make sense only as one divines the ruling ideal.

Pragmatic truth about a tradition can of course be limited to a primitive factual understanding: Shiite Islam is powerful in Iran, the Khomeini revolution controlling the country, but enjoys a complex relationship with the 40 percent of Iraqis who are also Shiite but traditionally suspicious of their Iranian brothers because the Iraqis are Arab and the Iranians Persian. But one can also rise to a sophisticated level of understanding of another tradition, its symbols, and institutions by seeing the ways in which they succeed in motivating masses of people, and one may appreciate their attractiveness without having to confront the question of whether they are, in the final analysis, true. The question of ontologic truth (or, as I prefer, the truth question) is raised only at the point one confronts the still relevant truth claims handed on, explicitly or implicitly, by a tradition. How to integrate the reality of what they do and what they teach in that other tradition into one's own understanding of Being, one's wisdom?

For such a truth question to arise, a critical shift must occur. Criticizing the relevant truth claims of other traditions makes the question of their translatability particularly relevant. One must be so steeped in the alien tradition that it is possible to see that tradition from within its own horizons of interpretation, a perspective that is difficult enough to attain when it comes to earlier epochs within one's own traditions. Only when this perspective is achieved, however, can the delicate task of translating begin. Incorporating the insights of the tradition into a global synthesis of one's own natural faith must avoid the hopeless deformation of the other's vision and instead recover the light it has to offer for growth in one's wisdom. Translation will prove less a process of forcing the vision and discourse of the foreign tradition to fit the limits of one's own than a growing together—both by discovering common ground and by expanding one's categories to accommodate fresh insight—as well as a purging of both traditions of inadequately spelled out elements and unsustainable parochialisms.

If one assumes a relativist ontology, he cuts off from the start all possible significance of translation. Assuming that things interpreted within one culture are only symbols, meaningful only within the horizons and set of symbols constituting that culture and somehow mysteriously working to make just that culture function, would mean that the symbols cannot transcend toward transcultural realities and cannot make sense in another set of horizons. Hence translation would be pointless.

In a work now nearing completion, I argue for a more objectivist theory of knowledge founded in a communality of human nature (changing so slowly as to be, for all practical purposes, stable on the short scale of human history) and in the independent existence of a world able to reveal something of itself as it is in itself. In the second part of this volume, however, we shall return to the possibility that one civilization has reflected critically on the possibility of universal truth and has pretended, in its science, to find the methods and the symbols necessary to search out and express universally valid truths about Being. With that, we shall fly in the face of every contemporary relativism. At this early phase in our work we are concerned first with the less overwhelming task of description. The categories drawn from our own tradition, which will be used in Part 2 to develop an understanding of how major traditions work within the world system, are intended to be formal enough to represent structures common to all human organization. As such, they are products of that universal science the West has claimed to be possible.

Still, we must from the start be on the alert for significant differences between traditions. Take, for instance, the rather formal claim that every enduring tradition demands a considerable explication of its founding experiences, which in turn requires a distinctive set of symbols through which the original vision is captured, elaborated, and passed on. This simple truth should not detract from the significant differences between such symbol systems, even within traditions of the same genus, such as traditions of revelation, like Islam and Christianity. A number of factors impose quite distinctive interpretative (hermeneutic) tasks upon anyone seeking to unlock the sense of what is claimed, and even the way in which it is claimed, as well as the way it is experienced and lived out in the different traditions: the ways in which symbol systems relate to the experiences that gave rise to them; the ways in which institutionalized, authorized guardians of the symbol systems look after them; the ways the law-giving and role-forming work of the resulting institutions mold human existence and the relative weight of institutions in the different traditions; and above all, the great difference separating kinds of symbols—poetic from mathematical symbols, for instance.

Consider the dissimilarity between the way Buddhism is institutionalized and expressed in symbols and the highly structured, centralized, very explicit institutional nature of Catholicism, with the Church watching guardedly over the Christian *symbolon.* Or contrast the freedom with which a Voegelin will rethink the Platonic myth of the creation with the credal and dogmatic constraints on the Christian theologian who wishes to remain faithful to the tradition as he reflects on the Johannine Prologue. To see the dogmatic constraint only in negative terms is to reduce the theologic to the philosophic and to miss the sense of revelation. In every tradition, the passing on of the acculturated needs and possibilities by the institutions guided by the symbol systems is affected not only by each act's diachronic position in the history of tradition, but by its synchronic setting as well: the reincarnations of the vision have to interact with the challenges and revelations of the surrounding eras, including foreign and competing traditions operating in them, to be effective.

The basic formal presuppositions of our Western method necessary for us to begin the first, easier, largely descriptive task of appropriation are not much more contentious than the kind of considerations we have just been raising. Even a traditional society with little sense of destiny—of going somewhere—can be studied from this existential, time-oriented viewpoint with an eye to understanding how it remains so stable from generation to generation, how incursions of the new are domesticated and successive generations are acculturated to a system stressing minimum aggression to the tradition's environment. The resulting understanding can be sympathetic. It need not function as a hidden imperialism.

A Space for Pursuing Authenticity

Ideational Balance

These last remarks should not lead to complacency. Authentic inquiry is an active critical process; an unoriented, indiscriminating acceptance of everyone's visions is not sufficient even for description, as it fails to challenge the other to present his best case and lacks a standpoint from which to judge anything. There is no understanding without judging, though judging does not always have to take the drastic form of the ultimate ontologic.

The project of authenticity is also rendered pointless by voluntarism. If anything can come of anything at any time, with no intelligible connection to what came before, then each separate act of one's will, each moment, each work of art stands in splendid isolation. No orientation is ever possible, so there is nothing to gain by studying traditions. Capricious leaps replace the hard work of development. Determinism is an equally fatal natural faith. There is little point in critical confrontation with the past if we are in some rigid way fixed in our course by it. How does the balanced position find a way between the extremes of determinism and voluntarism? This is important for understanding the suitable manner of appropriation.

How can we get sufficiently free of the traditions which, after all, have furnished us with the very instruments of analysis we must use in understanding them? How can we make of what is an intimate part of ourselves an *objectum,* literally thrown (*jacere, jactus*) against (*ob-*) another part of ourselves? A critical center of awareness and initiative somehow has to sit in judgment over a different aspect of the self: acculturated predisposition, habit, acquired capabilities, linguistic and conceptual tools, or other guiding forces.

To express the same dilemma in hermeneutic language, how can we ever step outside our own horizons of interpretation, our own world, to place those very horizons in question? Of course, we never completely overleap our own ground, so there is no hope of judging ourselves from God's world-transcending position. On the other hand, with every breakthrough in understanding there has to have been some leaping, some getting beyond what has heretofore been taken for granted. Otherwise there would be no real learning at all. Indeed, it is this newness which so impresses the voluntarist that he neglects to see the continuity. If there were, however, no genuinely new element in the event, materialist determinism would be valid and there would be no possibility of questioning and reflecting.

The key to escaping from this dilemma is that our interpretative horizons, our worlds, our traditions, and even our inmost selves are not, taken singly or together, all of a piece. We live in various times: astronomic time, geological time, biological time, macro-historical time, micro-historical time, existential time. Within existential time we are in many different worlds of concern, each with its characteristic rhythm, its unique hold on us. All of these worlds move at different paces, on different scales, and are experienced differently; all entail different modes of our presencing (our calling attention to ourselves) and distinctive aspects of our freedom to pay attention. Their distinctiveness is the root of their being able to call attention to one another.

Between these various worlds we enjoy some freedom to move. It is from the perspective of each that we may glimpse something of the others. The most difficult task is to recognize our all-encompassing horizons, the ground of grounds, interior to which all our figures appear. Later we shall explore the role of appropriating foreign traditions as a way of stepping outside our familiar world and taking up honorary citizenship in a distant culture, from which vantage point (not God's, to be sure, yet far from our own) we may be able to bend back (*re-flect*) on our Western world and objectify even aspects of its most englobing and characteristic horizons.

But even this difficult cross-cultural feat offers no guarantee that we can ever glimpse the ultimate horizons of our common humanity, the boundaries of human thought itself, as those post-Cartesian masters of transcendental idealism thought they could. The limits of our transcendental possibilities in the Kantian sense and their relevance to the quest for wisdom will have to be faced. Fortunately, the project of achieving some universally valid expressions of truth does not, I hope to show, depend on successful completion of a transcendental logic or an absolute phenomenology. But for the moment, let us look in more humble terms at the difficulties of appropriating one's own peculiar traditions.

Space for Self-Examination by Critical Traditions

As our traditions are not of a piece because the figures they produce—which do indeed hide their grounds as McLuhan insists—are multiple, changing, even competing as a consequence of being dialectically related, we get glimpses of the otherwise hidden ground. By standing out from it in different ways, these figures are also the way into the ground. They not only focus our vision but they send it scurrying along as well, glancing from perspective to perspective. Whatever remains constant through this kaleidoscope of ever-changing foci points to the ultimate horizons of the tradition, even to the natural limits of our knowledge. These limits are what get broken through, in the fundamental horizon-opening experiences of transcendence that found and orient historical traditions and establish new possibilities of science. Such breakthroughs permanently widen the horizons.

I note, in passing, that all questions are inevitably the offspring of a particular situation. They always stand in a certain relation to one another. This is particularly obvious in science, of course, but even the breakthrough that is revelation (which I shall turn to in the next chapter) requires the preparation of context before attending to the experience. Certainly, however, good reasons can usually be found *ex post facto* for why one sort of question tended to be asked before another. It is also always the case that only certain elites in particular cultures under discernible kinds of circumstances can hold open the space of a particular kind of questioning. The physicist, for instance, requires an enormous acculturation (we call it a formal education) and not every kind of person is suited to it. Despite such particularity of time and social class, all questions of science intend universality. I will discuss this further in the next chapter when I turn to the types of traditions available to us.

Not only are there in our local and epochal situation a multitude of competing traditions, but within any given historical tradition there are usually tensions between subtraditions that militate against taking any formulation of its claims, any symbol, completely for granted. There is always an ongoing struggle over what counts as *the* tradition. When one considers the dynamism of interpretation, it is astonishing that one set of symbols can ever be imposed by an all-dominating institution, as in the case of the tribe and in the Church's doctrinal orthodoxy, so that basically one way of looking at things becomes the canon.[6]

A monolithic society such as the tribal can only be found in a situation of isolation where it is able to maintain its cohesiveness because of a

6. Christians further believe that even the sustained, habitual movement of will (character) is a response to a redeeming divine grace not unlike that asserted in the tradition as being responsible for the unity of the canon. Whether there is any historical evidence for such a claim about the divine initiative is taken up, perhaps decisively, by Eric Voegelin. See especially *Israel and Revelation,* the first volume in *Order and History* (Baton Rouge: Louisiana State University Press, 1956–1985), as well as important passages in the balance of the volumes in that series and the whole of *The New Science of Politics* (Chicago: University of Chicago Press, 1952).

harmony with the physical milieu (or because of the tyrannical imposi-
tions of a narrow power elite). It entails a set of tight institutional
structures with stable roles. The struggle for orthodoxy in the two-
thousand-year history of the Church is a far more complex matter, which
I shall reserve for another volume.

There is a kind of unhealthy traditionalism to be found in the mass of
people in our rapidly developed societies. This is an astonishing phenomenon. They weave about themselves a cocoon of narrow self-interest,
they avert their glance from the other as much as possible, and they take
utterly for granted the larger situation, to which they relate through an
often rather illusory mythology of common sense mixed with elements
of religion and accepted morality. Traditional societies maintain themselves by being cut off; the egocentric individual does so through resolute
drowsiness.

But those who refuse to take refuge in mythologies and narcissism will
be challenged to reflection by the ongoing tensions of class struggle,
national conflicts, competing ideologies, economic competition, multiple and creative intellectual disciplines, and artistic traditions. The problem ought not to be one of starting a thinking process, but of situating
oneself in relationship to conflicting currents and clashing figures so that
thinking may follow some path. That both problems exist and that
initiating thought in most individuals is a challenge remains a reality
which should not be dismissed by invoking original sin or mediocrity.
The pathological grounds of defensive insecurity directly affect the way
Being is lived out in society.

Our Western philosophical-scientific and revelational-theological traditions have managed to open themselves up to critical self-examination
more than any other tradition. From their origins, they have emphat-
ically not been of a piece. As far back as Israel's struggle with the
surrounding cosmological civilizations of Egypt and Mesopotamia and
then with Greek philosophy's struggle to develop critical self-knowledge,
these traditions have, from their initial breakthrough to transcendence
and to *psyche*, put themselves in question.[7] Such self-criticism is not the
origin, but the fruit of an ideal of critical reflection, born of a break-

---

7. The first critical movement in history, with the sole exception of Akhnaten
and the revolt recorded in the Tell-el-Amanch Documents (1375–1358 b.c.), was
the prophets' revolt of the ninth century in Israel. See Eric Voegelin, *Order and
History* 1:355–59, and for his remarks on Amenhotep IV, 1:101–10.

through to the sense of interiority, soul, freedom, destiny, in both the Hebrew and Greek traditions. In the next chapter, we take up in some detail this claim, best developed by Eric Voegelin, that the Occident is so self-critical because of the opening of history in Judaeo-Christian Revelation, and the discovery of the soul by the Greeks. That this has, from the start, been the work of an elite is significant for situating today the challenge of authenticity. We might ask, What development and for whom? But first, we must pursue the question of the structure of traditions and how they are theoretically appropriatable.

Orientation: An Existential Focus

The Great Explicit Traditions

We see now why critical appropriation can begin, and our minds are somewhat tranquilized on the subject of using a scientific method, Western and recent in origin, but questions of method have barely arisen and the question of who is called to do this remains suspended, despite our precocious and optimistic suggestion that all are called to education and all educated people are called to authenticity. A first question of method can be addressed at once: what to do with the overwhelming richness of the materials to be assimilated? Keeping in mind our ideal of understanding, in terms of their contribution to present possibility, the formative influences that have made us and our situation what they are, I stick by my position that we need a view of great scope, a strategic view, indeed nothing less than the following: (1) Synchronically (in terms of what is going on now), our vision must encompass the whole planetary situation in its essential processes and structures, and (2) diachronically (along the line of historic development), we shall need to search far back into our tradition to discover the origins of the perennial influences that have "sedimented" into the implicit horizons governing our occidental interpretation of the world. Without the planetary overview, we are ignorant of the major forces creating the situation in which we must make our decisions. Without the radical diachronic understanding, we shall not understand ourselves and what is at work shaping our own view of things.

We come, therefore, to what is sorely needed in this situation—some orientation for our strategy for the pursuit of truth. There are at least

twenty massively-influential explicit traditions in the present world system (see Appendix C), any one of which can absorb the entire career of a
whole corps of scholars—Islamologists, philosophers and historians of
science, Marxist scholars, Christian historians and theologians, specialists
in Talmud, among many others. Two kinds of criteria must be found:
criteria by which to decide the study of one tradition more urgently than
another and criteria for a method of arriving at the essential among the
mountain of materials presented by each tradition.

In what sense do I mean essential? The genuine need of our time is for
appropriation grounded in radical critique. The kind of awareness post-
Enlightenment rationality imposes on us demands nothing less than a
return to beginnings. For Kant, rational critique reveals an ever-receding
ideal, organizing principles of the mind which never yield knowledge of
the thing in itself. For us, it will quickly become evident that hope of an
adequate grasp of the situation is also a guiding ideal more than a reality,
both because of its complexity as ongoing creativity and the hidden
nature of the depths of the subjective. Yet it makes sense to set such an
ideal goal to guide our appropriation.

When I undertook the methodic appropriation of one of the great
traditions, Catholic Christianity, the richness of this four millennial experience embedded in the treasure-house of Judaeo-Christian symbol and
the long history of institutional arrangements had somehow to be brought
to heel. Remembering Voegelin's warning that method is mischievously
developed in separation from actual researching, I timorously set out. My
efforts to disengage the essence were stumbling, anything but convinc-
ingly definitive, yet they have been personally rewarding: I see many
aspects of the tradition more clearly and my appreciation for its mysteries
has deepened. Throughout I struggled to keep the focus on what is
necessary to understand the central truth claims as they remain relevant
today. But has the resulting enhanced understanding helped me or anyone
to a better control over our situation? Whether the planet will be a better
place as a result is another matter. Factors other than just understanding
are involved in developing the world.

What about the vast influence on the individual of implicit traditions—all those transmitted, often oppressively, by family, friends, and
"tribal" peers—which may be in some ways even more important in the
life of the individual existentially than some of the great theoretic claims
of the explicit traditions? Nor should we forget that explicit traditions
are themselves incarnate through the implicit acculturation which ani-

mates all our action. The background of the explicit figure (what Heidegger terms *das Ungedachte in Was gedacht ist,* "the unthought in that which is thought") is an essential part of its meaning.

Exploration of the truth claims of explicit traditions demands that they be judged not just in terms of the institutional authority's pronouncements regarding the ideal, but also in the light of what is implicit in their being put into practice. The fact that practice ingeniously adapts the ideal while falling short of its nobility is significant in judging the truth of the ideal, which may have utopian aspects, and in any event the improvisations form a significant part of the reality (hence the existential truth) of the tradition in question.

These existential realities about how we live the truth must not be lost to sight as we seek to develop a direction and a method. I try at every point to keep this existential focus, with its moral dimensions, in the foreground representing the lived reality of everyday human experience.

The Explicit as Figure for Implicit Ground

The distinction between explicit and implicit is significant, but not hard and fast. By an explicit tradition I mean a recoverable history of the handing down of an express truth claim, carefully elaborated and preserved in an enduring formulation, or a historically traceable suite of formulations. The distinction between implicit and explicit traditions is not absolutely clear in practice because there is a certain ambiguity in the whole question of how truth claims are expressed. What people or institutions do is as revealing as what they say and is vital for criticizing what they say. The outside interpreter may correctly infer aspects of intention which the agent hides from himself. Moreover, human intentions are complex. For instance, a man may oppose pornography theoretically but never miss a chance to look at the pictures in the dirty magazines at the barber shop. His condemnation in theory is sincere, but he is weak in controlling desires he has not succeeded in penetrating with his larger, purer vision. This lack of integrity betrays a conflict of needs and desires, confusing the situation.

A person becomes explicit about what he claims when he takes the trouble (usually when contested or otherwise provoked by the situation) to formulate it, especially when the intention is that the formulation be received and preserved, as are most works of art, for instance. But many statements are not explicit at all. Many works of art, despite the care with which they are elaborated, make no explicit truth claim. What they are saying is only implied, and the interpreter has to assume the risk of stating explicitly what the work says. Some of the fertility of the work in stirring the imagination of the spectator lies in its not closing the field through explicit statement. Every explicit statement closes options according to its degree of definiteness. Rarely are statements so definite, however, as to leave little leeway for interpretation. "There will be no smoking on this flight" is an explicit order leaving no room for varying interpretations, because the things and actions involved are very limited and clear. The context is closed and narrow. Some works of art do make explicit statements—this is often the case with films and novels. The message may even be hammered out in a succinct formula one cannot forget and is often hinted at by the work's expressed title. A whole spectrum of possibility, moving from the merely suggestive to the deliberate and exactly formulated, confronts the appropriator of any tradition.

The trouble the founder or founders take to assure that the formulated truth is preserved and propagated often results in institutions mobilizing others either to preserve and exploit these precious insights (as for instance in the founding of an academy), to actualize them in community life (as in the founding of a church), or to utilize them to a practical end (as in the founding of an enterprise, such as a corporation, with a clear goal and a strong sense of identity). The way the institution plays its role will affect the truth handed down, both in its unfolding formulation and in its practical applications.

The institutionally transmitted "canonical" texts and their authoritative interpretations present the appropriator with pronouncements and reflections by spokesmen for a tradition down through the ages. From these, he can gain three things:

1. A first, relatively easy access to epochal horizons of interpretation situated at different moments of the developments of the tradition. The dynamic unfolding of the truth is thus made accessible. The historical series of figures giving some access to the ground, the epochal horizons, permit us to penetrate past these figures presented explicitly by the texts into the partially hidden grounds they are intended to reveal.

2. This ground is also partly revealed to us by the difference between what the texts explicitly profess of the ideal and what other

evidence indicates was actually practiced. The social and the psychological sciences can be of help here.

3. Appreciating what is at issue in the clash of competing positions
through the history of the tradition, including the persistence of
alternative orthodox subtraditions and persistent or recurrent heresies,
also illumines the ground and adds to the intelligibility of positions
maintained.

These few preliminary hints at the complex relations of the explicit to
the implicit and of theory to practice, along with a few dark remarks
about the illusive subject of figure/ground, suffice for now to indicate
why the core of the civilization-spawning traditions is explicit and why
formal appropriation quite naturally begins with a gathering up and
interpretation of the explicit formulations, including the formulated rules
of the resulting institutions. At the same time, the explicit (figure) stands
out against the background and is surrounded by an aura of the implicit
(ground). While there is not much that can usefully be said in a general
way about the dialectic of figure/ground in interpretation, we shall have
much to do with it when actual appropriation begins.

With Which Explicit Tradition Should We Begin?

We must now consider whether to begin with a particular explicit
tradition or a comparative study of the major traditions. I shall make
short shrift of the latter suggestion. Perhaps because my point here is so
simple, comparativists seem to miss it: how can you compare what you
do not know? A Cantwell Smith can validly bring Islam and Christianity
into critical confrontation because he has reflected, as a Christian, for his
entire life on his own Protestant tradition and has immersed himself in
the study of Islam for thirty years. But no one can do that with Protestant
and Orthodox and Catholic Christianity and Islam and two major traditions of Buddhism and the Hindi traditions and Jewish traditions and
Marxism and entrepreneurial liberal traditions, to name just a handful.

In arguing for an existential focus, I have something more philosophical in mind than just the practical issue of getting a sufficient hold on a
vast tradition to be able to make valid judgments about it. I am facing
another reality; the traditions which have most formed us are going to
affect our judgment of what is important. The hope is, however, that to
the extent the appropriative process succeeds in increasing one's critical

awareness of his beliefs and makes him more humble about the adequacy of his understanding of the underlying mysteries and of their call to open onto all experience, he will become less "triumphalist" in his approach to others' traditions, readier to acknowledge not just their pragmatic impact on the world situation, but the possibility that they have something important to contribute to the search for wisdom.

The very antithesis of an antiquarian interest, our existential concern with tradition is directed uniquely toward the truth as we are able to know it in the present situation. "*Response-ability*" is being personally and socially, psychologically and economically able to respond to the genuine opportunities and needs of the situation in which one is called to play a role.

All great traditions make claims about how it stands with the world, claims therefore about what is possible, far beyond the limited opportunities I personally have had to taste of Being. Yet under the constraints of the demand for action, I am constantly judging the truth of these claims, implicitly and explicitly, by the decisions for action I take on the basis of my natural faith. I write off whole traditions (consider how the average Westerner dismisses Islam, for instance). I will only admit into my world those things claimed by a tradition of which I can make sense in the light of my own experience.

There is usually little plan in this. Rather, such a response arises from within the unresolved, unexamined, shut-off hurts, tensions, and crises of my own past. The complex set of problems arising from pathology, including all the ways in which psychic damage prevents subjects from coming to grips with painful realities and the ways symbols are distorted to hide more than they reveal, cannot be ignored in appropriation. This lack of genuineness is best dealt with concretely in the critical movement of appropriating the truth of a particular tradition—for example, when examining the distortions introduced into practice (and perhaps even deforming the expression of the ideal) that result from not only pathology but sin, and that form the involuntary and the voluntary *pseudos,* as Plato and Voegelin call such distortion. I use the term *sin* here both from within my own Catholic tradition and also in a more generic sense of rebellion against the founding experience of Being and its demands, which lie at the core of any tradition (more on this in Chapter 3). But if we recall my earlier comments on freedom, the source of such behavior—pathological or sinful—becomes apparent for many of us. Most people are simply not free enough to stand against the exigencies of the practical world. For them, the demands placed upon them set the agenda. As a result, in the lives of most of us, there is little trace of any strategy for the pursuit of truth—we are simply too much stuck in the here-and-now of the world.

Being of the world, at its fullest extent, means looking for the sense of existence entirely within the time limits stretching from my birth to my death. Even history must make sense for me, now or before I die. Such a "secularist" (in the New Testament sense of *saeculum,* "world") refuses to look beyond what everyone basically experiences in the everyday world or to believe that the whole world derives its meaning from something beyond it. He is doubtful about the purported experiences that have supposedly happened to some and that are interpreted as signs of the transcendent origin, end, and meaning of the world. I am aware of the disturbing implications of what I here (most tentatively) advance.

In effect I am suggesting (and this sounds smug, if not to say "triumphalist") that he to whom has not been given the grace of belief in one of the great religious traditions may be, if not excluded from understanding them, at least severely handicapped in his efforts. To start with, he may well have no interest in really trying to understand what is going on in the synagogue, mosque, or church. Most secularists, in my experience, are themselves smug in their calm assurance that religious life has little to offer them. But the problem is as acute in other types of tradition, such as science. As any number of indicators—from astrological belief, to uninformed eco-activism, to Luddite-like anti-technologism, to settling for a technician's role as though it were that of the scientist—will show, the demands of science are as readily misconstrued and dismissed as unimportant by a similar type of "secularity." As a philosopher, this worries me quite as much as does the smugness of the religious secularist, and for much the same reason. Settling for less than one's own freedom and for less than the truth is simply being less than human.

Arguments have been offered for starting with the main line of explicit traditions, first because they have affected our sedimented implicit horizons in essential ways so that the study of their origins can give us perspective in depth on the present situation, and second because by being explicit they are more accessible than implicit traditions and the aura of the implicit which surrounds their own formulations and practice. In choosing from among the many traditions operative in our situation, an existential focus has been proposed. In Part 2 we shall analyze briefly the present world situation, the role of the specific major traditions in it, and argue for the importance of studying key occidental traditions.

Before doing that, I shall turn to some general considerations of the anatomy of explicit traditions. The differences separating the four genera of explicit traditions—the artistic, philosophic-scientific, associational, and revelational—especially the distinctive kinds of truth they hand on and the ways their respective institutions do it, profoundly affect our approach to their appropriation; within these genera, specific traditions confront us with unique claims which make their own kinds of demands. We shall consider how to gain access to them, how in a general way they interrelate, and what some large implications of their impact upon us are.

3.

The Structure and Kinds of Explicit Tradition

The Structure of Explicit Tradition

The last chapter focused on the individual, especially on the kind of personal space—education, motivation and attitude, character—necessary for appropriation. But I also stressed our social nature and hence our dependence on the transmission of truth by traditions. I advanced arguments for an existential focus to inquiry into traditions and gave reasons for beginning this aspect of the quest for truth with a study of the great explicit traditions.

In this chapter, we turn to the structures and kinds of such traditions. We shall explore how explicit traditions make objectively possible a certain "distancing." When the charge of implicit tradition is overwhelmingly dominant, development, in the sense of rapid modernization, simply does not occur from within. A certain kind of explicit tradition is, then, a necessary condition for development as it is understood and has occurred in the West. We have seen that this kind of development is linked to an attitude toward truth.

Why do only certain explicit traditions foster radical self-questioning? To answer this question, we must understand better how explicit traditions begin, how they get passed on, and how they relate to one another. Of the four kinds of explicit tradition, only one tradition has been central to fostering criticism. It emerges from the genus of scientific/philosophic traditions, for which it is the generator, but it is also cross-fertilized from a tradition of revelation that gave mankind the sense of history and that lays the foundations for the notion of development. Development, in other words, occurs historically out of a unique and complex interaction of certain traditions and institutions.[1] Our concern to foster sound per-

1. As previously noted, the historical sense required for this is uniquely Western. The Chinese clash of schools (Taoism, Confucianism, Mayahana Buddhism) does not generate a Western-style *internal* questioning.

sonal and social development demands of us that we seek to understand this unique structure.

The Foundation of Traditions

For a "handing over" to begin, something new, perceived as worth handing on, has to happen, or something preexistent must at last come to someone's attention as important enough to merit propagation. This time of awareness, of illumination or breakthrough, constitutes the tradition's founding experience. In most explicit traditions, some version of the unique experience is conveyed by "canonical" texts. Such breakthroughs, whether to new kinds of knowledge, a new idea of civic order, a new relationship with the divinity, or a new range of artistic expression, all open unprecedented possibilities and create properly cultural, as opposed to merely natural needs, if they are to be realized. They are moments of great privilege and fertility, and are often mysterious.

Even the most minor acts of creativity open fresh dimensions and produce therefore a small modification of the world, in a sense opening a smaller world within the larger one. This is so whether the event is the coming into existence of a material fact or a product of fancy. "He has been living in a world of his own," we may say of someone who has gone off into fantasy. Society is not concerned with personal, small-scale innovations that get passed on from person to person through direct contact based on common experience. The great traditions, by contrast, are founded in world-shaking breakthroughs that set significant portions of mankind on new paths. They generate unprecedented kinds of symbols—new art forms, new kinds of literature—as their apostles struggle to capture, in various expressions, a new experience of Being. New kinds of institutions are founded to pass them on as social forms appropriate to the new vision, which can mobilize whole nations to live it out.

Between these two extremes—of small scale personal traditions passed from one individual to another largely by imitation and monumental traditions that mold whole civilizations—one finds a spectrum of intermediate traditions, ranging from those animating local social clubs and the cultures of industrial and commercial companies to the traditions guiding governments and particular sciences, to the giant traditions whose institutions mobilize hundreds of millions of human beings and can endure millennia. Many smaller traditions assume importance in our personal lives because of the roles we play in particular institutions and because of personal interests and ambitions. Often they are obsessive, becoming obstacles to the pursuit of a more ample wisdom and hence requiring critical appropriation to free us from their possessive grasp and to put them in a balanced strategy founded in a larger perspective.

The event that initiates a tradition I shall call a *privileged experience of Being*. As there is no term more all-encompassing than "the transcendental predicate," *Being*, the reader must not expect it ever to be a very clear notion. Heidegger spent a lifetime showing how *Sein* obscures itself in revealing itself—it is not definitively capturable in any expression and is never clear and distinct. Being is always more than the truth we possess about it. My overall aim is to build up a description of Being and the ways truth illumines it, or rather the ways Being reveals and obscures itself in the truth when we remain faithful to the dynamic reality we experience as we seek to express it. Especially important in my endeavor is the distinction between being (*esse*) as the actual and potential existence of things and persons and Being (*Sein*) in the sense I mean in the present context: the light spread by opening horizons of interpretation.[2] So permit me to set down in a preliminary, very sketchy way what is meant when I use the term in the present reflection.

Being here means any particular set of interpretative horizons, the meaning-giving context that organizes phenomena and relates them to larger considerations, making them part of a particular world of meaning. The beings are the things and circumscribable settings of things that manifest themselves within the time-space opened by the interpretative horizons deployed. In gestaltist terms, Being is both revealed and obscured in the interplay of background (*fond*), understood as condition of cognition and previous experience necessary for the possibility of certain kinds of figures standing out, and those expressive figures through which alone we can glimpse the ground, but which, by their assertiveness, distract us from the enveloping illumination of the Being that is revealed. In exploring Being in the present work, we shall concentrate much attention on this interplay between the figure and the ground that it hides and that nevertheless allows the figure to have a sense.

---

2. I do not use *Sein* in precisely the sense Heidegger uses it, especially the later Heidegger. Although I am concerned with the "historicity of Being," I do not undertake any *Seinsmysticimus*. I intend in my next book to argue in greater detail for my own use of *Sein*.

Breakthroughs are new revelations through fresh figures, the very event of which enriches the ground that both makes them possible and feeds off what newly appears (*erscheint*) in the figures. The new experience of Being unsettles the old worlds and thereby demands the "decentering and recentering" of previous symbols to capture it and to evoke the altered horizons.[3] The fresh tradition motivated by the new vision at once enfolds an older tradition and goes beyond it.

What, then, is the difference between a great event that founds a new tradition and a less disorienting event that merely marks the start of a new epoch within an already established tradition? Obviously, it is a matter of degree. These are not precise distinctions: the historian has some leeway in deciding what is a new tradition, the start of a subtradition within a tradition, an epochal break within a tradition, and a significant event within an epoch insufficiently creative to demand recognition of a new era. Some breakthroughs are so world-reorienting it would be foolish not to see in them the start of a new tradition: The event on Sinai, the Christ event, the revelation to Muhammad, the Copernican revolution, the discovery of Einstein's new physics, perhaps even the founding of Edison's General Electric Company. The important factor is the enduring impact of the new insights, the persistence of meaning captured in the symbols that express them, and their ability to illumine reality for us even today.

What determines how broadly felt this influence must be and the degree of innovation that must mark it before we identify an epochal breakthrough is in part determined by the question focusing our attention. The birth of a new child is an epoch-making event for a family, but only the slightest statistical ripple for the great city. At the opposite end of the scale, our quest for the foundations of our traditions directs us to the very roots of a civilization.

But it must not be forgotten that these dramatic, world-shaking moments articulate with myriads of little, personal, local, and class worlds founded in humble events, each affecting directly perhaps only a few lives, but adding up eventually to statistical significance and forming together regional or even world processes that can shape history. The interaction between the mass of implicit worlds into which individuals are formed by imitation and the great explicit pronouncements of major self-defining traditions raises all the questions which lie at the juncture of history and

3. The phrase is from Maurice Merleau-Ponty, *La Phénoménologie de la perception* (Paris: Gallimard, 1947), 248.

social science. Being is not just theory, it is action. Being is incarnate not just in treasures of symbols, but in the habits forming character.[4]

The founding experience of Being is privileged because only those who enjoy the initial breakthrough will ever experience, in its pristine quality, that event of horizon-opening. Whether the breakthroughs come in a flash of philosophical intuition, an unexpected theophany, a conception of a successful experimentation, or a pragmatic response to a growing need, the pioneering moments are unique. Very often they are the result of a new kind of activity.

It is one thing to learn in physics class the theory of special relativity; it is quite a different experience to discover it oneself. It is one thing to live in a well-established American republic or Canadian dominion; it is another to fight the American Revolution and to hammer out the U.S. Constitution, or to retreat to Nova Scotia or Quebec as counter-revolutionaries on the way to building English Canada.

The situation in Canada raises an important question as to where and when a tradition can be said to exist. The tensions that exist within the Canadian dominion resulted from the three-fold tensions in its founding: those who stem from the settlement of *la Nouvelle-France,* for whom establishing the Dominion was a way to attain enough sovereignty to retain the traditions of that fragment of feudal order; those who stem primarily from America (known as United Empire Loyalists in Canada and Tories in the United States), for whom the building of a fragment of their vision of Britain was all-important; and finally the immigrant communities (originally from the United Kingdom, then more generally from the world), who owe allegiance to neither of the other groups and who consequently tend to expect the dominion to become a unit in its own right with none of the previously mentioned loyalties. (The third group is not a tradition in its own right; rather, it is a people in pretradition status.)

This example of traditions in conflict is a small-scale example of one

---

4. My methodological decision to begin by focusing on the great explicit traditions and what is most explicit in them—their canonical statements and the commentaries on those statements—does away with any of these problems of how explicit doctrine articulates with implicit practice. We shall address this issue in Part 2. This beginning, however, should gain some vitally needed insight into how these vaster structures have arisen, how they have maintained themselves, and the ways in which they remain effective while being incarnated through millions of daily lives carried out with obviously limited critical reflection.

kind of mixture and adsorption of experiences. The symbolization and primal founding experience—despite the existence of the dominion to-day—has not actually occurred. (That Canadians do not march in the streets as their provincial premiers and the prime minister manipulate the terms of the country's constitution to the disadvantage of their constitu-ents is among the best evidence that no Canadian tradition of association apart from an association of existing traditions yet exists.) Whether this will lead to the founding of a new tradition favoring association by and for Canada, or whether the fragments will retain their separate identities is not yet clear. What is clear is the contrast with the American republic to the south, where a new tradition of nationalism was clearly established and remains—though recently brought into question, especially in Span-ish-speaking America—and in the Protestantization of the Catholics of the United States over the past two hundred years.[5]

Canada's example brings us to a most important point: participants in a tradition do not automatically carry it on. Practical living, our failures in seeking truth—these expose all traditions to the risk of dying out. Moses may recount what happened on Mount Sinai, but only he enjoyed the privilege of experiencing it in those irreproducible circumstances in which it occurred. We who come along later to enjoy the fruits of a well-established tradition lack the sense of the unexpected, the creative, the leap in Being. This lack of experience on our part is one source of the mortal danger to all traditions as they sink into routine.

The Initial Expression of the Vision

Later access to a privileged founding experience is limited to an inter-pretation of the pioneers' initial symbolic expression of their vision. Sometimes, forged in the white heat of inspiration, that expression is so vivid, so poetically successful as to admit the reader or viewer into a successful re-presenting of the founding experience. (Some of the early suras of the Koran evoke that feel of immediacy.) More often than not, however, the early beginnings must be largely inferred from information that has been handed down, seriously recast by later generations.

The founding vision rarely emerges from the privileged experience of Being in the form of a well-worked-out manifesto, showing a clear-

5. I am indebted to Bruce Stewart for his understanding of the Canadian experience.

sighted grasp of the long-range implications of what is being proposed. The new vision of the world shatters old certainties, and its initial expression is often vague or ambiguous. What actually comes down to later generations is an elaborated formulation, showing traces of trial and error; it can be a process of formulation in which much of the suggestiveness of the earlier, more compact symbolism is lost. Such rectification and codification provide the glass through which we glimpse only darkly the pristine founding experience.

Normally, the institutions which have been evolved to put the vision into practice will have had a strong hand from their earliest days in developing this formulation. Knowledge of the history of the institution, of its needs and struggles to adapt to a perpetually changing situation, is therefore necessary to distinguish later adaptations in the canonical formulations from elements that flow directly from the founding experience. There is no justification for necessarily favoring the earliest (usually most compact) version of the vision. To be sure, there is often immense power in the source. As the tradition moves away from its origins and seeks to spell out its implications, some of the nuances of the compact original may be lost or the brilliance of a charismatic founder may become diluted. But a seasoned formulation of the ideal vision is based on living experience (which can include not only an element of dilution by mediocrity but also new experience) in an ongoing struggle to get at the truth conveyed by the accumulated and reformulated symbols of tradition, mixed with efforts to domesticate the vision to make it something one can live with comfortably. The creative efforts of each generation seeking to adapt the founding vision to the needs of a shifting reality can be little revelations of Being that join with the perennial sources of inspiration—the fundamental project grounded in the founding vision—to become one living tradition. Accommodations to mediocrity, on the other hand, can obscure Being, deepening ambiguity and hypocrisy.

Under the stress of evolving experience, the dense implications of the early, more compact symbolic expression are reflected upon and spelled out, "differentiated" as Eric Voegelin puts it.[6] About such an evolved, ventilated structure precipitate additional experiences. The tradition embellishes and enriches itself, growing organically in both theory and

---

6. Such a process—growing, falling away from earlier truths, then recovering and refashioning them—is the story of Eric Voegelin's *Israel and Revelation,* the first volume in *Order and History* (Baton Rouge: Louisiana State University Press, 1956–1985).

practice, but not forgetting, we hope, what the pioneers originally experienced, which may remain perennially valid.

Canonical Texts

It is only natural that the great explicit traditions accord a central place to their canonical texts. Islam has been called a religion of the Book. Judaism is the religion of the teaching (*ha torah*) which again is found in the sacred text. Christianity, while centered in the church as continuing mystical presence of Christ, treasures the whole Bible as the word of God. Taoism and Confucianism both revolve about great books, especially the *I Ching*. The Vedas are the central perennial animating source of the Hindu religion. Of the great world religions, only in Buddhism does the Master's Way, passed on by secret teaching and emulation assume a greater importance than any books (which, however, also exist and are not without their important impact).

Of the two extant political regimes with the greatest longevity, one is very much a religion of the book. The text of the U.S. Constitution has provided a venerable frame about which to weave a dense network of practices, some explicated in rules and laws, others more implicit. The case of the British Constitution, by contrast, is somewhat like that of Buddhism: a highly articulated implicit behavior which is at any moment on the threshold of expressibility. This example of sustained, evolved parliamentary and juridical practice supported by texts but grounded in no overall ruling canon (not even with Blackstone) is unique, meriting special study by those concerned about how traditions work.[7]

When the implicit is passed on largely by imitation but accompanied by a high degree of awareness so that the practitioners of the tradition can, at a moment's notice, explain the rationale for what they are doing, the threshold separating the implicit from the explicit becomes murkier than usual. The case of the oral transmission of secret teachings of the Buddha by certain strains of Tibetan Buddhism is again different because it is an explicit, but unwritten tradition. To be explicit, teachings do not have to be written, since differentiated symbols can be passed on orally. But in most instances, explicit traditions are written, which permits

7. The British Constitution, according to A. V. Dicey, is nothing more than "a generalization of the rights which the courts secure to individuals" (*Study of Law of the Constitution*, 8th ed. [London: Macmillan, 1915], 119). See also Bertrand de Jouvenel, *On Power* (Boston: Beacon Press, 1948), 311–22.

propagation over vast areas and assures exact continuity down through the centuries. Indeed, a concern for orthodoxy often instigated written records of the teachings in the first place. In the Tibetan Buddhist tradition, this same concern has led, on the other hand, to choice of the oral mode accompanied by the strictest admonitions against changing so much as a syllable of the pure teachings of the Buddha. In the absence of texts, if one were to be party to the secret doctrine, there would be no way of judging its faithfulness in fact. It should also be noted that in two and a half millennia, this particular tradition of Buddhism spread outside Tibet only after the recent Maoist invasions. It would be interesting to see whether the purity of the doctrine can now be preserved within its diaspora, but absence of a canonical text precludes anyone's ever knowing. It is symptomatic, perhaps, that the Dalai Lama is shuttling by jet to assure personally the purity of his scattered flock.

With written texts, however, diaspora is less of a problem. The evolved written version of the founding vision becomes then a central point of reference, divergence from which can be discouraged by the supervising authority if it seeks to impose orthodoxy. Attitudes toward the untouchability of the canonical text will vary widely, of course, from tradition to tradition, depending on the faith status of the text in question, the kind of truth the text is believed to contain. The Koran, believed dictated to the Prophet by a messenger from God, provides a kind of *cas limite* of absolute untouchability, in which every character became sacred once the Caliph Uthman's redaction became almost universally accepted. Judaeo-Christian texts acquired a Koranic untouchability only after a long period of consolidation, a complex process of redaction followed by a distinctive process of canonization.

Whereas the priests of David's and Solomon's courts and even the Deuteronomic reformers of the seventh century B.C. did not hesitate to undertake a massive reworking of earlier materials in the spirit of what they believed to be the living essence of the tradition, by talmudic times no pious Jew could countenance the change of an iota of the Tanakh. Already in the legend of the translation into Greek by the Seventy, a story widely believed in the century before Christ, the text is seen as coming from the mouth of God and hence so sacred that the seventy scholars, working independently, were inspired to come up with absolutely identical translations.[8]

---

8. See Voegelin, *Order and History* 1:366–67. Note, however, one change: the books of the Protestant Apocrypha were once canonical in the Tanakh (at the time

The case of the New Testament is also complex. Each of its books was written in response to a local need. Scripture scholars attempt to discern the nature of the different local doctrinal and ecclesiastical preoccupations lying behind each of the versions of the gospel. The Evangelists felt free to shape and refashion oral and even earlier written material to fit their ideational scheme. (They surely would not have wanted to change the sense—the truth—of anything received from Jesus or from the Scriptures, but they did not seem to consider themselves bound to the exact letter of the expression.) St. John, at the end of his gospel, says Jesus taught and did many things not recorded in his book, so much that the world could not contain all the books needed to tell of it.

In the decades following their first circulation, not all of the books eventually considered part of the New Testament were everywhere accepted, though at an early stage the three synoptic Gospels enjoyed wide circulation among all the communities and nearly universal acceptance (except among the Marcionite gnostic heretics), while the early acceptance of John's version was spotty. Yet by the middle of the second century at the latest, when the canon was largely set and widely accepted, the texts, now called "Scriptures" just as the revered Old Testament had been, took on the untouchable status of sacred texts.

In the development of explicit traditions then, canonical texts, if they do arise, become watersheds. From the time they become set, they serve as a central reference point, a link to the experience of the early community, a measure for later evolution of doctrine, and a perspective on the present generation's experience. Archaeologists can dig in the transmitted canonical text for signs of its evolution, looking for traces of the most primitive forms of expression of the founding vision, seeking to reach indirectly the privileged experience of Being which gives the tradition its *raison d'être*. Consider an example: the constitutional history of the American republic divides into the story of how the Constitution was formed, and a subsequent history of constitutional application, amendment, and interpretation. The experience of the need that gave rise to the republic is inferable basically from the Constitution itself, supplemented by the recording of debates preserved in *The Federalist*. The Constitution—the

---

of the Septuagint), but were subsequently removed from the Jewish canon and therefore were not to be found in the Tanakh when the Protestant founders updated their translations of the Bible from the Vulgate.

authoritative, canonical expression of the founding vision—does not express exhaustively the entire vision of the founding fathers. The many glimpses which we can obtain from *The Federalist Papers* are helpful, even though they have no institutional, canonical status.

Knowing the origins and changes in canonical texts is all to the good. But the appropriator must recognize the significance of the canonical text in its mature version and try to understand what its final redactors intended, what the tradition reveres. Ultimately, one must face the critical question of its truth status. To get at the truth of a whole tradition, it is essential to understand the degree, definitiveness, and sacredness of canonicity of its texts and to appreciate critically the reasons for these qualities, which amount to the validity of the truth claims which have been transmitted from the beginning.

An explicit tradition that does not produce canonical texts will inevitably be more fluid. It is obviously a tradition founded in less absolute, more pragmatic or probabilistic truth claims. (Where the canonical text is unwritten but remembered and passed on orally and secretly, as in Tibetan Buddhism, innovation is particularly restricted.) Lacking a definitive formulation, orthodoxy will not be the same: it will take the form of adaptation to an ongoing consensus, as in many traditions of association, such as companies and clubs. Or it will adapt to the latest formulations of the accepted institutional authority, without strict check from the past or perhaps even much concern for the old ways.

Influential interpretations of the canonical texts and authoritative teachings based on them may be preserved through the centuries. Some can be of such influence as to mark distinct epochs in the history of tradition. When a prophetic figure takes up the central vision of the canonical text, attempts to think it through in the light of his own epochal situation, and perhaps, as saint or hero, to incarnate it fully in his life, a further differentiating and enriching of the tradition occurs. Those affected by the later text usually consider it a faithful interpretation of the founding canonical text, a kind of appropriation of it that is valid for them as well. The texts in which such later efforts are recorded can assume, as we shall see, an authority second only to that of the founding text. The later appropriator of the whole tradition has to evaluate this faithfulness, coming to see whether the "gloss" enriches the essential vision or deviates from it, and if the latter, whether justifiably or not.

Other Sources

Manuals and law codes constitute a class of authoritative teaching that deserves special mention for its considerable role in the institutionalization of tradition. They are usually the work of the bureaucratic leaders of the institution. It is easy to disdain them in contrast to works of prophetic inspiration, but it is a mistake to ignore their importance in the development of civilization. They may unavoidably be levelling, but the spirit of the founding is not confined to working only through the great charismatic shakers and movers. Einstein is passed on from generation to generation through textbooks written by assistant professors seeking tenure.

Nor should one ignore the ingenuity that goes into adapting the inspired and prophetic to the humble pressures of everyday life. It is an essential, if somewhat disquieting part of the work of acculturation accompanying inevitably the spread of any great tradition. Part of appropriation consists in recovering the inspired core of the tradition from inauthentic institutionalizations of it. But without those adaptations to daily life, there would be little handed to us to recover. The Baltimore Catechism's answers have stopped many a questioning, but its pat formulas have also served as a starting point and guide to many a reflection. The future heroes and saints in any tradition are first nurtured by the mothering structures of homely institutions. The perennial struggles between prophet and priest are part of the motivating force of every tradition.

There are many other ways in which traditions are formulated, including liturgies, folk mythologies, and art works of every kind.[9] Some of the towering literary expressions of Christianity, for instance the *Divina Commedia* and *The Brothers Karamazov,* not only take up traditional Christian symbolism, they also propose new understandings of the collective experience. In fact, one of the problems is an *embarras des riches:* there are so many expressions of Christian worlds in so many forms, any one of which offers us the grace of a little *cosmion* worthy of years of reflective

---

9. Some, like the Gothic cathedrals, are texts of immense complexity, requiring such a long effort to be deciphered in all their magnificent symbolism (portal statues, *feuillage* of the capitals and bosses, stories in the windows, bas relief on the screens) that a person could spend a lifetime discovering the interwoven meanings that the artists, with help from theologians, have built into monuments like Notre Dame de Chartres.

recuperation, that the appropriator, limited to just one lifetime and pressed with the need to come to grips with several major traditions, is forced to a heartbreaking selection.[10] How does one select? There are no easy rules or categories to apply. Although art, literature, and liturgy remain central vehicles for preserving the life of the tradition, they now play a peripheral role, losing out in the competition with the more explicit statements of theology and philosophy—especially the official statements of the institution—for the appropriator's attention.

Every text and work of art in a tradition is an effort at explicit self-definition on the part of someone or some group within the tradition. Texts and art works are not, of course, the only way of discovering what the people living a tradition have understood it to be. Practice also provides a clue to their values. When one acts in a particular way, it must be because he thinks effectively that the action is most worth doing, whatever he may profess to the contrary. And believing that the action is worthwhile implies an acceptance, at least operationally, of an interpretation of the world in support of the action. One may profess that cigarette smoking is folly, condemning it explicitly. But one who smokes anyway is implicitly affirming either that his present pleasure is what really counts, that this is reality rather than the menace of future suffering, or that addiction has a freedom-destroying grip so that he cannot do what he thinks ought to be done, a possibility that complicates interpretation. But the man who professes that our relationship with God is most important but spends all his time making as much money as he can complicates interpretation just as much and in the same manner.

In seeking to understand an explicit tradition, one must juxtapose the ideal expressed by all the authorized texts with whatever can be observed about actual practice, as it in fact has been and is now—the existential or sociological reality of the tradition. The tradition ought not to be reduced to stirring statements of its ideals; nor is it found only in the acts of saints and heroes; rather, it has to be seen in the tension between the stated ideal that drives it forward and the reality of everyday practice, heroic and tawdry, much influenced by implicit traditions, which gives it presence in the world and potentially offers many glimpses into the Being that is

10. The term *cosmion* is Voegelin's borrowing from the Greek word for "orderly," "modest," "well arranged." The link between a *cosmion* and the idea of horizons of interpretation in the understanding of Being presented here should be clear.

revealed in living the tradition. (Being is revealed, as well as obscured, in the mediocre as well as in the exalted.) Disengaging truth from the complex of idealized symbol systems, both compromised and enriched by the sociological reality of flesh and blood as found in the institutions, is an arduous challenge for the appropriator.

Traditions and Inquiry

Conditions for Criticism

It is the complexity of explicit traditions, the fact that they are not all of a piece, that provides the space for reflection and hence is in part responsible for high civilization. It is difficult to break the hold of an implicit tradition, to get the distance from it necessary for reflection, because an implicit tradition exists as a fabric of largely unreflected habit spontaneously triggered by typical situations. Deployed almost automatically in a way that makes the agent part of a system of operations rather than the commander of the situation, they relieve us of the need to reflect. When playing the piano, I am lost in the music, the operation flows through me without calling attention to me. Only when I begin consciously interpreting the music do I stand out. This is only possible because the explicit tradition, the text of the music, invites me into another historical space: it comes to me from the composer's different world. In contrast, when I am lost in a baseball game, there is no space for interpretation, nothing "over against" me, and perfect style is impersonal and automatic.

Now it is precisely the distance separating spontaneous, acculturated practice and formal, perhaps textual or iconographic presentation of the vision that may, under the right psychological and social conditions, permit us to question one or the other. I say "may," because even explicit traditions are lived by means of acculturated habits guiding our action implicitly, and we may be swept along by acculturated structures too fast for much reflection. One rather negative way of being jolted into reflection can occur when we notice a serious discrepancy between institutionalized practice and the stipulation of canonical text. Or a difference may be perceived between the letter of the canonical text and the official interpretation, or there may come to be a conflict of authoritative interpretations. Put positively, the recorded and transmitted symbols bring with them a perspective on the world different from the immediately acculturated horizons of my unquestioning everyday role playing. It is like the challenge of a friend who accuses us of not questioning aspects of our view of things that may indeed be seen a different way.

Although the space opened by explicit statement is a necessary condition for critical reflection, the absence of such self-criticism in many explicit traditions shows that it is not a sufficient condition. The space of inquiry is partly dependent on the nature of the revered texts, especially their authority, which is based on the kinds of truth they express and the kind of authority acquired by their interpreters. This will vary not only between the different genera of tradition but between particular traditions of the same type. Take, for instance, the traditions of revelation: the way a Chasid, steeped in Talmud, approaches the sacred letter of the Torah filtered through the interpretations of the great rabbis, is very different from the way a modern scholar would approach St. Thomas's commentaries on the text of Aristotle. For a believer any discrepancy between the authority of a canonical text and the authority of a later interpreter will be an issue. For a Catholic the scriptural interpretations of the *Magisterium* are most telling because the authority of the teaching Church is divine and the Scriptures themselves attest to Jesus' institution of its authority: "Whatsoever ye shall bind on earth shall be bound in Heaven."[11] A fundamentalist Protestant, on the other hand, believing interpretation to be the work of the Holy Spirit through individual Christians, attaches ultimate authority to the Spirit's interpretation of the letter of the holy text in himself. These are questions touching the very nature of truth. As we shall see, they put the appropriator's own natural faith to the test.

This example of Protestant-Catholic disagreement makes the point well, since two different traditions of interpretation have drawn from the same canonical text. A Catholic must be mindful of an explicit tradition of interpretation, contained in the writings of the fathers, the teachings of the great doctors, the letters of the Popes, and the pronouncements of Councils down through the centuries. A problem of consistency presents itself, raising its own questions. The Protestant fundamentalist, on the other hand, takes up an implicit tradition of interpretation, learned from his community. He may accord some authority to a great interpreter, a founder of the sect perhaps, but this may or may not be a constant source

11. Matthew 18:18.

of reference the way earlier authorities are for an Oecumenical Council, which will cite them in the course of its arguments. If it moves beyond them, it will seek not to contradict them.

Consistency is possible for the Catholic Church because authoritative texts exist in great number across the ages. Where, on the other hand, the main interpretative force is lived, implicit, communal experience, as is the case to a lesser or greater extent with all Protestants, there is little record to check for consistency, and therefore, in a sense, the problem disappears from view. Who can challenge the consistency of present interpretation with those of the seventeenth century if the earlier interpretations, being merely oral, are no longer available? The Protestant fundamentalist has only the letter of a two-millennia-old text to exercise control.

Some canonical texts motivate the institutionalization of their own interpretative authority. This will be the case for any well-drawn constitution. Other texts demand respect because of the origin they claim: pronouncements of God are not to be tampered with. But many founding texts ground their authority in the breakthroughs to new insight that they communicate. Einstein was only a low-level patent office official when he elaborated his great text on special relativity; it is not who said it that counted, but the insights communicated by the founding vision, establishing a new direction of research, a new way of conceptualizing the world. Of course, a text whose authority ought to reside only in the quality of its visions may draw authority it does not deserve from the great prestige of its author. Einstein writing on theology enjoys such a dubious authority, and had Aristotle edited a manual on chariot repair, it would have assumed importance in the Middle Ages even if his instructions could not get a single axle to turn.

Certain interpretations acquire such universal acceptance within the tradition that they become attributed to the prestigious founder himself. Thus the entire Pentateuch was long attributed to Moses, many a later Hadith to the Prophet, and a great variety of sayings to the Buddha. One hesitates to label as "pseudo" such authority by transfer. In general, it seems rather to be a case of an insight perceived by those living the tradition to be in accord profoundly with the founding vision. Although it is in fact a later differentiation or perhaps even a new discovery, it is linked to the founding source, more to consolidate than to establish its authority.

There are thus many different kinds of explicit tradition; not only do they hand on different kinds of truth (as we shall see in subsequent chapters), but within the same genus, their differing authority structures account in part for the fact that critical self-examination does not develop in all of them. In sum, each major tradition has its own peculiar version of founding and interpreting authority, and a specific way in which its members take it up and carry it forward; hence it has its own space of critical inquiry or its own structural grounds for lacking one.

The Unique Space of Criticism

The uniqueness of nations, peoples, and cultures proves an obstacle to a generalizing science of development. The very idea of a generalizing science is itself the product of a single unique tradition. Unusual features of certain occidental traditions merging into a central tradition of critical science has provided the reflective space of historical consciousness and with it a process of colonization that brought the concept of development in its train.

This is not only a theoretical issue: the imposition of the techniques, machines, and mind-sets on nations of radically different culture whose traditions are not critical in the European way is at the origin of what we today call "the Third World development problem." The development crisis is not first and foremost an economic issue. It is a clash of cultures, rooted in radically different experiences of the truth. So even when it is introduced from the outside more or less by force, such critical, developmental thinking can be resisted. This shows us how unique it is. If the recoverable space of explicit traditions is a necessary condition of critical self-examination, why is it not by itself also sufficient? Why have not all great explicit traditions developed scientific appropriation of themselves? If it is a question of kinds of authority, what kind of relationship between authorities has to prevail for critical questioning to begin?

To answer this question, the origins of criticism in our Western tradition must be understood. Such an effort goes hand in hand with development of a theory of Being and truth. Once we have begun to understand this occidental discovery of truth as reflective and critical, we have to ask, as we have started to do, how legitimate it is to detach this critical consciousness from its Western origins and apply it to the human experience of the whole world. If we claim there is ultimately a single wisdom based on Being's revelation of itself through human consciousness as one, we shall have to establish our means of knowing that and its implications for the synthesis of many kinds of truths from many traditions. I shall sketch these issues in the present volume only summarily, leaving to the two volumes now being completed a more serious reflection on the development of this freedom and a more developed theory of how it is possible.

Something unique happened at the inception of Greek philosophy, with its acute sense of the need *to search* for the truth. The word *historia,* which means "researches," was first used by Herodotus. There was born mysteriously in Greek thought a sense of truth that somehow juxtaposes the vagaries of the individual *doxai* (positions or opinions) against the absoluteness of the source of Being. This sense was not lost to the fathers of the Church, who transmitted it to the Middle Ages through a rejection both of gnosticism, with its tendency to total possession of Being by explaining everything in one fantastic intellectual scheme (contrary to the spirit of *historia*), and of the opposite temptation, anti-philosophy, an escape into fideistic spiritual life.

But how was the sense of history created in this tradition, not just as searching, but as destination, the sense that mankind is coming from somewhere and going toward an end? How did the West come to conceive of truth as universal and transcendental? And what led to such an acute sense of individual responsibility in the search for truth?

The answers will begin to emerge as we study the different ways agents in each kind of tradition relate to the founding truth. As we investigate each genus of tradition, we shall discover the distinctive kinds of truth each hands on, and we shall explore the complex ways in which they relate to being and how they might relate to one another in an englobing wisdom. This will clarify why a sense of historicity, development, and authenticity emerges from certain traditions only. Understanding of what it means in each instance to take up the tradition and carry it forward—to repeat its possibilities in a new situation and to extend them—will prove vital to our later consideration of the nature of truth itself when we confront the challenge of moving toward an ecumenic wisdom.

Four Genera of Tradition

My ultimate task is to show how research into the traditions forming ourselves and our situation can help us advance in self-responsibility, thereby progressing in our search for truth and in managing our own development and that of the world. Consideration of the ways that possibilities from each kind of tradition can be taken up and carried forward therefore raises the truth question in effective, dynamic terms. The search for truth requires theoretical criticism of these possibilities—ontological judgment of their genuineness—but first it also necessitates interpretation through correct understanding of how they are formulated, preserved, and evolved, and finally how practically they are to be lived. In the course of this analysis, we shall be almost continuously preoccupied with the role of symbol systems as incarnation of traditions. We live first and foremost in the spoken and written word, hence the importance of ideational symbols more than artistic ones; idea words, rather than icons, will occupy most of our attention.

The power of ideational symbols lies in the way they fold the past into themselves. Mysteriously, an explicit idea making a universal claim invites us to relate the thing critically to the whole world of Being. Expressed in that uniquely powerful symbol, the theoretic word (*Logos*), the scientific proposition has become a central structural member of our civilization. Relating the word of science to the *Logos,* St. John's Gospel reveals, "was in the *arche,*" the origin, and the claim of Jesus of Nazareth to incarnate that Word has been, and remains, the greatest stumbling block to the project of ecumenic wisdom. I shall do my best to make a bit clearer how the theoretic word can do what it claims to do as we consider below the nature of philosophic and scientific discourse. We shall prepare the way by inquiring into the different kinds of repeatability, starting with the ways concrete works of art can found a tradition, which they do by being in their own way repeatable. All traditions reveal aspects of how truth is lived. Eventually we must seek to understand how the various forms of repeatability relate to one another in the full fabric of life.

Artistic Tradition

There are three ways in which a work of art can reveal a sense and thus call for a critical response to that sense as a kind of truth claim. First, a work of art is a little world (*cosmion*) of its own, its parts forming a cohesive, balanced, expressive, intelligible whole. It is constituted by the artist as a being, contemplatable and enjoyable in its own right, as it is given its own coherent time-space. In this way it founds a new possibility for transmission through repetition, calling for co-creativity—in painting and sculpture, through appreciation; in music and drama, through performance. Works which demand completion by performance invite a most active kind of co-creativity, in which the performer must enter into the world sketched out by the composer's symbolic instructions to complete the work in a way faithful to those pointers, while adapting it to the circumstances in which it is performed. For instance, in the adaptation of a Greek tragedy to the tastes of a contemporary English audience, the degree of co-creative effort in the final product can be very high. In that case, the carrying on of the tradition demands a maximal creative investment.

All such activity is a reminder that truth is not just theoretical or caught only in static formulation. It is to be found in living and acting out, just as a true vision demands a putting into action. Appreciation, though at the lower degree of co-creativity, is also active in its own way: in studying a painting or reading a novel, the appreciator must gather up the symbols,[12] without which relational act the sense of the whole would not manifest itself and would not come to be in the new situation. The coming to be of truth in an individual consciousness is always the result of activity. The little world opened by a work of art has to carve out a place for itself. It must manage to impose itself on the ongoing world of everyday life and create its own audience and its own imitators. The possibilities for the viewing and expression of Being opened by a seminal work are taken up and exploited when new works in the same style appear, when performances are repeated, or when the work is taken up contemplatively by appreciators.

Second, a work of art may reveal a sense through explicit statement in the following ways:

1. A work—play, novel, even oratoria—may contain explicit propositions. To that extent the art work is open to criticism according to the canons of philosophical-scientific truth. Such truth is characteristic of the next genus, the philosophic-scientific, the tradition that produced the critical attitude. *Une oeuvre à thèse,* a work with a message, should be integrated into a reflexive universe of discourse through application of the criterion of universality to be discussed in a moment.

12. *Legere* and *legein* come from a root that means "to gather up" or "to pull together," as in *intel-legere,* "intelligible."

2. A work may invoke or represent a thing, presenting for perception one of those discrete, familiar concretions of Being which we call a thing, or perhaps painting in words a concrete personality. In both instances, the truth of the representation is its success in revealing the thing or person as the author intended. In a historical work the author intends, for instance, to capture the personality of an important figure as he really was. In fiction the author creates an interesting personality, perhaps as illustrative of a type. He succeeds if his creation manages to communicate the desired effect.

3. More fundamentally, though, the essential role of art is to disclose new aspects of reality that otherwise would pass unperceived, thus opening new horizons of significance: it reveals Being on levels of experience other than the praxis-oriented ones of our everyday commerce with people and things. Art seeks to penetrate this surface to reveal the dynamic subcurrents of being, the deeper frameworks, what Merleau-Ponty so felicitously (and untranslatably) terms *les épures de l'être*.[13] Artists, both in teaching us to see aspects of things we may not have noticed before and in opening us to new levels of acoustical, visual, psychological experience through their creations, play a pedagogical role. When an artist breaks through to a new kind of expressivity, opening new horizons, he founds a tradition. Artists who come after him and use the new language he has forged, contemplating the levels of being he has opened up, can prolong the exploration of those horizons.

Third, every work of art reveals something of the sense of its situation. As a historical phenomenon, it inevitably tells us something about its author, his time and position in the traditions within which he works. This is a sense the historian must gather up diachronically by looking back at what preceded and forward to what followed the particular creative work he is attempting to place in its setting, but it is also synchronic as well because the historian places the work in its contemporary context. Here the question of truth is extraneous to the work of art itself, but it is part of the task taken on by the historian as he seeks to situate the work correctly and by the art critic as he gathers up whatever clues it offers about its author.

13. See my *Merleau-Ponty's Critique of Reason* (New Haven: Yale University Press, 1966), 133–50. The dictionary gets closest to Merleau-Ponty's meaning with "working drawing," which is still too stilted and mechanical.

The complex ways—religious, philosophic, national—that an artistic tradition can stand in the service of another and that artistic traditions are themselves influenced by other traditions is a subject for endless exploration. The reading of works of art accompanies our efforts to reconstruct the horizons of many traditions; the works are often unique expressions of worlds, of epochs now past, of milieux within an epoch, of the little worlds of unique personalities. Incarnations of what Hegel called "objective spirit," such symbols capture in their existence as things the time-space horizons that gave them birth, mysteriously freezing another time and another perspective until someone comes along to read them, thus unlocking the old world and making it present in the interpreter's new horizons. Artistic expression adds the force of revealing Being to the uttering of founding visions and orchestrates the mediations of those who appropriate and pass on the tradition.

The focus of our research explains why artistic expression will not occupy the center of our concern. Concentrating on the still relevant truth claims the traditions make on us, we direct our concern first toward the more explicit among its various expressions—the credo rather than the liturgy, the constitution rather than the mechanisms of bureaucracy, the scientific treatise rather than the laboratory manual. This is a methodological decision, only the beginning, not the end, of the quest for wisdom. Guided by propositional truth as a kind of framework, the appreciator should eventually move beyond it to participation in the glory and darkness of Being's revelation and dissimulation of itself, not only in the chiaroscuro of artistic expression but in the ambiguities of practice. When we are seeking to understand the truth as it was lived, the less differentiated symbols of the work of art express aspects of being which can slip from sight in the critical, analytic propositional work of science.[14] Who would want to separate, for instance, the formal statements of the *Summae* from the artistic statements of the great Gothic cathedrals when attempting to reconstruct the thirteenth century as actually experienced by those who lived in it? Dante's vision, rich in propositions, is also structure, color, and music, without which the texture of his experience of the divine would be missed.[15]

14. Eric Voegelin has coined the useful terms "compact" and "differentiated" for symbol systems that are of different degrees of explicit, analytic "spelling out." See *The New Science of Politics* (Chicago: University of Chicago Press, 1952), 62.

15. This aspect of the shining forth of divine glory in a work of art is explored in the context of a theology of beauty in Hans Urs von Balthasar, *Herrlichkeit* (Ein-

Scientific/Philosophic Tradition

A work of art may be the vehicle of a philosophic or scientific proposition. When that is the case, it must be judged, as we have noted, not only aesthetically but propositionally. Aesthetically, it lets Being shine forth with its glory and its shadows. Propositionally, however, a work of art that goes beyond the disclosure of Being to judge its object does so by critically situating things in relation to one another, positing an explicit truth claim: this is how it stands with this thing; this is its nature; this is how it relates to this other kind of thing. To such an extent, *oeuvre à thèse artistique* also belongs in the genus of the scientific/philosophic tradition and is more than a work of art.

In the privileged moment of first scientific or philosophic insight, as with the creation of a significant art work, a new vision of being opens up. Once enjoyed—whether in the god-possessed trance of Heraclitus or the cool labor of Sir Alexander Fleming—and expressed, this gift can be shared with less inspired mortals in the form of teaching. What distinguishes scientific or philosophic insight from other kinds of founding experiences of Being is not that it is taught, however, but its explicit claim to some form of universality accessible to the properly informed mind. Since it refers to a structure of nature or to a formal truth (as in logic and mathematics), it is repeatable without reference to the particular circumstances of its discovery. The grace of *e-vent* is not part of the reality it holds up to view. "Science," teaches Aristotle, handing on just such an insight, "is of universals."[16] An event, a single act, a particular tree, or a person is not as such universalizable; each can only be experienced in its immediate particularity, one on one. These things can be testified to, but not in any sense proven.

It is the ability of the verbal and mathematical proposition to express not only the particular (the proper name, for instance), but the universal as well, thereby placing the word at the very center of our search for truth. That is why the appropriative enterprise begins and ends in words expressing universals and large encompassing structures, that is, in self-critical prose, a language always seeking to understand its own limits.

---

siedeln, Switzerland: Johannes Press, 1961–1964). This work has been translated into French: *La gloire et la croix,* 7 vols. (Paris: Aubier, 1965–1981); and the first three volumes of an English translation have now appeared: *Glory of the Lord* (San Francisco: Ignatius Press, 1982–).

16. Aristotle, *Metaphysics* A, 982a5–19.

Artistic insight, too, can to an extent be detached from the historical circumstances of its inception: Monet's *Nympheas* can speak to us, provided we have been initiated somewhat into its language, without our knowing anything precise about how the aging painter was fascinated with the glory of water and sky. Still, the more we can situate the work, the greater our understanding and appreciation. Shortly we shall examine two other kinds of tradition in which the founding experiences cannot be detached from the historical circumstances of their creation without losing their significance—the traditions of association and of revelation.

But even in the case of the universal insight of science and philosophy, this ability to be detached from history is more a formal possibility than a reality. One can detach the formal intelligibility of a philosophical position or of a scientific discovery from its human ground and from its concrete expression but one does so at the price of losing some of its meaning. There is even a risk of distorting what the philosopher or scientist—who may also be a poet in the invocation of both the concrete and more tendential aspects of what the critic formalizes—meant. So the truth of any proposition is not exhausted when its reference is limited to a state of affairs existing independently of the knower. Since any theory is an imperfect approximation calling for constant revision, we must take into account its pointing to the experiences it expresses and its situation in relation to positions held before and after it, which are struggling to invoke adequately the same or similar experiences.

Of course, a certain core of what has been discovered can be taught as an utter truth, at least theoretically, if its claims can be verified at any time. This kind of verification can be done by empirical observation or controlled experiments when the proposition is about the kinds of things which are so repeatable. Natural science strives to achieve total repeatability by abstracting its objects and carefully discerning limits fixable as perpetual systems. In due course one comes to recognize that the supposed invariable states are in reality stable only within a certain time frame. Even the solar system, often the very symbol of the unchanging for primitive man, came into being and will go out of being within the larger evolution of the galaxy. Stability of any system turns out to be a practical consideration in relation to a certain scale of human experience that corresponds to a certain level of questioning. Within a certain scale the mathematically abstracted objects are perfectly repeatable, and correspondence limits may be perfectly respected. The fact that more often than not, instead of such verification, students learning science and even scientists reading reports accept on authority, believing on faith, reports of earlier observations, takes nothing away from the essential verifiability in principle of this kind of founding experience, at this level of abstraction.

The drive for ever more adequate expression of the structures of things and the state of affairs of the systems relating them carries philosophy and science forward, making them developmental in the strongest sense. The retention and taking up (*Aufhebung*) of earlier formulations into larger and more differentiated syntheses is the very movement of occidental science. It is not just a matter of larger constructions accommodating earlier discoveries, but of the revelation of becoming: we are progressively recognizing that smaller and larger structures belong in not only an expanding context of understanding but in an expanding universe of evolutive complexification in the course of time. The gradual realization of the complexity of the concepts of repeatability, universality, and evolution came to dominate our tradition. This failure of other traditions to develop an adequate concept of truth is central to the present clash of cultures we call "the development problem." This and our tradition's core concepts, especially universality, have profound implications for the search for truth, as we shall see in more detail below.

Tradition of Association

A third kind of privileged experience of Being is that enjoyed by those who found an association. From the original perception of a need follows the conception of an ideal, the expression of a goal for the realization of which new means must be created. The means will include new symbols to express the ideal and appropriate new institutional structures to carry it out. There is always something astonishing about beginnings; such insights appear inspired from beyond. When the breakthrough is great, it is experienced as a divine manifestation occurring with a suddenness that catches everyone unprepared. In acts of associative foundation, the human power to bring something out of nothing can be awe-inspiring. That is why the founding moment is often represented mystically. Hannah Arendt has written, "It is the very nature of a beginning to carry with itself a measure of complete arbitrariness," and she quotes Augustine, "*Initium ergo ut esset, creatus est homo* [that there be a beginning, man was created]."[17]

17. Hannah Arendt, *On Revolution* (New York: Viking Books, 1963), 207. She quotes *De civitate Dei* 12:20 (see *Basic Writings of St. Augustine,* 2 vols. [New York:

Once a course of action has been set and institutional structures for pursuing it have emerged, they then have the weight of authority behind them and are passed on as already having been achieved. They are themselves aspects of Being. "*Principium* and principle are co-eval: the way the beginner starts wherever he intends lays down the law of action for those who have joined him in order to partake in the enterprise and to bring about its accomplishment. As such, the principle inspires the deeds that are to follow and remains apparent as long as the action lasts."[18]

The ancients were so impressed by the uniqueness of the privileged experience of Being lived in the founding of a *polis* (city state) that they could scarcely conceive of it as other than the grant of one great genius, the original law-giver. Plato, in recognition of the sanctity of the beginning, said of the *arche: "theos en anthropois idrumene sozei panta."* Arendt paraphrases: "For the beginning, because it contains its own principle, is also a god who, as long as he dwells among men, as long as he inspires their deeds, saves everything."[19]

Nevertheless, a tension lies at the root of the life of the polity in the permanent possibility of coercion—the restriction of human freedom by force, the coercion of individuals by each other, of individuals by groups and vice versa, and of groups by groups. To counter this possibility, the "divinely inspired" polity is led to formulate ideas and institutions which will balance or negate the threat. So long as the measures instituted by this response to harsh reality remain themselves coercive in nature, the polity faces a tormenting internal dialectic. Between the need and the ideal, between the courageous attempt to found a new *socius* and the living political entity that results, falls the shadow of hypocrisy.

This is an important factor in every institution where authority is exercised. By hypocrisy, I do not here mean a particular vice, a matter of a failure of responsibility between private individuals in their dealings with one another. Rather I am referring to the disjunctive tension between word and deed: the ideal is more easily stated than respected in action. Ideals may have nuances, but action often requires decisions that preclude

---

Random House, 1948], 2:200–203). My own discussion of association owes much to comments offered by Hugh Miller. I am especially grateful for his vision of hypocrisy.

18. Arendt, *On Revolution*, 24. Arendt points out that the very notion of *auctoritas* for the Romans was rooted in *augere*, "to increase": that which increases the Being of state is authoritative (Ibid., 202).

19. Plato, *Laws* 6.775e. Arendt, *On Revolution*, 207.

nuances. One either performs the action or does not; the demands of action tend often to be abrupt.

The effects of this structural hypocrisy are manifold and widespread, often surfacing in unexpected disturbances of the public order and revolts within all kinds of institutions, and hence they are a source of practical critique in all kinds of tradition. In an association as fundamental and inevitable as the state, the tension of hypocrisy is not felt between the word of the founders and the actual policies of the government (between a divine ground for coercion and its political practice there can be no tension), but between the founding act or vision and the idea of God or the gods. This implies some differentiation, not just between one putative divine act of law-giving and another, but between the revelation of divinity in its essence and in its historical (or mythical) aspect—between, in other words, religion *per se* and civil religion. This condition is an unlikely one, for reasons which will be made clear below; nevertheless, it is not impossible. As the mass of participants in the polity remain tied (*religata*) to the divinities of the civil religion, the reaction will take root and grow in individuals or small factions. The classical example is, of course, the trial of Socrates on the charge of "believing in deities of his own invention instead of the gods recognized by the state" (*Apology* 24b).

The manner in which the institutions of the founders deal with this tension is crucial to the longevity of the polity. Let us hypothetically postulate two starting points: either (1) coercion is a necessary ingredient of any possible *socius,* or (2) it is not. If the founders accept the first starting point, how do they deal with its existence? Their institutions will reflect the view that some degree of coercion is justifiable by reference to the ideal: the gods, as it were, approve. But the gods cannot approve of an indefinite degree of open and violent coercion. The speech of the Athenian envoys to the Melians would never have been uttered at home; even Hitler was forced to conceal atrocities, and the final destruction of the Jews was a state secret. In general, it can be said that such regimes are obliged to maintain a complex balance. Too much public display of coercion and the body politic will begin to doubt the veracity of the founding event itself; too little, and others who can make similar claims of divine justification are likely to attempt a new instauration. Such regimes become more unstable the more the founding event and the living concerns of its founders recede into the past. As the initial conditions first become dissimilar to the present ones, then strange, and finally incomprehensible, despite the best attempts of propaganda and political hagiography, only force remains as the cement of the social bond.

Such despotisms may in fact be quite long-lived, but they are never secure. Thus Machiavelli comments on principalities obtained by iniquity: "Those [cruelties] can be called well used (if it is permissible to speak well about evil) that are done at a stroke, out of the necessity to secure oneself, and then are persisted in but are turned to as much utility for the subjects as one can. Those cruelties are badly used which, though few in the beginning, rather grow with time than are eliminated. Those who observe the first mode can have some remedy for their state with God and with men, as had Agathocles; as for the others it is impossible for them to maintain themselves."[20]

Another possible solution to the problem of coercion, and one still in keeping with the postulate of its necessity, is the claim that it is progressively ameliorable. To use our theological expressions, the gods may not approve in principle, but for us it is a temporary expedient and therefore permissible in certain contexts. Such a polity will remain stable so long as conditions are seen to be improving and coercion to be decreasing. Here hypocrisy becomes possible on a public scale: present conditions can be justified repeatedly by the inceptive ideal. Given a prosperous domestic economy, an acceptable division of labor and distribution of wealth, and manageable foreign relations, this kind of polity can maintain a steady-state equilibrium. The forms of coercion may become increasingly refined, more civilized, and less openly violent. The continually perceived harmony of the founding ideals with the present reality may lead to greater stability in the form of an inner, psychological prophylaxis at the level of the individual. It becomes difficult for the individual to recognize breakdowns of the social system or injustices. But when conditions change (through the arrival on the scene of a foreign adversary or corruption, for instance) and coercion to maintain order is increased, tension is greatly magnified by the apparent contradiction that has arisen between the founding ideal and the contemporary policies of the current institutions. These institutions, now on the defensive, may react in a wide variety of ways, from denial to outright suppression of dissent. In any event, what had turned out to be a factor in the stability of

20. Niccolò Machiavelli, *The Prince: A New Translation,* trans. H. C. Mansfield (Chicago: University of Chicago Press, 1985), 37–38.

the association, its promotion of justice over force, becomes in the end a source of public revolt.

The person born into an association, living habitually its customs and laws (*Sitte,* in Hegel's sense) can be said to be more possessed by the nation, tribe, or association than possessing it. But if participation is ever to be mature and authentic, he will need a critical understanding of the constitution of the nation, enterprise, or association. This cannot be achieved without reference to the circumstances of its founding, the grounds of its legitimacy, and its continuity to the present moment. Where the past is hidden in obscurity, where the founding acts are remembered only mythically, the critical task demanded by the quest for authenticity is obviously going to be troubled. But even demythologiz-ing need not necessarily lead to disaffection—only to a shift in the nature of one's adherence, a growth in responsibility we call maturing. The individual's act of adhering, whether unreflective or critical, is nev-ertheless a kind of repetition of the founding act, and hence a participa-tion, however indirect, in the original founders' project.

With these kinds of considerations—raised by Hannah Arendt, Eric Voegelin, and other political thinkers—in the background, let me try to state as precisely as I can the kind of truth question involved in the repetition of an associative tradition. Basically, two kinds of issues are involved: genuineness and legitimacy. The question of genuineness, in its most general form, is this: does the association, through its vision and its institutional forms, and despite a given degree of hypocrisy, continue to respond sufficiently to the needs, as presently perceived, of the actual situation it is meant to address? An example may illustrate this. The Parti Québécois is not questioning the legitimacy of the present government of Canada, despite its perception of that government as having been im-posed by the conquering *Anglais.* What it questions is the genuineness of that regime for Quebec. The present structures of government do not seem to respond to the Québécois' perception of the need to preserve their culture. This example allows us to probe the difficulty in determin-ing whether a tradition of association suffers institutional hypocrisy or a falling away from the founding experience.[21] My assistant, Mr. Bruce

21. Both Europeans and Americans of my acquaintance express their sheer incomprehension of how Canadians have reached the present impasse, and despite a son-in-law who is *un vrai du vrai* from the heartland of Quebec *séparatisme,* Lac-Saint-Jean, and more than two decades in Canada, I do not really comprehend it either.

Stewart, points out that the two main interpretations of the problem operate on different levels, one dealing with institution and the other with fidelity to the tradition, and that most of the debate follows from nuances and variations within one position or another.

The institutional viewpoint emphasizes the growth of the provinces into positions of separate action at the expense of a unitary outlook (as represented by the regional institutions of parliament). In this perception of the "feudal fragment," Quebec is reacting to the inability of "English Canada" to honor the founding nations' bargain of confederation. This situation is due to both the rise of the provinces and to the "immigrant fragment's" attempt to devise a unitary tradition of association—a single Canadian nation—out of the Dominion. The interpretation that stresses fidelity to tradition, on the other hand, sees Quebec as having transcended its origins via *la révolution tranquille* of the 1960s, so that fidelity to *l'ancien Québec* now means Quebec is as a self-determining nation with its own vernacular state, just as elsewhere in the liberalized West. Such a state may have institutional supranational ties, but it is otherwise *maître chez eux* (the rallying cry of the 1960s) and willing to restrict its role to itself.

The Pierre Trudeau's centralist view married the institutional-regional conception of Quebec as guarantor of the French fact in Canada with the institutional-unitary conception of *une province comme les autres* ("a province like the others"), and assumed all provinces follow a national agenda. Contemporary Quebec now views itself as a separate French nation in North America without concern for other French-Canadians, leaving open only the question of whether the province of Quebec and the region of Quebec (no other province is also wholly a distinct region and *nation*, in the French sense) should be joined, or whether the full leap to *un état comme tous les autres* ("a state like the others") should be made. Perhaps the truth here is that there are problems from both the institutional and fidelity-to-tradition perspectives, and that they are made worse by the difficulty in reconciling Canada's various traditions of association with its single, highly elaborate institutional framework.[22]

The more elaborate the institution, the more maintenance it will

22. I am indebted to Bruce Stewart for his analysis of the Canadian situation. In offering a seminar in early 1991 on knowledge of large-scale systems in which we used the Quebec situation as our research case, Mr. Stewart and myself were neither able to bridge the differing perspectives of institution and tradition described here, nor to move much further in prioritizing the arguments.

demand, the more it will tend to take on a life of its own, to some degree in hypocritical tension with the founding goals of the tradition which spawned it. An institution may altogether outlive its original purpose (a student of mine was once hired for a summer by an ongoing institution, a YMCA in a moderately sized Canadian city, to find it something to do!). The question of legitimacy arises when the institution exercises governance over basic aspects of human life, as does a state or religion: in the name of what, and by what authority does it rule?

The mass of people is not usually able to hold open and examine this difficult space of questioning—at best, a "public opinion" is formed quickly and takes on a life of its own, helping to close down serious inquiry and self-examination. Yet whole classes have been known to revolt, their mass act constituting an implicit questioning of the legitimacy of the regime. The masses are usually driven to revolt not by hypocrisy as such but because primitive needs have ceased to be met. What Guglielmo Ferrero calls the "efficacy" of the regime falls so low that desperation becomes general.[23] Such an outbreak goes nowhere, however, unless an elite surges forth to take control, giving the mass movement an expression and direction. A blind movement becomes a tradition-founding event when the masses' perception of the need for a change is transformed into a privileged experience of Being by an elite that can express a vision of what is to be done. Getting the masses acculturated to this vision so that generation after generation will work smoothly within the new structures is the process of legitimization. Ferrero explains: "A government is legitimate if the power is conferred and exercised according to principles and rules accepted without discussion by those who must obey. There are still people who, without knowing the abstract theory of legitimacy, yet recognize in the respect for these rules and principles the source of the right to govern."[24]

Once a government is so accepted, once legitimacy is unequivocally established, a hypocritical "legitimacy veils the inevitable flaws and errors of government." To get the masses to this point of tolerant acceptance, the enthusiasm of the elite has first to be secured. Ferrero sees the importance here of the trappings of government: "art, monuments, gold,

23. Ferrero uses this term throughout *Principles of Power* (New York: Putnam, 1942).
24. Ibid., 135.

jewels, military parades, etc."[25] Even the greatest artists can be enlisted to play this essential role for the regime.

The highly developed regime, if it is to survive for long, must evolve a means of regulating its complex institutions, of integrating people into their offices, and of systematically inculcating the spirit of that particular sophisticated society. In all of this, the creation of adequate expressions—constitutions, laws, administrative rules, slogans, captivating symbols—provides a mass of explicit materials, with the help of which we can begin to reconstruct the evolving visions the regime expresses through its very existence. These instruments of self-definition along with details of actual practice reveal something of the truth of that regime, that is, they afford insight into its unique being. Comparing, for instance, the written Soviet constitution to the actual practice of dealing peremptorily with dissidents would tell us much about the nature of that regime—until, of course, its recent evolution.

This existential truth that molds the lives of millions and contributes substantially to the shaping of civilization is often underplayed by philosophers, who, for the reasons explained, tend to concentrate on symbolic expressions. It would be a mistake, however, to neglect what I would call the great pedagogical role of the major institutions, state and church, and what they reveal of the human being as social. By exercising pedagogy through institutional innovations, a Jefferson, Bonaparte, Adenauer, MacArthur, or de Gaulle had a formative influence on the destiny of the country that was constitutionally transformed, the sense of which has often been explicitly symbolized long after the pedagogical action.

Just as art is involved with the great associative institutions, providing them with instruments of acculturation, so do associations and the institutions affect other kinds of tradition: academies and royal courts influence what art is turned out; universities and research laboratories shape philosophy and the sciences (the departmental structure, for instance, institutionalizes a positive mentality of specialization, creating a "multiversity" that works effectively to block the cooperative, cross-disciplinary search for truth); revelation is passed on by the Catholic, Orthodox, Anglican, and Congregationalist churches differently. The impact of a scientific or philosophic text is much affected by the nature of the associations, which either grow out of renewed interest in the text or, when

25. Ibid., 141–42.

preexisting it, integrate its vision into the living fabric of existence in the way the Chinese imperial bureaucracy made use of the Confucian classics.

My earlier position bears repeating: the philosophers' focus on ideas in the important texts is not a perverse exercise. Institutional history can also be pursued with only slight attention to the ideas the institution exploring them serves; interest in the dynamics of administration for its own sake can prove a fruitful specialization. But anyone concerned with traditions' formative influences on us and the situation, and in exploring their truth, will have to study the interaction of idea and institution, as well as the artistic and rhetorical forms of their acculturative expressions. Joachim Wach has put it very well:

> The sociologist, no less than the historian, is interested in the intricate rela-
> tionship between the ideal and the real. . . . Two fallacious doctrines have
> distorted our understanding of the true relationship between these factors as
> they have worked themselves out on history. The first is an excessive spir-
> itualization of history which neglects the effect of harsh reality on ideas and
> programs, overstressing the latter and taking fine plans for actual achieve-
> ments. The other is superficial materialism which equally reduces history to a
> mere consequence and result of "material" conditions and divests it of any
> inherent value and effectiveness.[26]

As he shows throughout the *Critique de la raison dialectique*, Sartre has understood this much better than some Marxists. There is a development that goes on within the sphere of ideas rather independently of institu-tional development, sufficiently separate at least to make the study of the history of science or the history of theology possible with only slight reference to institutional development. But the whole truth requires the study of the development on the level of ideas, the struggle on the level of institutions, and the interplay (with all its hypocrisy) between the two.

Tradition of Divine Revelation

The fourth kind of privileged experience of Being is the rarest in number of distinct traditions and has wrought the most profound and widespread changes in human history: traditions founded in a special kind of encounter with the divine, which those traditions have termed

---

26. Joachim Wach, *Sociology of Religion* (Chicago: University of Chicago Press, 1944), 53.

revelation. Among religious traditions, two subgenera can be distinguished: (1) those founded in a vision calling for cultic enactment and for the exponent to "put on the god," living out the deistic-moral-social reality into which he is inculturated, usually from birth, and which constitutes a whole fabric of existence and implies a massive set of truths about Being; and (2) those claiming to be founded in a vision that is a revelation in the strict sense. The "hardest" and most demanding sense of divine revelation is found in the Abrahamic family of traditions: Hebrew-Jewish, Christian, Muslim.

Both kinds of traditions confront the seeker of wisdom with stumbling blocks. It is difficult to grasp what religions of the first kind are about short of living in the sacred time-space of a society formed by their vision and struggling to live it out. Religions of revelation in the strict sense are difficult to come to terms with because they demand supernatural faith in the witness to the event or events in which God calls forth a people, revealing some innermost secrets of His being and His plan for them. In later works I intend to elaborate on this stumbling-block dilemma with particular attention to the Abrahamic traditions of revelation because they have been formative of our own tradition in the West and because I am more familiar with them. The reader can, by extension, see for himself what the dilemma is regarding the religion of the East. For now, we shall proceed as though the claims by these traditions to hand on revealed truth is worth taking seriously in their own terms. It is in their own terms, without critical examination at this point, that we shall state their kind of truth. These traditions exist as massive realities in the world system, so we must deal with them one way or another.

As inspirations of every sort have struck their recipients on one occasion or another as visits of the divinity, one must distinguish the kind of event that is reported by adherents to a tradition of revelation from all sorts of philosophic, artistic, and scientific inspiration. Like any inspiration, the revelatory event is visited from without in the sense that it breaks into the heretofore familiar horizons of interpretation, forcing the context to open out to embrace an aspect of reality previously unsuspected to exist, at least in the precise form it now assumes. Unlike scientific work, what happens is not really prepared by what came before (at least as something to be refuted). In a theophany, an appearance of the God, the unthinkable happens: a principle transcending human capability and imagination confronts a prophet, a commanding presence teaching with authority, and calls into existence a people. After the theophanic event, one does not look back on what was known before and recognize that what has happened simply throws light on structures that were there before, perhaps unnoticed. On the contrary, an initiative is created and a new age begins. The Incarnation of Christ is nothing less than "a new creation," as God brings a people into being.

Like scientific intuition, the religious event issues in a teaching that has both theoretical and practical implications. We are told that this is how things are, and consequently, this is what you shall do. But unlike scientific intuition, verification is not just a matter of attending to the phenomena in the way in which the teaching presents them in order to repeat for oneself the intuition. For the sacred event of the commanding presence is not a repeatable intuition, nor an experience each individual can have for himself. Rather, it is a demand issued on a specific occasion by what is purported to be a superior cognitive-voluntary center of initiative, made at its choosing. In this, it resembles more the legitimacy of the founding act of those who establish a constitution, with the obvious difference that a nation or an association is founded by people in response to the needs and desires of a potential or actual community of people.[27] The divine relationship, on the other hand, is established between man and a transcending principle that graciously condescends to turn toward us, on its terms alone but in cognizance of our limited ability to relate, and while offering a saving direction, it commands acceptance of a law the justification for which is only partly verifiable in ordinary human experience.

Of course, some aspects of the divine teaching are natural, in the sense that in them claims are made about man and nature which we can then verify in the experience of everyman. This is what has permitted rational appropriation of parts of revelation by men who no longer believe in their divine origin. (In this way, the Christian sense of the dignity of every individual has become part of common Western humanist belief.) But other aspects of the teaching, those which reveal mysteries about the divine One itself, surpass understanding. While they may prove harmo-

---

27. According to Wach in *Sociology of Religion*, religions founded in revelation are merely a subset of founded religions. Wach tends to confound revelation with the formulation of any experience of the holy, though later in the book, he does distinguish the prophet from the founder of religion (341). The kind of theophany that results in the issuance of an explicit command and teaching formulated by divine authority grounds a tradition with a source that the adherents are related to in a unique way, a point Wach insufficiently recognizes.

nious with the totality of a man's experience as he interprets its sense in the light of belief in the revelation, they can never be directly verified, only accepted on the authority of the divine source as its teaching is expressed in divinely chosen symbols, which are transmitted to us by the prophetic human witnesses sent forth to bring us the good news. All prophecy purports to be apostolic (from *apostolein,* "to send forth"), and the prophet's claim to an authoritative mission furnishes the ground for his being believed. How the genuine is to be discerned from the false prophet is, of course, the heart of the truth question in this domain.

Some of the traditions of the first, "less hard" kind emphasize more a kind of reasonableness of the teaching about the "Way." This would be the case for the more exalted traditions of Buddhism, Taoism, and Confucianism. Islam presents an interesting diversity in this regard. Many subtraditions of the Shi'a Ali and some types of Sufi mysticism emphasize the uniqueness and transcendence of the Koranic revelation. But there are also many in the central tradition of Islam, of the Sunna, that advocate the reasonableness of the teaching, seeing it as a kind of summit of human wisdom to which we have been guided by the divine, a teaching all men should be able to embrace with their minds. Orthodox Judaism, Catholicism, and the Orthodox Christian traditions stand with the Sufis and Shiites in witnessing the mystery of God's revelation, which illumines reason and which the mind is invited to explore theologically, but which has depths of mystery that appear ever more inexhaustible the more one embraces God's word and sets out to explore them.

Consequently, the mode of appropriating a tradition of revelation obviously has to be quite different from those of appropriating science and association. A scientific tradition is appropriated ideally by repeating the cognitive operations that present the object to one's attention and doing so in a way that makes possible a perception of its evidence and the logical steps of deduction from principles abstracted from that evidence. In the case of association, after consideration of the grounds of the association or state's legitimacy and its genuineness, one agrees to adhere (or to continue to adhere) freely by associating oneself through an act of will, thereby assuming responsibility for carrying forward the vision of what is to be done. Ideally, this is a function of a reasoned assessment of how the association fits into one's situation and knowledge of Being, and through facing up to one's desires.

But divine revelation advances claims going beyond anyone's ability to verify. Such claims are accepted on the authority of the sources because

God says so, as His prophet and Church report, and the believer accepts these things as true and acts in consequence. The resulting good fruits are the only additional supporting evidence. To bolster the divine authority, the tradition remembers and records the teachings of the prophetic apostles and the wondrous acts that accompanied them. The living community putting these teachings into practice is the best testimony to their reality, just as mediocre religious practice presents the greatest obstacle to belief.

Even though appropriation in the service of the project of authenticity demands that an inquiry into tradition focus on present relevant truth claims and therefore that it be aimed more at explicit doctrinal statement than what the sociologist terms the dynamics of social integration, it must never be forgotten that (1) without the implicit integrative factors, there would be no tradition to criticize and (2) the truth of the tradition, as I have repeatedly pointed out, is to be found neither in the explicit, dogmatic statements alone, nor in practice alone, but in the relations between the two. I acknowledge the general truth of Pauline Vislick Young's statement in her monograph on a modern religious sect: "No amount of theological doctrine could probably have the effect that their comparatively simple ritual does, of producing in the individual participant a sense of the reality of his religious faith."[28] What is later formulated dogmatically is first lived dynamically. But in the process of appropriation, what may have remained implicit must first be stated, rendered explicit, in order to be judged philosophically. Appropriation, because it is authentic, is critical; because it is critical, it must be explicit. There is operative in appropriation a kind of reverse *épochè:* everything is required to show its claim to existence.

There is a common misunderstanding, which many of my students have echoed over the years, to the effect that anyone who would write about traditions of revelation has as his real goal apologetics rather than the search for the truth. I disagree—indeed, we cannot hope to command the truth if we are unwilling to face the claims of the traditions of revelation. Compounding our difficulty here, though, is the whole issue of explicit claim versus implicit practice. What was said earlier about an almost inevitable hypocrisy in the state applies to every tradition of

28. Pauline Vislick Young, *The Pilgrims of Russian Town* (Chicago: University of Chicago Press, 1932); cited in Wach, *Sociology of Religion,* 40.

revelation as it is lived out. The mediocrity of the masses' incarnation of the ideal and the downright misuse of the symbols for ends of earthly power gives bad witness. This quite naturally invites a sort of gnostic reaction in those who cannot stomach the fact that human beings tend to help themselves freely to the power potential that is to be gained by manipulating the noblest symbols. No great tradition, only their minority gnostic sects (for example, Puritans, certain Shiite extremists, the ultra-orthodox, the Pharisees, holier-than-thou Pentecostals, and to quote Ontario's treasurer addressing the leader of the New Democratic Party in the House, "socialists with headaches from tight haloes"), has ever thought that the good can be kept clear of all evil in this world. The truth has to be won laboriously from the midst of the reality of mediocre and even evil practice.

Conclusion

In the following chapter, the question of truth of traditions will be pursued in more depth, with emphasis on the way one remains faithful to the truth in each kind of tradition as it is handed down over the years and on the distinction between genuineness and goodness, something that needs clarification on the way to the pursuit of truth. This is a question of fitting the vision to the facts about the real world in which it must be applied and of keeping the ideal in touch with operational reality. It will move us a step closer to a formulation of the truth question more adequate for our ecumenic age.

4.

The Truth and Faithfulness
of Traditions and Institutions

The handing down of traditions by institutions is neither a smooth nor unambiguous process. The light and shadow, the fits and starts, the tension between soaring ideal and vested interests are the inevitable result of the finitude of human existence. It is an essential aspect of that obscuring which occurs when Being reveals itself, as Heidegger says, through "*Da-sein,*" the existent as being-there. Man's struggle to realize potential not only makes possible reforming, recreating, and adapting to new needs, but may also lead to the deforming of greater possibilities to serve egoistically narrower, short-sighted desires. That is why critique, in a strong sense, is inseparable from the search for truth. We are therefore not concerned only with how traditions work but about how truth is revealed and sought. Here I will use tentative steps (to be methodically developed in later volumes) toward ways of thinking that are better attuned to the dynamic character of Being than is classical Platonism and that are more respectful of the "known once for all as it is" aspect of truth than is post-Kantian thought. Modern man still has to learn to think, properly, of concrete possibility.

In pointing out that traditions are founded in privileged experiences of Being, breakthroughs that are positive events, I may have left the impression that traditions are in some simple sense progressive developments. A darker side is also found where possibilities handed on by the tradition are misused: mythology and illusion can dominate. Moreover, the notion that any one tradition in a given genus holds a monopoly on the truth should not be allowed to grow. The historical dominance of entire cultures by persistent, rich, overpowering traditions can give that impression if one's view is foreshortened. Two examples come easily to mind, but others are not hard to find. Our occidental tradition of physics can easily give the impression of displaying a smooth, unilinear development and of being the fundamental truth about nature. The more our biology becomes biochemistry and chemistry becomes physio-chemistry, the stronger this illusion becomes. Many valid truths about nature are to be found in philosophies of nature and even in traditions of revelation that are not synthesized into the richest possible wisdom by the enthusiastic proponents of science, legitimately proud as they are of its ability to unlock many secrets of nature.

The other example is the "catholicism" of the great traditions of revelation. Christianity in the East and West, the traditions of Judaism, and the branches of Islam all lay claim to a fullness of truth that invites one who is ensconced within such a tradition to view everything in the world as being adequately illumined in the light of the Gospel (to a slightly lesser extent, the balance of the Bible), the Torah (again, to a slightly lesser extent, the Tanakh), or the Koran. One tends even to play down the seriousness of the schisms within the respective tradition in question.

A basic tenet of the natural faith underlying my project is the belief that all great old traditions transmit experiences representing the living out of reality, thereby confronting the searcher for wisdom with the challenge of integrating the truths they have to offer into the most adequate understanding of Being. For this reason, it is important to view clearly the existence of parallel traditions and to see that within every epoch truths are discovered that may become dimmed in the excitement of later epochs.

I would emphasize now the fundamental ontological point that there are inevitable limits to every formulation of truth that comes to being in time and space and that later formulations tend to obscure earlier insights. It is essential to distinguish this inescapable veiling effect of our finitude from the role of moral perversity—the finitude of all interpretation from what the old rabbis termed "sinfulness." Sin and error may be related, but they are not the same. Moral critique and the reform of institutions is not the same as the recovery of Being from ground-hiding symbols.

Genuine Being: Possibility and Illusion

Because every privileged experience of Being is an experience enjoyed by finite, situated, human agents, error is attendant at the birth of all creative intuition. Of the four kinds of privileged experiences of Being, the first three basically consist in the experience of a comprehensible (*comprehendere* means to be able to get one's fingers about it) reality, resulting in the formation of a circumscribable noetic structure, the expression of which is a closed figure. Even the cosmos of early philosophy and of modern astrophysics is a finite structure—enormous, to be sure, but one which can be expressed by a figure. The fourth kind of tradition, very rare revelation, purports to result from an encounter with the Absolute, the incomprehensible as such, a confrontation with the ground of grounds in which it takes the creative initiative. This insight is experienced as something that cannot be expressed adequately by a closed figure, an expression that would absorb attention into itself. Whatever figure is offered by the inspiration and initiative of the source itself is meant to function essentially as indicator, literally a "pointer towards." The figure may be a messenger of the transcendent, whose very life becomes a dynamic figure, or it may be a divine appearance (theophany). Both are usually accompanied by a word from the most high, giving a glimpse into the depths of the mystery. According to Christian revelation, the Word made flesh, the ultimate figuration of the infinite source, ends in the silence of death, a total emptying out (kenosis).[1]

Even in the second instance, in which the appearance or the Word presents itself as an initiative of the transcendent source, the human interlocutor's inability to grasp all at once and to express adequately the inexhaustible sense that is offered in an overwhelming glimpse of the infinite mixes intellectual and moral darkness with the peculiar light of the divinely offered symbols. That is why the founding moment of any tradition, even the most limited, must of necessity be only the beginning of growth rather than the definitive positing of a set of answers to ultimate questions to be preserved, sense unaltered, on tablets of stone.

We shall consider first the easier kinds of founding experience, involving comprehending circumscribable figures, and then the rare but civilization-founding kind purporting to arise from an encounter with the Absolute. Each produces its own sorts of tensions that carry us along in the stream of existential time while erring and developing in truth.

The Figure Hides the Ground

No matter how dense an intrinsically circumscribable structure and hence rich in possibilities for unfolding sense, it is nevertheless always

1. See Hans Urs von Balthasar, *La gloire et la croix,* "The New Covenant," 3: 76–82.

only a part of a larger system. The larger, only liminally perceived, context functions as hidden ground for the understood figure. The ground holds not only the causes, but is part of the very meaning of the figure. By structure I mean any whole (figure) with parts that belong together in a way one can grasp. A structure, then, is an intelligible assemblage. In order to be able to comprehend such an assemblage as a whole, rather than as a *mixtum-gatherum* of randomly heaped-together items, one has to see that the parts do indeed belong together in a distinctive, intelligible way, whether static or dynamic.

Some processes are dynamic structures, such as the orderly, intelligible growth of an organism, which reveals the structuring operations of an organizing principle. Not all processes are structured, since some, like increasing population, are mere statistical aggregates of similar actions that are not intrinsically related but enough alike to produce an overall result, an ongoing change we are able to perceive. It becomes possible with either static or dynamic structures, once one has had an insight into the sense in which the parts (or moments) belong in the whole, to abstract the formal sense of this belonging and to symbolize it, thus holding it in the form of a general type of structure or process. This may occur even when an exemplar of such a type does not exist, for we can also make up forms imaginatively.

Given this ability to circumscribe structures in the world, it must be that reality itself is so constituted as to permit and indeed found such an operation. If that is so (and all experience confirms that it is) and if there are self-standing things and kinds of things and processes intelligible in themselves, why insist that there is always a ground, that every such circumscribing is also a taking out of context? If one is talking about pure formal intelligibilities, such as mathematical objects, there would seem at first glance to be no such problem. Upon reflection, however, this is not so. It should be noted that there are no pure triangles and no number *seven* in the world of experience. Moreover, even the most self-evident, freestanding mathematical notion has its hidden ground, the unthought presuppositions upon which it depends for its sense, which have only gradually come to be understood down through the history of mathematics—often with startling results, such as the discovery of all the possibilities opened by non-Euclidean geometry. Our belief in the self-standing and obvious reality of threeness and triangleness represents one of the last major, generally unquestioned stands of Platonism. Philosophers of mathematics and mathematicians are aware of this, but the average public school teacher continues to teach mathematics to children—hence, to the average layman—in this "Platonic" fashion.

When my son was barely eleven months old, he looked out of a streetcar window toward the showroom of a boat store and exclaimed in the only language he knew, "*Bateau!*" The only *bateau* he had until then known was a little plastic canoe he played with in the bath. A baby's mind had proven capable of recognizing a certain relationship between shape and function and then of seeing it in an object, far from water, larger by a magnitude of ten thousand, and different in shape. The works of Piaget and his students abound in equally astonishing examples. The interesting thing is not just the mind's ability to have such insights and to achieve such abstractions, but the makeup of a reality which founds such possibilities in truth.

The ability of the human mind to recognize types of structure, static and dynamic, to abstract from the concrete circumstances in which the formal type is first recognized, and to relate and recombine the types enables it to rise out of the flow of temporal experience into an imaginative timelessness. This timelessness of formal insight fascinated the Platonists and distracted the search for truth away from the dynamic, from thinking adequately about possibility. None of these fixed notions is able to stand on its own absolutely as an intelligible whole; there is no concept without connections beyond itself, with "nothing more to be said about it," as Hegel saw so well.[2] But while such autonomy (*Selbständigkeit*) is partial, it is also a defensible, meaningful, useful characteristic, as far as it goes. The kidney has its ultimate sense only in the larger cardiovascular system, yet it is certainly a subsystem *sui generis* that can be understood in its basic function of filtering.

Obviously, the degree of *Selbständigkeit* enjoyed by a bodily organ is less than that of the individual human being, who nevertheless, while capable of self-direction, is dependent upon a society, and draws air and sustenance from nature. But if the thing expressed does indeed enjoy a

2. Hegel shows this from the very start of the *Logic*. To be sure, he was in too much of a hurry to demonstrate the place of all things within the all-comprehending structure of Being, what he termed the "Absolute Idea." This reduced the incentive for him to give full weight to the various degrees of *Selbständigkeit* to all the things that in ordinary experience enjoy stability relative to our normal, human, *ek-sistential* time scale. Hegel not only overstated our ability to show all the dialectical relationships, he played down the considerable reliability of slowly changing things and the intelligible abstractions made by the human intellect.

degree of relative autonomy, the expression is true in itself, as far as it goes. If its relative autonomy is mistakenly thought to say more than the perception authorizes, the fault lies with the one judging. Depending on the intention behind the question that has given rise to the answer, a given expression may go far enough to found adequately a limited course of action within a definite context or to satisfy a particular need to know.

If the meaningfulness of a less than absolute *Selbständigkeit* is justified, why insist on the potential deceptiveness necessarily accompanying any founding breakthrough? Since a breakthrough is necessarily only a beginning, it ought to invite us to seek more experience, but our expressions of the insight tend to seem final and unquestionable. Figures tend to close completely, becoming dogmatic and thereby effectively hiding ground instead of pointing the way toward it. This happens because of the demands of action. Action has something terribly definite about it—either you do or you do not, and if you do, you either turn left or right. So we often need definite answers, more definite than the data frequently allow.

One cannot perceive ground directly because, both perceptually and imaginatively, we always focus on a figure. Figures provide the only hint of their grounds, of the contexts of which they are part. The effort to comprehend a context directly only produces a larger figure, a structure, if only of a setting, with its own still more comprehensive ground. The dialectic between figures, each offering only profiles and hence part of the truth, provides by implication glimpses of ground; the dialectic of the figures points to the larger contexts within which they are only moments. Profiles always suggest more, both spatially and temporally. In spatial terms the facade of a house implies the interior and other faces. Temporally, each figure shows itself to be in essence the product of something else and of a set of conditions, figurable by another set of conceptual determinations. The house is the product of architect and builder and is the result of an analysis of market conditions, among other factors.

At the same time, every profile also hides ground for a simple reason. An expressed figure is what has now become intelligible. It draws all attention to itself and away from the larger, still obscure issues which as ground are lurking on the horizons of awareness. The figure also distracts attention from the as yet unresolved and unexplored internal articulations lying below the surface of understanding.

Often the unthought presuppositions and the possibility of alternate explanations or competing models will have to be advanced by others outside the tradition that is handing on the symbols in which the figures are captured and expressed. Our interests are heavily invested in the symbols of our traditions. Disciples become narrowly acculturated into thinking only in terms of already acquired symbols, and their methods do not encourage them to probe beyond their limits. In seeing something clearly, one can also fail utterly to appreciate what he does not see directly or even to acknowledge that there is more to be seen. He may become so comfortable with a way of viewing things suited to an institutional role, how he lives his life, that he may be terrified of hearing a new point of view that may cause him to put matters in question and perhaps change an aspect of his life.

An interesting example from the practical realm is given by Martin Buber. Theodore Herzl, obsessed by the insight that only the recovery of a homeland would allow the Jews to become again a people like other people rather than a marginal alien presence in European society, proceeded to develop his grand scheme for *aliyah* to Palestine as though it were an empty territory. In *Der Judenstaat,* though he descends to such details as the desirability of the seven-hour workday, he never once mentions the word *Arab.* Buber relates that Herzl's friend Nordau, having just realized the terrible fact that others were going to be disputing the territory of the Jewish homeland, rushed into Herzl's office, shouting "Herzl, the dream is over! There are Arabs there!" The story may well be apocryphal, but it serves as an excellent symbol for the point we are here considering.

The internal clarifications and transformations forced upon the Zionist project by alien forces competing for the same space is a paradigm of the kind of evolution through which every living tradition must pass as it is obliged, little by little, to discover more of its ground. The appropriator has to take into account the compressive pressures of the competition working in each synchronic situation, marking each epoch. The genuineness and richness of the privileged founding experience of Being can only be inferred by criticizing the ability of its official, handed-down expression to inspire adaptation, continued growth, ever-deepening insight without the need to renounce or to reformulate drastically the initial vision.

Wisdom demands that we avoid overemphasis on either the negative or the positive aspects of this finitude. To fail to see in the elaborated treasure of symbols of a great tradition an irreplaceable possession, to emphasize only the dogmatism that follows from trying to make such an inheritance into a source of total security would be to indulge in angelism. Such a sanguine view—whether in favor or opposed—fails to ask what truth may be in the tradition's symbolism. Recall our finitude: we see things as they are, but partially and only in profile. The critical work of seeing what *is* there, in context and against what ground, requires an openness to possibility that makes knowing the scope of the field in advance unrealistic. On the other hand, to fail to recognize that some formulations represent perennially valid insights into structures that are stable within the time frame of ordinary human history or that they represent insights into formal intelligibilities with an *a priori* truth is to invite the mistaken notion that everything is always in every respect open to revision.

Encounter with the Ground of Grounds

The point of the mystic's *via negativa* is his awareness of the incomprehensibility of the Absolute, the ground of grounds: no human predication can capture finally the source of all possibility. Mystical technique calls for an emptying out of all figures. The whole world of experience is recognized as inadequate for representing the ineffable. Thinkers from Plato through St. Thomas to Heidegger have recognized, however, that the figure is also the way into the ground. This is certainly evident in the succession of philosophical and theophanic figures down through the long history of Being's revelation-dissimulation of itself in the occidental tradition. There is no figureless way. The condition for the possibility of a *via negativa* is a *via positiva*.

To be sure, each figure has the potential to become an illusion if taken to express the Absolute exhaustively. Nor can we discover some sort of definitive revelation of the Absolute simply by gathering up all the figures through which it has allowed itself to be expressed. Only by attempting ever anew to gather up the hints of the hidden "unthought" in what has been expressly thought can we "dwell in proximity to It" (*in der Nähe des Seins weilen*), enjoying hints or glimpses of it that Heidegger calls *Winke*.[3] Only by taking "the step back behind" the whole history

---

3. Heidegger, *Sein und Zeit* (Tübingen: Niemeyer, 1953), ¶22. Eastern mysticism, with its persistence in emptying the mind of all figures, stands in contrast to Christian mysticism.

of Being's revealing-dissimulating of itself will the dynamic relationship of Being to man begin to be hinted at, in all its richness and mystery.

But for those who believe in revelation, that is not all there is to the story. According to the longest and most fertile Western traditions—Judaism, Christianity, and Islam—the beginning was not always a case of an inspired thinker's breaking through to a new depth of ground, caught fleetingly in a complex new figure, a reaching toward transcendence from below.[4] The assertion of all Abrahamic faith is that from the depths of the Absolute came, to the encounter with the prophet, an unexpected, incomprehensible initiative, not an inspired intuition on the prophet's part, but a call and a presence through the gracious offering of a divinely chosen and ordained figure, a gift of the transcendent from above. This divine icon, an authorized and unsurpassable Gestalt of the Divine, would be a rallying point for all future contemplation, an invincible center of focus resistant to all *Aufhebungen* ("reversals," "canceling-outs," or "higher syntheses"). Indeed, in a supreme instance, this figure would be no mere symbol or story, but an acting presence dwelling among us as a living teacher—not just a truth, but a moment in history come to speak as the truth, the truth that is the Way and the Life itself, God acting as His own exegete. The revelation offered through Moses, Christ, and Muhammad comes in divinely guided events, manifestations of divine life in our midst. In the case of Jesus, Christians claim for this continuing mystical presence a perfection that cannot be surpassed.

Whereas the merely human thought-figure expressing an intuition of the divine is illusory if mistaken for an adequate expression and is explicitly recognized as inadequate by the mystic, the witnesses report that the living divine presence (to Moses on Sinai or Isaiah in the sanctuary of the Temple, in the person of Jesus of Nazareth or in the *ruach* of the Pentecost) is no merely human expression, but the *kavodh,* the *shekhinah* of the most high, the divine glory shining about us. The symbol representing this experience—a sign inspired by the divinity—stands for and invokes the memory of that presence or, as with Christ in His Church, continues it. Each theophany (and the God-inspired *symbolon* which commemorates it) is a unique and unsurpassable grace of God. Just as for

---

4. Western Christianity is, of course, the direct development of Divine breakthroughs in the Abrahamic line. Here, however, I am concerned with the relation of all of these as branches of one type of tradition of revelation. Obviously, Judaism, Eastern Christianity, and Islam have also had their impact upon the course of the West.

Christians the fullness of the revelation in the concrete event that is the Christ will never be surpassed, so Muhammad is the seal of the prophets for Muslims, and the Koran contains the fullness of what Allah has graciously ordained to reveal through the angel Gabriel about himself. The revelation to Moses remains eternally valid. For those who believe in the event of these revelations, there can be no progress beyond Moses, Jesus, or the Koran.

It is interesting to note, in passing, that Heidegger himself is loath to reduce the manifestations of the holy to figures of thought. He treats the holy for the most part as a dimension of Being, of the "fourfold" (*das Geviert*), preferring to pass by in silence the great theophanies which have formed and shaken the Western tradition more than any formulation of Heraclitus or Hölderlin. Is this reverential or does he think that with the "death of God" the details of His manifestations have become uninteresting? Only the Greek gods receive Heidegger's serious attention, and while as figures they are to be remembered, they are also to be surpassed. As Eric Voegelin has shown, appropriation of the Western tradition cannot proceed responsibly in silence regarding the Hebrew, Christian and Muslim experience. As we shall see in the second part of this volume, the question confronting the appropriator is this: What is the critical thinker to do in the face of such claims, the effects of which are massively present in the world situation, and which the Christian tradition itself presents as a stumbling block? The question will be addressed directly in a later volume.[5]

For someone in a tradition of revelation like those of Judaism, Christianity, and Islam, the question of illusion is more an affair of faithlessness. Illusion for the believer occurs when one has been given the grace to see the light revealed in the divinely vouchsafed figures and then through moral failure has turned away or deformed them into idols. That this can happen is no surprise to the man of faith, for "even the just man sins seven times a day."[6] Even the greatest saint is unable to sustain for himself

5. If Heidegger does think the "withdrawal of the God" and the "fulfillment" (*Vollendung*) of metaphysics (included as little more than a chapter of that field) render the theophanies irrelevant, then he has committed a tragic mistake. In setting the theophanies aside as matters of faith (*Glaubensachen*), he may be indicating that appropriative thinking about them must not be metaphysical. But he himself did nothing to show the way into the proximity of the holy as invited by the grace of faith.

6. Proverbs 24:16.

the intensity of his openness to the divine presence, and after a time the Almighty, Jesus, or Gabriel withdraws. As Martin Buber insists, even the most satisfying *Ich-Du* ("I-you") experience comes to an end, to be held thereafter only in a pale memory, inevitably in *Es* ("it") form.[7] From such memories however, we can return to the direct presence of the *Du*.

If the founding experience reveals the presence and the promise of an ultimate reality which itself takes initiatives, calling a people into existence and setting them in motion along a way leading to a designated promised land, then one is dealing with a reality that is less to be appropriated than appropriating. God chooses Abraham, calls out this people, designates the destination, and above all leads the people through his prophets. Each Christian is individually called in baptism. A task remains for those who are called. It consists in opening their minds and hearts to the call, accepting the divine leadership, following on the way. Rather than essentially a call to theoretical understanding, it is the mutual giving-accepting-appropriating of love. It is rather like that joining of wills that occurs in any association, except that the call to join the Kingdom comes from on high and with an unsurpassable authority, both implying a condescension by the Most High and demanding a surrender like no other.

In all this, the Abrahamic tradition insists, the mystery of grace is central. That is why Christ links truth and life. This is where the problem begins for those seeking universal wisdom, the problem of the particularism of the traditions of revelation, particularly marked in the "hard" traditions. First, it is given to a tiny number in the whole history of mankind to experience directly the divine presence in the founding theophanies—a few prophets, a few apostles, a few companions of the prophet. Second, it is not given to all to hear (though billions have) those who are sent forth—*hoi apostoloi,* the prophetic teachers of the Jews, the immams of Islam—to witness the *e-vent.* Third, not all those who hear are moved to accept the witness. The traditions of revelation do not view that as a perfidy or even a lack on their part, but as a mystery of grace and election. Even among those who believe upon hearing, there are enormous differences in the degree of loving appropriation, and there are painful differences in understanding. There are even many apostasies.

The dilemma facing the person who does not believe in theophany and in such intimate love relationships with God but who recognizes the

---

7. Martin Buber, *I and Thou* (Edinburgh: T. and T. Clark, 1937), 8–9.

challenge of appropriating these influential traditions is perhaps not as unusual as at first appears. The problem of coming to know foreign traditions that claim one must live them to understand them challenges all appropriators. Even the man embracing a tradition of faith finds himself confronted by the obstacle of alien faiths, even though he is open at least to the idea of revelation. While trying to understand and to respect what we can, one must withhold final judgment as to the nature and genuineness of the most intimate experiences of others when they remain a closed book to us. The intellectual life, the pursuit of wisdom, requires humility of all.

It is disturbing to the scientific person to know that there may be important human phenomena which he perhaps does not understand very well. But is this really so surprising? If these traditions are centered in a kind of experience in which one must participate to begin to understand, is this so different from claiming that there are limits to the ability of the man who has never played an instrument very well to understand what it is to perform a great piece of music, or from admitting that the person who has never loved will understand little or nothing of this fundamental human reality? It might be answered that one can always decide to learn to play an instrument, and one can always learn to love. But is that always true? It is not given to all to enjoy intense, intimate friendship, and musical genius is rare.

Authenticity demands that we become as aware as we can of our own limits, of what we do not understand. This is always difficult. The pursuit of wisdom has been considered from its first thematization by the philosophers and the authors of the Wisdom Books of the Old Testament the most difficult of challenges, demanding discipline and special gifts. Each advance in understanding one tradition, of whatever type, gives us something more to bring to the dialogue with others. Beyond that, one can only strive to be receptive to all that is. The freedom discovered at the heart of Being means that none of us elects to appropriate everything available to us; nor, perhaps, are we elected to do it.

The Kinds of Truth

I have been emphasizing a plurality of kinds of truth. Combining radically different kinds of experience of very different kinds of entities into one wisdom, a global view of being is not something that goes without saying. I admit that in placing this emphasis more on the many than on the one I am seeking to guard, right from the beginning, against reductionism. What is important at this point is merely to recognize that an emphasis upon plurality is more likely to reveal the existence of an unpresumed unity than an emphasis upon unity is to reveal an unreduced, real plurality.

Different kinds of traditions evolve different kinds of symbols to express the distinctive sorts of truth they hand on. The moment has come to address in more detail this question of the quite different senses of truth to be found in each of four kinds of tradition because this affects the ways in which they are passed on and how they relate to one another. Understanding how the different kinds of tradition pass on differently the various kinds of truth is a necessary first step toward describing the demands of the wisdom we seek. In examining each genus, we shall relate a particular kind of truth to a kind of expression, and then, since the issue here is the passing on and preserving of truth, address the question of what forms would be faithful to the vision and which would deviate from it.

The Truth of the Work of Art

The sense in which a sonata of Bach is true is quite different from the sense in which the mechanics of Newton are true. The inspired poetry of the prophet transmitting the experience of the divine presence is true in a way closer to the successful work of art than to philosophic propositions couched in terms of closed figures. Analogy in natural theology is conceptually closer to the evocative symbols of revelation than to the formal figures of a mathematical formula.

One might question whether it is advisable to speak of the work of art as true when one does not mean its reference (the sense in which the film *Mon Oncle Antoine* is faithful in its portrayal of rural life in Quebec, for instance), especially as an abstract painting or a string quartet may have no reference to any recognizable thing. The sonata posits, even by implication, no definite proposition whatever. For the sonata, true means *echt*, in the sense that it is "the real thing." What does it mean to say of a work of art that it is genuine (*echt*), or conversely, that it is phony (un-*echt*)? What do we mean when we say of a new building that it is a piece of real architecture and of another that it is not, or when we call a painting pretentious? It is not easy to describe in general terms, but it is that which entices artists to perform it or to imitate it, to take up its new challenge and grow in the greatness opened by it. The work of art is expected to *dis-cover* new Being-possibility, offering new insight into reality (including the internal, spiritual reality of the artist himself and his lived horizons of experience) and adding to the arsenal of expressions with which a culture celebrates the world.

At its greatest, art reaches the essence of a classical situation by becoming a statement that is unsurpassable within its own order (Racine's *Phèdre,* the Parthenon, the *Chaconne* from Bach's Second Violin Partita), exhausting the possibility of the genre. We can go back to admire such works and draw sustenance there, but artists cannot directly build upon them with the hope of surpassing them. It is as though certain figures by their perfection open us more directly onto the ground itself. Instead of attracting attention to themselves, they admit the listener or spectator into a new and unsurpassable region. One wants to return to this privileged gateway rather than try to construct one's own. Architects could develop the Lever House's discovery of gracious curtain-wall construction, and we may witness the progeny of the Haydn symphonies. But who would even think of trying to go a step beyond Homer or to better Beethoven's Opus 127 Quartet?

This mysterious ability of the greatest art works to invoke the unsurpassable is similar to the opening out toward the transcendent by divinely inspired figures through revelation. Here again Hegel failed to capture the sense of such a movement beyond the dialectical interweaving of notions, the dynamic movement of which reveals, according to him, the Absolute Idea. In the breakthroughs of the greatest works of art, it is precisely their power to indicate the incomprehensible, the "Encompassing" (*das Umgreifende*), as Karl Jaspers calls it, which is mysterious and instantaneous.[8]

But to what is a work of art true? Basically, it is true to itself. This means more than harmony and balance of all its parts in the whole. It means fulfilling its express function successfully, achieving its essence fully: the *dis-covery* within itself of a kind of being. Ideally, it should reveal possibilities as they have never been before, achieving a perfection in its particular order that radiates inexhaustibly.

---

8. Karl Jaspers, *Reason and Existence,* trans. William Earle (New York: Noonday Press, 1957), 52.

It is this new radiating-opening that founds not only new possibility but new cultural needs. The epoch-opening but less than classic work grants a new vision of what is possible; from the interior depths of the artist's soul interacting with the mystery of his chosen material, it opens a new way for exploration; and it offers at least the beginnings of a new language. Therefore, it cries out for exploration, for fuller development, for communion. The first Doric temples were like that. But when the summit was reached in the classic temples of Pericles' time, there was nothing more to say in that particular order: with that vocabulary, beauty, and harmony, grandeur itself stood before the contemplating Greek, as much as it is possible through a limited thing. Homer had imitators, most mercifully lost or forgotten; only the *Aeneid* can stand comparison, an audacious *tour de force* that won Virgil everlasting fame. Indeed, it is not just the dimensions of the *Ring des Niebelungen* that prohibit its imitation.

But even the classics, however successful they may be in evoking the ground of grounds, remain human creations, figures bearing the marks of their time and of the souls of their creators, creatures in a world evolved. It is anachronistic to imitate the Parthenon or to resuscitate the pseudo-mythology of the nineteenth century *à la* Richard Wagner. On that side of their being, even the classics are dated. The divinely authored figures of revelation, on the other hand, are never dated—the Burning Bush is not typical of thirteenth-century symbols, nor is the Baptism of Jesus in the Jordan what you would expect in Mithraic times. They are not susceptible to successful imitation either. Works of pseudo-revelation attempt imitation, but with pitiful results (the Apocryphal Gospels are a good example, as are Masonic liturgies).

Encounters with the Divine

Some religious traditions, the less "hard," are founded in experiences closer to the second type of tradition, that of philosophical intuition. Journeys of self-discovery and methods for emptying out the self (Nirvana) until the ultimate principle sustaining us from within is blocked by no obstacle are experiences of Being as ground that are discoverable deep in the soul. Toward this "no thing" the disciple is guided by the teachings of great masters, much as the philosopher or the scientist guides his students toward the correct grasp of the universally valid structures he has sought to express in new symbols.

Why then does a tradition like Buddhism merit being called a religion rather than a philosophy? Because not only does it, like metaphysics, seek to confront the ground, but it also flowers into a way of life—complete with ritual, disciplines of ascesis, even monasteries for spiritual development—and holds out a devout morality to be practiced. We are reminded of the Neoplatonic Academy, which was not dissimilar in the way it functioned but was rather more religious than a modern philosophy department, or the Academy of Plato himself. Where philosophy passes over into an institutionalized way of living, it becomes truly religious.

But revealed religion claims to be grounded in a privileged experience of Being with an initiative that comes from the divine personality. For this surprising moment of grace there is no preparation. The transcendent is not experienced as an abstract principle but confronts the prophet as an infinite intelligence and will—a person. Its surprising intrusion from beyond into the sphere of human experience demands of the one confronted a faith—a confidence, a free commitment—not to be found in the more philosophical religious traditions exploring the depths of the soul. The prophets' resistance to the call is a signal of this otherness and personal concreteness.

The vision held up to the prophet explicitly includes a command for action that—though it has implications for an overall vision of things and therefore helps to ground a theology—is not intended as a science but as a *praxis,* an affair of love and a way of salvation. Nor is it all interior: the ragbag confederation of Hebrew tribes becomes the historical Israel under the Almighty's prophetic leadership, following him to the conquest of Canaan;[9] the apostles follow Christ by taking the good news of his Kingdom to the far corners of the world, becoming the historic Church; the soldiers of Islam, submitted to Allah's will (the meaning of the past participle, *muslim*), ride across the desert to conquer all for Allah, to forge under the Prophet's inspiration a people, the *umma* (the faithful, or elect) of Islam. That is why such a commanding presence resembles in its founding effect the will-act bringing about an association. Through acceptance of the command, one becomes a member of the community, the "people of God" with whom one marches under God's leadership.

9. The confederation of Hebrew tribes, which formed the new people of Israel after the Sinai experience of Moses, faithfully recalled the extraordinary privileged experience of Divine Being that lay at its origin. Not every people recalls a founding experience and none so remarkable a one as this.

Hence the teaching cannot be disassociated from the historical circumstances of its revelation and the way the resulting divine authority is transmitted.[10]

From all this it is clear that truth in theology differs from truth in philosophy or positive science. The theologian embraces from the start and with the intention of never "going back on them" the divinely given symbols manifesting in their unique way the Ground of grounds, who has chosen the time and manner of the mediation of its saving revelation to finite man. Instead of producing a conceptual scheme constituting an all-embracing, vast but nonetheless closed figure, like those of Parmenides or Einstein, the theologian strives to express what his faith presents of the commanding, incomprehensible Ground in a conceptual scheme as open, "transcending," "analogous" as possible.[11]

The tradition of faith can never reach back beyond the original revelation. Instead it deepens its appreciation of the internal articulations—the relations between finite things and individual moments—within this graciously granted all-illumining and enduringly open horizon. Even so radical a transformation as St. Albert's and St. Thomas's switch from Neoplatonic to Aristotelian metaphysics to articulate their theology takes place within the fundamental apostolic, patristic, and finally Augustinian horizons developed within those originally opened toward the transcendent divine source in a unique way by Jesus' teaching.

Such has been the way of truth in the Jewish, the Catholic, and the Islamic traditions. In the Catholic tradition, for instance, the apostolic teachings, which constitute the expressed founding vision growing out of the privileged experience of Being in the Jesus event, provide an ultimate set of interpretative horizons within which any advance in theological formulation and discovery must present itself if it is to be orthodox, that is, fully faithful to the truth. There can be no surpassing the apostolic teaching, or the Koran or the Pentateuch in the way Newton surpasses Copernicus and Plato can be seen to go beyond the *aporia* of Parmenides and Heraclitus. The revelation is normative. The truth is sought by remaining true to the theophanic revelation of the Ground of

10. For Judaism and Islam, a different language is appropriate, but the underlying ideas of prophetic event, content of prophetic messages, witness, and broadcast are present.

11. Plato the theologian strives likewise to point us toward that which to us is absolutely incomprehensible. But the sense of the source as creative, wise, and providential is much stronger in the Christian reflections.

grounds in the person, the teaching, and the acts of Jesus Christ; in the Lord's commands to Moses; or in the angel's dictations to the Prophet.[12] Nor can the patristic teaching ever become simply outmoded any more than the teachings of later prophets of the Old Testament or the Hadith of Islam can. The core of the apostles' main theological insight or the example of the Prophet and his companions is to be respected, recovered, taken up perhaps into new expressive schemes that must be molded to the demands of orthodox formulations or to the vision contained in the most universally accepted Hadith. That is the only way orthodox theology can be done.

This sense in all branches of the Abrahamic traditions of the fullness of revelation or "the sealing of the prophesy," as Muslims express it,[13] repels the modern scientific spirit, which has as a central dogma of natural faith the possibility of unlimited progress in every order of mind. We encounter here a fatal clash of faiths. A philosopher of history like Voegelin (who is never to be confused with a Christian theologian) will be tempted to relativize every claim of revelation and to insist that revelation is not closed—there will certainly be other inspirations to come. Such a move effectively removes the stumbling block and paves the way for universal science.

But it achieves this, the believer will protest, in an unscientific way, by turning its back without good reason on what the Jewish, Christian, or Muslim man of faith claims: that God has granted a saving revelation to a particular people, destined to be brought by them to all men. This is the sticking point for the man of universal reason. For the man of faith, the Font of the Living Word is the beginning and end of all wisdom. Faith seeks understanding, as Augustine said, but the formula cannot be reversed, as Voegelin would have it: intellect does not found faith, that is, relativize it through its subsumption into a scientific wisdom. Such reductionism, in the theologian's view, turns out to be a sophisticated rationalism despite its willingness to respect symbols of transcendence.

12. The root of the word *truth* is the Old English *treowe*, which (like the German *treu*) means "faithful," a thought-provoking connection for us here. Heidegger, in *Vom Wesen der Wahrheit*, develops the sense of *Wahrheit* as preserving (*wahren*) "what is." In the pursuit of authenticity, which requires adaptation to changing circumstances, this creativity, the preservation of what is unsurpassable, must be reconciled with the innovations that have become necessary.

13. Muhammad, as the Seal of the Prophets, is proclaimed as the completion of the message.

They are fine, replies the theologian sarcastically, so long as they do not reveal something to which the philosopher must submit (again, the meaning of the word *Islam*). The great Voegelin of *Israel and Revelation* was already just ambiguous enough that, when he revealed himself in the time of *The Ecumenic Age* to be a poor *Muslim,* careful students of his thought, especially the believers, were not all that surprised. The challenge of the stumbling block is so daunting that it causes trouble for even the most respectful of "scientific" thinkers.

Remaining faithful to the founding experiences of Being involves, consequently, distinctive approaches for each of the two types of religion, the philosophical-mystical and the "hard" revelational.[14] For the philosophical-mystical religion, fidelity consists in handing down the method of discovery, along with a vocabulary of symbols as well as cult and ascetic practices, from generation to generation, from Master to disciple. The truth is manifest when the disciple, after immense personal effort to perfect himself through the method, becomes an "enlightened one." Although there is much an enlightened one can tell us about how it stands with Being, the only interesting thing, ultimately, for him, as a religious person, is *to be* (or should we say consciously to *cease to be*?).

To simplify the contrast with revealed religion, let us concentrate on Christianity as our example. When Christ declared to his disciples, "I am the way, the truth and the life," he made it clear that the Kingdom is likewise not primarily a set of dogmas, but, like Buddhism, a way of living. This way does not lead, however, into one's self as it does with Plato or the Buddha, whose followers may follow a method (*meta ton hodon,* "along a way") for removing egoism as a block to an adequate identification with ultimate reality. Rather, the way leads out of the self through the Christ, in whom the personal God emptied Himself (*kenosis*) and who achieved our redemption through His emptying-out obedience to the Father unto death. This way leads to love of oneself as child of God and to loving interaction with others, hence to peoplehood under the inspiring guidance of the Spirit, when "there shall be but one fold and one shepherd" in an existential, social state of affairs, partly in this world, partly in the next, the realization of the Kingdom of God.

14. In choosing not to follow the terminology of the early Heidegger, I obviously have certain convictions about how the ultimate source reveals itself that are quite distinct from those of the German thinker. It would be pointless to pause here to pursue the question of the differences, a topic I will address in subsequent volumes.

The Church does not understand itself simply as an institution invented to assure that teaching about the Way is passed on from generation to generation.[15] As the Mystical Body of Christ, it is meant to be the vehicle to the truth. Its goal is the fulfillment of the ultimate Being-potential of all its members by uniting them perfectly with reality, grounded in the divine will. Truth, therefore, is a living unity within this body—communion in a full sense, the loving, hoping faithfulness to Christ as the Word, centered in charity, Eucharist, and prayer. Dogmatic expressions of this state of affairs are inspired conscious grasps of the structure of reality as illumined by the collective, living experience of this community animated by the Holy Spirit.

Faithfulness for the Christian, then, is simply being one with the mind and heart of the true Church and acting in consequence. Dangerous as the distinction between the institutional Church and the Mystical Body is, some such distinction has to be maintained. In the so-called Church militant, a sinful humanity operates within the Mystical Body as its most visible but unpurified manifestation. One can easily say the unenlightened preaching of a parish priest is not the Church, that a flat editorial in a diocesan newspaper cannot be taken as an expression of the mind of the Church, that pogroms in the Middle Ages carried out by Catholics were contrary to the very essence of Christian teaching. Nonetheless, people inevitably see such things as manifestations of the Church, not without some justification. Yet God cannot be defiled. How does the Christian cope with this enormous dilemma, the Christian form of the hypocrisy challenge?

The Christian would reply that those aspects of the worldly social body we call the Church that manifest the living teaching in its unity and goodness are fully and unequivocally of the Mystical Body. Individual acts of deviance, whether an immoral act, a faulty teaching, or any patent organizational inadequacy leading to injustice, is simply not of Christ. Thus, while sociologically of the institutional Church, such sins are theologically or mystically outside the Church no matter who commits them, even if it is the Pope.

The problems, however, lie between the extremes of Church holiness and bad human acts. This massive and hierarchical institution exists under varied conditions and with a multiplicity of substructures, includ-

15. I oversimplify here to introduce a difficult issue that I will elaborate in a future work.

ing dioceses, ecclesiastical offices, religious orders, organs of publication, schools, and hospitals. Each has its own inertia, its own center of gravity. While they are inhabited by Christians often attempting to conform their minds to the spirit of the Church, there is inevitably a certain centrifugal pull to these distinctive organizations, each tending to some extent to go its own way without regard to the center. Nevertheless, teaching is transmitted by these organizations, each to some extent in its own fashion, though all may wish to be orthodox.

A serious problem of fidelity poses itself for each of these distinctive subtraditions. Down through the ages, the infidelities of some have provoked the great crises which have wracked Christianity: the selling of indulgences, for example, was a serious infidelity on the part of one sector of the Church.[16] Though the main abuse was largely confined to Germany, the roots of the evil were to be found in certain widespread excesses of the late Middle Ages when many institutions of the Church had become so entangled with those of the feudal system that the dismantling of feudalism brought catastrophic conflicts for the Christian Church. The unity of that existential social reality was destroyed, and the consequences for European civilization weigh heavily on us to this day.

The other side of the coin, however, is that to the extent that a Christian community—whatever its hostility to the conception of a central body (its separation from Rome, as Catholics perceive it)—remains faithful to the living teaching, the Second Vatican Council affirms that it is included in the Mystical Body even though its participation in the truth is not total.[17] The holiness of the Mystical Body does not constitute the whole Christian tradition; it is only that part of it which is

16. Jacques Maritain, in *De l'église du Christ* (Paris: Desclée de Brouwer, 1970), distinguishes between the Church as a mystical entity, the divine *Corpus mysticum,* and the "personnel of the Church," the latter being capable of sin and illusion (see Joseph W. Evans's translation, *On the Church of Christ: The Person of the Church and Her Personnel* [South Bend: Notre Dame University Press, 1973], 135–51). If that distinction is allowed, one must separate the truth of the Mystical Body from the ungenuine acts of certain personnel of the Church when undertaking the critical recovery of truth in the tradition. The fathers of the Oecumenical Council, Vatican II, appear to admit some such distinction. For instance, in speaking of Christian disunity, they ascribe the blame "to persons of one or the other party" (*Decretum de Oecumenismo, 3*).

17. "Nevertheless, justified by the faith received in baptism, incorporated in Christ, they are by right called Christians, and the sons of the Catholic Church recognize them as brothers in Christ" (*Decretum de Oecumenismo, 3*).

faithful to God's express intention. To the Christian, the Mystical Body is not a sociological entity, but an object of faith. It is "Emmanuel," God-With-Us. It is the fruit of a promise, the promise of divine fidelity to the people: "the gates of Hell will not prevail against it."[18] The tradition finds the wheat mixed with many cockles. Both grain and cockle are to be allowed to carry on and do their best to produce, entangled, to be separated only at the Last Judgment. Meanwhile the poor witness given by Christians is itself untruth, turning people away from truth and the full union in living communion with Christ. But faithfulness, for the Christian, consists in holding onto Christ's promise and believing that, despite massive human failing, a current of sanctity keeps alive Christ's presence in the world and thus sustains the truth.

The task of the participant in a tradition of revelation who is pursuing authenticity is first and foremost to distinguish in the People of Israel, in the Church, or in the *umma* of Islam the divine from the sinful will, the truth from unfaithfulness which produces living untruth. While the theology of church may not be developed in just this way in the other Abrahamic traditions, Orthodox Judaism and Islam each have their similar conceptions of how faithfulness to Torah or to the Koran constitutes effective membership in *Am Israel* or in the *umma*. Theoretical truth is here clearly linked to faithful practice in union with the People of God seeking to do God's will. When we return to the question of stumbling-block, we shall have to face, among other issues, the fact that there are three conflicting claims as to who this people is: Israel? the Church? the *umma*? For the nonbeliever, this very conflict may seem reason enough to reject the whole idea.

The Handing Down

The Genuine and the Good

I propose to consolidate now what we have ascertained about genuineness from reflection on examples from the four genera of traditions, and then to situate genuineness in relation to the more traditional notion of goodness. What is at issue is the truth that guides traditions, giving consistency to human existence and permanence to our orientations, the foundations of all good order. I am reminded, however, that good order

18. Matthew 16:18.

must reflect reality. To prepare the way, I make several distinctions drawing on a theory of knowledge and Being evidently objectivistic.

Earlier I introduced the term *genuine* and its converse, *ungenuine* or *illusory*, to supplement the traditional terms *good* and *bad* because these have obscured a useful distinction. *Good* has been used both as a synonym for genuine in the sense of an appropriate response to a particular situation or need, but it has also been used for those enduring structures of being and human nature expressed as principles valid in all situations. An adequate expression of the good in that sense is at all times genuine, and an ideal which is an appropriate response to the need to realize the good remains valid under changing situations.

The intentionality of consciousness penetrates through three distinguishable layers of significance: (1) the utterance of the expression (*expresses*, "presses out," into the public domain through incarnation in the matter—sound or written character—that carries the symbol); (2) the experience itself; and (3) the state of soul, external object, or structure of being that is experienced. To judge an expression to be genuine, then, is to make a judgment about that expression's success in conveying the sense of the real contextual situation it tries to bring to light. Every successful expression will therefore direct our attention to that which it expresses, properly understood in its setting and in full recognition of its context. We have already seen an example of this in working out the difference between a tradition of revelation and its operative institutions, which required that we begin from the acts performed by adherents of the tradition in their roles under an institutional tradition of association.

As with every kind of judgment, the issue of how we know it is true, the question of evidence, can only be dealt with concretely. There can be a general science of kinds of evidence, such as that attempted by Husserl, but in the final analysis every show of evidence is a concrete affair. In each disputed case, accusations of genuineness and illusion have to be adjudicated by discussions of the evidence. Attention is called through discussion—a further cooperative manipulation of symbols—to whatever is purported "to show itself," "it" being this *manifestare* that motivates ultimate decision about the genuineness of the expression at issue.

The limitedness of every experience and expression of being does not mean that every expression should be considered partly illusory. *Illusoriness, ungenuineness,* and *mythology* are terms I would reserve for more patent flights from the constraints of reality than the fundamental ontological kind of error attendant upon all human efforts to express the things we perceive. I shall use *genuine* to refer to the application of a vision to a particular situation. *Good,* on the other hand, will designate the vision of an enduring feature of Being, the essence of some kind of thing, including some essential feature of man—anything then having a universal applicability and hence capable of being applied in many, if not every, conceivable situation.

As a foretaste of the usefulness of this distinction, consider this humble truth: a good tradition in which enduring principles are well expressed could be misapplied (thus be without genuineness) by agents who mis-read a concrete situation to which they attempt to apply an ideal. They could well be authentic persons—they would then be responsible in their efforts to grasp the sense of the ideals for the realization of which they are working; and they may be persons of integrity as a result—the hypocrisy in their case is minimal. But they could also be mistaken in their estimate of a concrete situation and hence make poor decisions because of the lack of genuineness in their judgments of the facts of the case. The subsequent discussion will show the utility of making these distinctions and marking them in our terminology.

Good and Bad, Faithful and Unfaithful

At one end of the spectrum of possibilities, visualize a good tradition handed down through faithful institutions genuinely responding to each successive phase of an evolving situation. Such perpetuation depends ultimately on the good individual, the person of good faith (hence of minimal hypocrisy) who, working together in the corresponding institution with other good people, consistently tries to live up to this vision of the good as confirmed and enlarged by his own experience.

This does not of itself make him authentic. To exist authentically, the individual must be aware of his responsibility in taking up the challenges held out by tradition and of his responsibility to be aware of present situations and foresee those in the future. Authenticity requires a broad genuineness and heightened self-awareness, reaching strategic dimensions. Authenticity without goodness is impossible, for first among our respon-sibilities is a genuine concern for fundamental human needs as manifest in our concrete situation. Goodness, as it is popularly used to mean genuine responses to particular, narrowly circumscribed situations rooted in some sort of fairly adequate ideal, can exist without authenticity. Indeed, such is most commonly the case. For the elite who have begun to grasp the strategic needs of the present planetary situation, goodness without authenticity is now impossible.

At the opposite extreme, the nadir is reached when a bad tradition, grounded in the illusions of an ignoble mythology, is handed on by a faithful (therefore bad in this case) institution and is perpetuated through being taken up by an individual "doing the work of the devil." Obviously, such work is not genuine because of the illusory element making the bad tradition unreal. An attempt to realize illusion is inevitably destructive of genuine elements in the situation. The faithful may be in very good contact with reality in other regards however. For instance, may it not have been that Foreign Minister Joachim von Ribbentrop at the time of the German-Soviet Non-Aggression Pact of 1939, while in the service of a bad tradition (National Socialism) and its bad institutions (the perverted bureaucracies of the Third Reich), enjoyed in many other respects a correct appreciation of the situation in which he was working to incarnate the National Socialist ideal? This is what made it possible for him to achieve an extraordinary coup, rendering the Nazis a great service in keeping with their distorted perception of things. His accomplishment eventually contributed to the destruction of much good in the European situation of the time.

The ungenuine elements in any tradition can never harmonize satisfactorily with the genuine Being-possibilities in any situation. Therefore, a person who projects faithfully a bad tradition—though he may successfully circumscribe a small practical situation as Ribbentrop did—will inevitably be out of harmony with other, more basic genuine aspects of himself and with all the good people operating in the situation. He cannot persist in such a bad course without remaining resolutely uncritical about much that is going on. Self-delusion is essential to the pursuit of evil.[19]

A thoroughly bad tradition cannot perpetuate itself for long. A moment's reflection will show this principle to be analytic and not an expression of pious ontological optimism. What it states, to put it colloquially, is that you may be able to fool some of the people in some respects some of the time, but that you cannot fool all the people quite fundamentally all the time. Or, put another way, it simply affirms the primacy of Being over non-Being, without denying temporary and some-

19. Fantasy and illusion can also be generated when basic needs are ignored.

times grave disruptions brought on by ignorance, bad faith, cowardice, and other abuses of power.

Strife is not always a struggle of good against evil, however. Bitter antagonisms pit illusion against illusion. But there can be a conflict of goods, of legitimate interests, when the agents' perceptions of what is good are too limited. Even in situations of severe, unavoidable scarcity, class struggle or naked competition in the negative sense of a dog-eat-dog fight for the largest share of a scarce resource is not a genuine solution and lacks perception and concern to the point of stupidity and evil.

Someone with a normal natural faith in Being sees evil as sterile because of its fabrication of non-Being as constituting Being for that particular situation. This immediately leads to misjudgments, no matter how good the work that follows. Adolph Eichmann's program in Nazi Germany represents one such example.[20] But we can find many others closer to home. An unwillingness to consider more fully the consequences of one's demands upon the planet have led to architecturally sterile cities and the impending ecological breakdown of the planet. Selfish behaviors have led to a breakdown of public politeness, courtesy, and road safety, to the detriment of all. The refusal to accept responsibility for one's actions has led to governmental bankruptcy in both the economic and moral senses. All this is merely to say the obvious: bad institutions attract righteous enemies; false courses of action self-destruct.

But bad elements can accompany good, vital forces that sustain traditions, parasitically draining some of their effectiveness. It is most important to understand that traditions and the institutions that carry them forward are concatenations of goals, drives, concepts, images, rules, and roles, as well as physical and managerial instruments, organizations in which various kinds of elements sustain each other and conflict with one another, sometimes canceling out each other's effectiveness. In such a messy network, grave errors can be borne along through the force of

---

20. The Eichmann transport system was a good organization only in the sense of achieving efficiently what it was meant to achieve. But since what it was meant to achieve—the collection and transport of innocent people destined for destruction in Hitler's extermination camps—was monstrous, this good means to a bad end is most justifiably termed bad in the final analysis. Eichmann made many genuine decisions, that is, ones showing a firm grasp of the concrete realities of the situation. But all of his hard and efficient work took place within horizons that themselves were bad, founded as they were in illusion, mystification, and rank perversion—grounded in evil.

those things which translate vital realities and keep people of goodwill going despite the groundless images, the individual perversities, the routines of role-playing, the destruction of human relationships, and the wasting of opportunity that compromise the result to some extent without necessarily rendering the balance destructively negative.

The good extreme in our spectrum of possibilities is purely ideal. Institutions are always used by the members to some extent for self-seeking purposes. Not only do we tend to ignore the needs of the other, but our avidity and insecurity causes us to neglect our own deepest needs. The hypocrite is his own first victim. If the forgotten deeper vision was indeed an expression of lasting structural needs, new expressions of it will eventually emerge, either through reform movements within the withering traditions, or through altogether fresh privileged experiences of the neglected structures, thus founding new traditions responding to the same basic needs.

I would like to conclude this first part by suggesting a confrontation with a popular concept of tradition: tradition as synonymous with reaction, with an unwillingness to change. Searching for authenticity, we have assumed that life as such demands development. Does not tradition most often retard and perhaps even stifle development? Or does tradition, properly understood and provided it is good, not rather furnish its very ground?

 **5.**

The Bad and Good
Senses of Tradition

Inauthenticity and the Bad Sense of Tradition

In the 1968 Royal Commission Report describing the future of Ontario education, Justice Hall and Mr. Dennis employ the term *traditional* in an obviously and uniformly pejorative manner.[1] "Traditional methods" are portrayed as being handed down without thought and therefore failing to change with the times. Conformism, rote, a total lack of creativity are the hallmarks, according to the authors of this report, of tradition. Similarly, in anthropological jargon "traditional societies" are those stuck in a paralysis of nondevelopment. The term is not always intended as a dirty one, however; many an anthropologist, wary of the culture shock to which wild dynamism has brought our century, casts an envious eye on cultures with people who maintain an equilibrium with their surroundings—a traditional society flavored with a dash of mythology to help digest unexpected *e-vents*.[2]

Societies pay a high price for such harmony. The kind of social stability achieved by traditional society impedes the full development of human potential, both individual and social. (In saying this, I am aware of my very Western assumption that man has the potential to unfold and so is meant to develop.) But in recompense, because implicit tradition is passed on by imitation and such acculturation requires institutional forms guaranteeing intimacy, especially that of the extended family and tribe, traditional societies achieve a degree of inevitable fraternity that our lonely

1. Justice Hall and Mr. Dennis, *Living and Learning* (Ontario: Queen's Printer, 1968).
2. Mircea Eliade describes this function of myth in primitive societies in his *Le mythe de l'éternel retour: archétypes et répétition* (Paris: Gallimard, 1949). See the translation by W. R. Trask, *The Myth of the Eternal Return, or Cosmos and History* (Princeton: Princeton University Press, 1971), especially 93–102.

116

urban civilization of alienated individualists can scarcely even imagine.[3] The paradox is that, while much human potential is sacrificed, there is often more humanity in the personal relations of more stable societies. (Note the further implication: certain kinds of development, while unfolding some potential, can at the same time destroy important aspects of the essence.)

The fraternity of traditional society often strikes modern man, who is accustomed to doing what he pleases, as tyrannical. An intellectual from Zaire recently confided to me his despair at returning to his country and having the whole family descend on him to live off the fruits of his brainy labors. There was absolutely nothing he could do about it. The individual caught in the tight weave of stable social structures in a stagnant low-productivity culture is offered little choice. He enjoys a sure knowledge of what he is because he has little chance to become something else.

Be this as it may, nothing like the life of traditional society lies in the future of high-technology man. Any move on the part of industrial nations toward equilibrium will have to be on the basis of a formally educated, highly conscious, self-directing citizenry seeking authenticity. I certainly mean to imply in that last statement an "or else": witness the twentieth century's attempts to roll toward equilibrium on the wings of social engineering and ideologies. Unless as a community we consciously and cooperatively seek truth and make a corporate effort to understand how to humanize our society, its instability will lead to a breakdown (starting with demographic decline) accompanied by all the evil fruits of anomie. This anomie, reaching a point of such decline in the quality of life that it becomes intolerable, will result in an iron order being enforced from above by a few gnostic tyrants with a simple-minded plan of salvation. Instant traditions will be fabricated and imposed through terror by oppressive institutions, though this has been tried before and found not to work.

In this chapter we shall concentrate realistically on the situation facing those who live in advanced societies. For such societies the attitude expressed by the authors of the education report mentioned above is understandable. It is true that the individual or institution stuck in tradition and hence failing to progress is both a menace and is itself menaced. Borrowing a term from popular psychology, I call such unresponsiveness

---

3. This is beautifully described in Richard Critchfield's remarkable *Villages* (New York: Doubleday, 1981).

to changing reality a *complex:* an outmoded form for making sense of experience—one which refuses to yield at the proper moment to a new one more in harmony with the data of an altered situation.[4]

We always draw on memories of the past to interpret the present. But when a hurtful moment of the past takes a possessive hold on us and will not yield a proper place to what is new, when it will not take its own proper place as over and done with, distortions in judgment occur. Complexes block receptivity to fresh data by conflicting with what the individual or group has emotionally invested in and hence chooses to hang on to, despite all evidence.

Masses of complexed people grouped in powerful institutions can become fanatic in their efforts to make over reality to fit their dream and in their vicious refusal of alien elements. In our time, fascism and conservative Soviet communism have provided instructive examples of such tragic reaction. In all periods, religiously driven fanaticisms have wreaked havoc. The surest (though not the only) index for recognizing such a complex is violence, in all of its forms, from the child's temper tantrum—substituting what he wants for what is and then trying to annihilate reality by dissolving it in tears—to systematic persecutions by the *Schutz-Staffel* (SS), the Gestapo, or the *Komitet Gosudarstvennoi Bezopasnosti* (KGB), who have also been skilled at rewriting history. What brings about violence is a refusal to acknowledge the right of the other to exist as other, and hence a refusal to adjust one's vision of things to include him as he really is.

The bad person or institution will seek to absorb the other, either annihilating him or breaking his resistance. Where the other is innocent, only trying to be himself without forcefully imposing his own style, the good individual and the genuine institution will adjust to tolerate the other to the extent that minimal social order permits. Such is the code of commonsense liberalism. If this other errs seriously in his difference and does indeed menace good order, then persuasion respectful of his conscience will be used by the good person and institution to induce him to adjust his stance.[5] Reality is a bit messier. Violence begets violence, and it is difficult for the most liberal of lambs to lie down with the lion.

4. I am not using the term as employed technically by certain schools of psychiatry, but as popularly understood in everyday human observation.
5. I. *Sein und Zeit* (Tübingen: Niemeyer, 1953), ¶26, Heidegger distinguishes inauthentic and authentic solicitude (*Fürsorge*) on the basis of helping the other to be fully himself.

Even good tradition, if its truths are not appropriated, can breed insecurity when the traditional person is challenged. Passively absorbing the roles molded by institutions a bit out of date whose agents are anything but paragons of authentic critical self-understanding, the child or the student is putty in the hands of the institution. The child conforms to the family's image of what he should be. So long as coherent dynamics of the tribe are unchallenged, creativity is at a minimum and the individual is very little responsible for himself; indeed, his self is more their vocabulary for expressing a self than a center of genuinely creative initiative.

Where the handing down is reinforced by an entire milieu in which everyone is similarly formed, the situation for which the child has been molded confirms what he has been taught to expect. No generation gap occurs, peer acceptance is high, and the society maintains itself steadily from generation to generation. Thus, nothing in the situation invites the individual to critical discovery. He has only to follow the rules of the game, which nobody questions. His only problem is to discern as he grows up the exact role that best suits his temperament and his circumstances. The question of truth is largely reduced to understanding what his immediate society expects of him.

In our urbanized world, the peasant tribalism, bourgeois solidarity, or patrician smugness achieved in less-dynamic eras is becoming rarer. Yet even the damaged and conflicting institutions of our time continue to form the young. The individual still finds the patterns of his existence proffered by "them"—"because they say so," because "that is what they are all doing"—even when "they" dictate a difference of fashion every six weeks and elements of society seek to influence masses of people with mischievous ideological wares. The individual is motivated by a kind of project of success. Confused about who he is, acceptance by the dominant peer group of the moment becomes vital. The rewards, depending on one's station, include all of society's benefits—above all, security—so long as one remains skilled at following the arbitrary twists and turns of "their" line.

Massive pursuit of success in the midst of such confusing pluralism creates a fragile situation. That is why society is gun-shy about questions. They distract attention from the absorbing task of keeping the machine of modern living running. The intricate institutions require unswerving devotion. As this dense interweaving of traditional patterns forms a partially interlocking system, the balance of independent forces (the processes that are not under good hierarchical institutional control) is precarious, so it is dangerous to undermine credibility in one vital part of the structure while most of the rest goes unquestioned. Because no one is responsible for guidance—not even of a national system, much less that of the world—society is at a loss to know how to reclose the Pandora's box of doubts about vital parts of the system once questioning begins.

But our world has been widely and fundamentally questioned, and it is showing signs, if not of coming apart at the seams, at least of increasing volatility.[6] As public approval of intervention by the Prince of Wales into civic architecture and preservation of rural and urban landscape shows, the average person is somewhat overwhelmed in the face of the visible volatility of society. Most feelings of disempowerment have some root in a sheer lag between what one learned (the past) and what is expected (the future). The rise of a technical elite to manage an ever more complex world system and the prevalent feeling of being out of place in the emerging world are other major roots of public malaise.

People like Justice Hall and Mr. Dennis, as they contemplated Ontario's educational system, set out to find new modes of acculturation fit for future society. In their view, creativity is the magic word, as each student is encouraged to reach into the magic hat of his inexhaustible personal resources and pull out a rabbit, symbol of the fertility of new ideas allegedly at the disposal of all. But Hall and Dennis are victims of a common mistake, that of taking creativity to be a froth of superficial inventiveness and imitation of someone else's supposed self-expression.

Nietzsche, a truly creative thinker, warned that creativity is the fruit of long discipline, which he thought was grounded in arbitrary, but nonetheless necessary, codes of law.[7] I was present when, at his eightieth birthday party, Buckminster Fuller answered a young disciple who asked how he had been able to foresee so many developments: "When you want an arrow to fly far, you pull the bow string back as mightily as you can. I always started with the Greeks." Depth of vision and breadth of

6. Objective measures are not reassuring. Annual crime statistics published by the Federal Bureau of Investigation show that reported major crimes in the United States increased 281 percent from 1960 to 1982, while the population rose 28 percent. In that time, divorce rose from 2.2 to 5.3 per one thousand (*World Almanac,* 1983), and illegitimate births increased from 5 percent to 18 percent of all births (United States National Center for Health Statistics, Annual Reports).

7. Friedrich Nietzche, *Beyond Good and Evil,* in *The Philosophy of Nietzsche* (New York: Modern Library, 1954), 476–77.

perspective come through hard work; the habits of concentration, of being able to hold large fields of information together and to work through them methodically, are not acquired easily. Yet there is nothing in the Hall-Dennis report to suggest hard work and discipline.

Most of us are destined to live off the creativity of a tiny elite of innovators, those who—having amassed a personal culture and self-discipline that permit them to live out certain possibilities to the hilt—challenge Being at the outer limits of the familiar. The basic choice facing most of us is not conformity versus creativity. It is between a conscious participation in the possibilities proffered us by traditions that draw on the creativity of those who have enjoyed the great experiences, on the one hand, and an unthinking participation in the nearest forms, held out by institutions intent on exploiting us, on the other.

The Source of Essential Possibility

Conformism is an easy target for ridicule, but without the imitative transfer of cultural possibilities that induces conformism, we would be nothing but animals. The higher animals, in fact, also owe important aspects of their capabilities to implicit tradition, though even the highest—the most splendid cats, the cleverest chimpanzees—possess only the narrowest of cultures compared to man. They show marvelous instincts and proven adaptability, but no perceptible progress is made from generation to generation. Instinct is much more restrictive and rigid than tradition. Cat tradition is too poor to open any space for critical self-awareness. All that a mother cat teaches her little ones about keeping themselves clean, descending trees, or catching mice is negligible alongside the culture transmitted by the most backward tribesmen of New Guinea. The tribesmen may not progress much either, but the lives they lead, made possible by the inculturating process, include systems of symbols, ceremonies, dress, and social forms, all of which constitute a wealth of possibilities. The savage may know nothing of the project of authenticity, but he is a person, a center of initiative enjoying a vocabulary of self-awareness sufficient to found some degree of responsibility in the pursuit of the good.

The higher the civilization, the more formal the transmission through elaborate institutions of a culture that is increasingly analyzed, with its technical and theoretical symbol systems and its elaborate institutional arrangements. Higher culture demands that critical analysis go beyond a mere imitable surface to express principles—of grammar, government, science, religion, music, cuisine. Education, then, does not demand rote imitation, but a raising of consciousness, finally to the level of auto-criticism, so that the new generation in turn will be able to reflect on the principles of the arts and sciences it inherits.

The towering edifices of modern culture rely on the methodic, analytic handing down from one generation to another. Weakening the quality of the education required to pass on these principles will soon compromise the society. Modern philosophy inherited many of its questions and techniques of inquiry, virtually unchanged, from higher Greek culture; the latest scientific discoveries are founded on the transmission, highly condensed in undergraduate courses, of the fruit of millions of hours of labor stretching back to the beginnings of Egyptian and Babylonian mathematics; the American Constitution was forged by practical gen-tlemen philosophers who meditated on Roman and Greek political phi-losophy; and the Abrahamic roots of the great family of monotheistic religions still nourish the culture. These debts are widely recognized, but the enormity of the dependence and something of its antiquity have become obscured. The more imitation is concentrated on the latest fash-ion or on the most recent discoveries, the less one is aware of absorbing the fruits of an old culture and the less the knowledge of the roots necessary to an understanding of who we are. The ancient culture con-tinues to have its influence without one's being aware of it, and therefore without one's being able to criticize or orient its effects. The original founding experiences could provide ever-renewable vitality to the tradi-tions' co-creators if we troubled to return to the texts that still hold valid insights and then study the evolution of their influence over the ages. Without a certain sense of tradition, one either follows dumbly along the course of conformity, or, when he becomes tired of the old routine, plunges into the excesses of voluntaristic pseudo-creativity.

Are these not the two poison fruits of contemporary mass education today, which obscures our debt to the past? It is difficult to say which is more deadly, the disruption of those who revolt or the glassy-eyed herd-following of those who have decided to play the game of success. As long as education remains too close to the imitative level, passive acceptance of models as ends in themselves will prevail. In science education such passivity takes the form of a kind of dogmatism. The wonder of discov-ery is hidden from the student; the contingency of model-imagining, the leaps of intuition, the conceptual revolutions, the research process—all are dissolved in one immense, flat "this is how it is." The dynamism of the search for truth is lost. In religion the wondrous invasion of the Divine and the struggle of the evolving tradition to express the mysteries in ever-renewed form can be hidden behind the creed and behind the "this is how it is" dogmatism of catechetical teaching and unthinking, routine practice.

Some well-meaning teachers try to remedy this flatness by throwing in a little history. Disaster. The usual result is a "this is how it became" dogmatism, giving the impression of a suite of necessary moments, meaningful only because they bring us as quickly and efficiently as possible to that superior stage of progress that we have the honor and delight of occupying. A past *Aufgehoben* ("overcoming") in a present that supersedes all that came before is not a real past at all but a subservient moment of a factitious present.

In the sciences, where what is perennially valid is taken up into the more adequate model, the sense that the newer is better is largely justified. But the nineteenth-century tendency to take the physical sciences as the paradigm of all serious knowledge ignored the differences between kinds of objects of knowledge and hence the need for different methods. Even in the sciences the importance of the past is now more widely acknowledged. Students should understand that no discovery in any line of tradition had to have happened, that founding inspirations do not automatically occur and in static societies rarely do, and that great breakthroughs capture structural aspects of being that are inexhaustible in their meaning, a heritage to be synthesized in increasingly richer structures of understanding which respect the differences between kinds of experiences and objects.

How then can a teacher arouse the sense of personal indebtedness for something that counts, a genuine gift of the past that one must care about personally and be willing to work to save and pass on? Two pitfalls must be avoided: on the one hand, a voluntarism that thinks we must ourselves create whatever is worthwhile, and on the other, a certain conservatism, an unwillingness to question the continued validity of what is venerable and to see the creative element of necessary renewal.

The media have contributed to creating in our time the phenomenon of instant traditions. A tiny group of exalted youth in California organize a movement on Tuesday, and by Friday it is being imitated in Aix-en-Provence. For all its electric instantaneity, this still represents a tradition, since a possibility discovered by one group is handed on later to another which reincarnates it in a different situation. But the speed of propagation gives the impression of spontaneity. The participants think they are acting creatively and in harmony with their inner selves when in fact they are following someone else whose lead happens to be close enough to their own vague aspirations to serve as a means of crystallizing them. A few may indeed be inventing, and what inventing it is—a froth of voluntaristic self-expression, a self reduced to feelings and will. This imitative froth fills a vacuum because the roots of greater possibilities in the civilization, which require discipline to be re-created, are ignored. A factitious, instant culture invented by rootless people is promoted as "the American way of life," and finds instant popularity among the rootless all over the world.

Impoverished, these instant traditions are nevertheless not destitute. Many recent creations continue to draw on a tradition of jazz, of expressionism, of dada, of anarchism and nihilism, even of gospel and Hindu ideas, often without regard for their genuine sense. And they are also borne by the cumulative effect of the rapidly forming and widely transmitted new traditions, representing an enormous activity all over the Western world.

But the neglect of our roots leads to the necessity of reinventing painfully what has already been learned before. The impossible is attempted again and again, an error that is no wiser than its opposite, the fear of trying anything new, the sin of the traditional in its negative sense. Everyone today is impressed by the successes of the most daring pioneers. Successful creativity is always exhilarating. Less attention is paid, however, to the needless suffering and waste brought on by mindless ventures: the communities that broke down in bitterness and hatred, the demonstrations that only widened divisions, the thousands of companies that failed for every huge corporation that succeeded, the Vietnam War, the art works that are more trash than *oeuvre,* and the worst of all—the thousands who end up on drugs or committing suicide, the sour fruit of a mad effervescence of rootless, directionless activity, an escape from self usurping the discovery of self. Most ironic of all is the effect this has on the majority of young people: they question their self-worth and become unadventurous, understandably frightened of the failures they have seen at close range, especially the breakdown of marriage.

Each society and each individual has its optimal rhythm of development. Below that limit, its potential is not fulfilled, and frustration can build up, as in the Soviet Union and its satellites. Pushed to develop too rapidly, the strain can bring disaggregation and breakdown. But healthy development also demands sound direction—the ideal must be genuine. History is an invaluable source of information about limits and genuinely possible directions. Consider the positive side of limits. First, we have personal limits because we are a particular kind of neurophysiological organism, one with enormous but definite capabilities, impressive but finite energy. Our limits also come from our being in a particular situation: resources have been developed and society has been organized in a certain ways; people look at things from particular angles and have limits to their conceptions; there are conflicts of interests, and so on. But each of these aspects of the situation constitutes a set of possibilities. The resources are at our disposition, not in limitless quantities, but in a way that generally puts far more energy at the command of someone living in the West than that available to most in underdeveloped countries. The organization of our society provides possibilities for self-direction, for career selection, for the contemplation of truth, which, while by no means infinite and certainly varying for each individual, are nonetheless without precedent in the history of mankind. This organization has provided material well-being, has communicated information, and has permitted the existence of a world population of five billion plus (whether our planetary population is sustainable within the ecosphere is, of course, another question). It constitutes an inexhaustible inheritance of concrete possibility. Possibilities are indeed so open for many of us that we become directionless and spoiled.

Our conceptions are also limited, but compared to any other population that has ever existed, a greater number of people and larger proportion of them are more aware of more dimensions of human existence than ever before. Much has been forgotten, and much is yet to be learned. The whole level of societal understanding must be raised quickly, for we are rushing toward what may be absolute barriers (for instance, the thermal barrier could be reached in the next century). These are the more dramatic implications of the negative side of our limits, but the concrete possibilities are now more far-ranging and challenging than at any time in the past.

These personal, societal, and epochal possibilities of our situation are specific invitations to co-creative activity. Earlier in this chapter, I played down the idea that many of us are usually called to a life of breakthrough-achieving creativity. Breakthrough creativity, resulting in true and lasting extension of Being, is the rare effect of exceptional individuals and presupposes long and arduous formation. But it requires more than just hard work, and I shall argue in subsequent volumes that there is at least an element of natural grace involved.

The rest of us are called to the important role of co-creators. We are the receptors and appreciators of the great initiatives and the co-workers who develop their possibilities through little steps. (One of the great strengths of high technology is the way it allows armies of small creators to work under the guidance of larger creators in developing complex machines, such as the Boeing 767, with its sixty thousand parts to a single wing, the design of every part requiring some input of disciplined, creative intelligence.) We gather together the possibilities our predecessors and contemporaries proffer and develop them in our own lives; we teach the sense of them (and respect for them) to our children.

This is a sufficiently engaging and exhilarating task to fulfil any person. But it is not enough to ensure that the society will endure. There are no prescriptions for forcing the evolution of Being, and we are reduced to respectful anticipation and to saying our prayers.

In Quest of the Origins of Genuine Creativity

In these times of rapid and radical change, we must be ready to adapt. The success of the Israeli army, claimed Moshe Dayan, was due to its being a response to a local, quickly changing situation rather than an imitation of the Prussian or British army. Being overly traditional in the wrong sense can be fatal, especially in the electronic age. But the abruptness of change is related to the growth of historical consciousness: the modern situation both grows out of such consciousness and enhances it. Never before has it been so possible to learn of the whole scope of human existence as it is today. Such a perspective can be enjoyed only through a synchronic movement outward to embrace all the civilizations on earth, which have been thrown into intimate confrontation within the emerging world system, and through a diachronic movement to encompass the ancient beginnings of the major traditions, which alone allows us to discover the profound sources of our civilization and to measure the acceleration of transformation and discern the direction of our destiny.

As we turn in the next part of this study to an examination of the synchronic context—the emerging world system and the role of the major traditions in it—we shall be seeking the perennial wellsprings of Being as they are seen effectively influencing the continued creativity of the traditions and through them the actual situation we find, here and now, in the world. How should we go about finding them? How can we put some order into the seemingly limitless affair of investigating the way the traditions draw on their sources of power, the origins of all good tradition?

II.

The Place of Traditions in the Emerging World System

6.

The Elements of
the World System

Goals in Studying the World System

I shall seek in this part of the study to determine, through a study of the existing world system, the relevance of the principal explicit traditions and their potential contribution to the development of an ecumenic wisdom. In the examination of large systems, one inevitably proceeds in a dialectical manner, moving back and forth from reflection (guided by our natural faith) on our understanding of the largest context to an attempt to strengthen our grasp of certain parts. Knowledge of the large scene directs our more specialized efforts, and our deepening comprehension of parts enhances our knowledge of the whole. The present volume belongs to the first movement—reflection on the (vaguely grasped) whole. There are two distinct aspects to this always provisional study of the large scene, reflecting the two kinds of truth: (1) the pragmatic impact of the traditions and their institutions on the planetary context of our action, and (2) getting some sense of their potential contribution to theoretical truth. In the present chapter we shall clarify the relationship between explicit traditions and other elements that make up the emerging world system, including processes of change, institutions, symbol systems, and events. We shall consider how processes of change are to some extent guided by the institutions that traditions develop to assure the pursuit of their goals and their own transmission. These pragmatic concerns are not as divorced from the theoretical goals of ecumenic wisdom as one might believe. A central aspect of the incarnation of the traditions is their formation of symbol systems. The institutions' use of symbol systems to guide action will be considered, as well as the impact on questions of theory. In the next chapter, still concentrating on pragmatic concerns, we shall briefly survey the major explicit traditions (or subtraditions—the distinction is in some cases not clear), seeking criteria for discerning their

131

relative importance in the world situation, one key in deciding where to begin methodic appropriation.

From this pragmatic discussion, one cannot arrive at even a preliminary estimate of the potential theoretical importance of the various traditions, that is, their eventual contribution to an ecumenic wisdom. But from our provisional survey of the planetary situation, we shall gain enough of an indication to mount some kind of an argument for a starting point in our own appropriation. I do not expect everyone to be overwhelmed, but at least we shall be set on the road to a more methodic pursuit of wisdom than casual appropriation in the midst of everyday experience.

In the first part of this volume, I argued that the planetary reach of the situation makes it imperative as a condition for genuineness that the individual and the society develop a strategy for the pursuit of truth. No single individual can cope with the claims of some twenty major explicit traditions operating in the world system I shall outline below. We need reasons for deciding what to appropriate methodically and how we are to go about it. Entire institutions may be consistently underestimating the importance of certain aspects of the situation and of our past that require study and appropriation.

The world is engaged in a planet-wide cooperative effort of economic and social development. This activity is inevitably mixed with a desire to improve fundamentally the human condition and is accompanied by a strong emphasis on human rights. A strategy of development is everywhere under intense debate. Why not go the further step and recognize that the condition for the possibility of a healthy strategy of development is some collective advance in ecumenic wisdom?

The need for cooperative work among experts to prepare the building blocks for an ecumenic wisdom seems compelling and obvious to me, whatever dark thoughts I may harbor about pathological grounds for the lack of human cooperation. Such building blocks exist. Studies of individual traditions, works like Marshall Hodgson's *The Venture of Islam* and the first three volumes of Eric Voegelin's *Order and History*, with their appropriation of the biblical and classical sources of Western civilization, are examples of invaluable contributions in this regard. I shall show in a future work on the Catholic tradition a further example of the kind of sweeping critical study I believe is necessary. A community of scholars, in an exchange intended to bring the fruits of such studies into a wisdom, must arrive at a partially common natural faith that contains elements of agreement about knowledge and truth. My dream is that this forum will provide a theoretical framework for the practical project of reasonable, peaceful coexistence on a dangerous planet.

With the goal of ecumenic wisdom in mind, the importance of traditions will be measured according to the two criteria mentioned above: in the pragmatic realm, how much influence a given tradition has on the emerging world system—the degree of attention we must give it in seeking to understand what is happening in the world; and in the theoretic domain, what light is thrown by its treasure of symbols upon Being. The theoretical consideration may in fact be out of all proportion compared with the tradition's current pragmatic impact. Contemplative monasteries may figure little in a defense headquarters' estimate of the situation, but authentic persons may still be found attending intently to the sweet sounds of their choirs, straining to catch an echo of the eternal.

The pragmatic-theoretic relationship cuts two ways. Without doubt, pragmatic power considerations weigh heavily on what gets onto the world's theory agenda. Do not believe for a moment that dominance of the academy by certain intellectual modes and ideologies, of the media by certain political tendencies, and of the churches by certain viewpoints has no serious and lasting impact on what is researched and thought about theoretically. Of course it does. But there is something at work other than the manipulation of power: the truth. And truth, perhaps in the effective form of supernatural grace manifesting itself as inexplicable love, has a way of bursting on the scene against the weight of worldly probability.

The Emergence of a World System

The emerging world system is a network of interacting planetary-scale institutions incarnating great traditions. The rapid development of high technology has accelerated a process that began in the Middle Ages with the spread of empires—Arab, Turkish, Mongolian, Moghul, Christian. One of these, drawing on Arabic science, Turkish administration, and Christian thought, with the help of modern navigational techniques and the capital emerging from an expanding system of trade, was audaciously carried across all the oceans of the world by modern Europeans in the sixteenth century, establishing the most far-flung empire the world had ever seen.

The oldest vehicle of Westernization is an institution spawned by the most ancient of continual traditions, one which by its nature is not supposed to be so exclusively Western, yet to this day remains heavily European in character: the Catholic Church. Despite the great antiquity of its traditions—it is almost, with its Hebrew roots, four millennia old—the institution has remained quite modern. The Church has been involved in the founding of universities (there are some twelve hundred Catholic universities in the world today) and in scientific research, and it is at home with contemporary forms of mass media. Just as it moved out from Europe with the force of commercial and colonial expansion, it is joined now by increasingly international operations of certain Protestant and Evangelical Churches following contemporary American neocolonial activity. (Similarly, Islam continues to spread in Central Africa, fueled by Arab oil money, though hampered by the failure of the nearby Arab Muslim lands to modernize as effectively as the Christian societies of Europe.)

The Marxist countries have been very active ideological missionaries, seeking to form the mentality of the rising elites of every country where they have successfully planted their influence and to spread their influence in many quarters of the world. The pragmatic failure of communism economically and politically in the home countries has had the interesting theoretical effect of sending many materialist true believers searching for a more authentic form of Marxist doctrine.

The most pervasive institutional influence, however, is that of the European, American, and Japanese banking, industrial, commercial, oil, computer, and service industries. The principal forms of exported symbols in this regard are films and popular music, along with scientific and technical literature. (Boeing maintenance manuals are in some circles as assiduously devoured as the Bible.)

There are, indeed, a plethora of freshly minted institutions and a froth of inventive symbols. Behind all the semiconscious missionary activity (the main goal being to train people to function as agents in the spreading economic machine, which requires some change of mentality), back in the home countries of Europe and North America, we do not find a well-thought-out ideology, such as Leninist socialism, but a loose set of traditions, which we can lump together under the awkward rubric of a democratic entrepreneurial-social welfare mixed economy. (*Democratic capitalism* is shorter and more convenient, if we ignore the fact that Marx transformed *capitalism* into a pejorative term.)

For the first time in history, a great historical movement is not constituted (by contrast to the subtraditions of Islam, Catholicism, Marxist
communism, and the imperial governments of Alexander, the Romans,
the Persians, and Turks) as a well-articulated, consolidated, explicit central tradition around which cluster a community of subtraditions. This
fact accounts in part for its strength. Because it is not centralized, it is
flexible. It does not run the risk of collapse from the center, but works
from millions of centers of initiative and seeks, after the fact, to consolidate itself through pragmatically developed planetary-scale institutions
that are created as needed, such as the International Civil Aviation Organization, the World Health Organization, the General Agreement on
Trades and Tariffs, and so on. This loose and dynamic mixture of implicit
traditions, attitudes, and knowledge, not the least of which consists of
the cultures accumulating in these slowly evolved governmental, educational, economic, and industrial-commercial institutions, represents, along
with the vast education absorbed by the masses who have been caught up
into these developments, a social capital of unprecedented proportions, a
force that sweeps all before it.

The Five Kinds of Elements

World and Regional Processes

I started by mentioning the planetary-scale institutions and the traditions they incarnate. But these are only two of the five elements interacting to produce the present world system. What role do the other three—
world and regional processes, symbol systems, and events—play in the
appropriation of the truth of traditions? Two of the elements, processes
and events, are principles of change. On the other hand, symbol, institution, and tradition provide some stability, since mankind seeks through
them to achieve a degree of consistency, a modicum of security in the
midst of change.

Because human action is the motivating power of development, let us
begin with world processes. These are large-scale, ongoing changes,
mostly of a social nature but sometimes, as in climate change, physical
ones that are impressive enough to call themselves to our attention. This
concept, you will note, is phenomenological: it implies *perception* of
change. There are surely processes at work, deep down in nature or

energized by millions of individual human actions that have thus far escaped attention. What you do not see may hurt you, but such hidden forces are a fact of life. Our estimates of the situation are never quite completely true because much that is going on and that will ultimately prove significant we have not yet discerned.

Processes are the structured energy of social existence. The great stabilities presented by largely unchanged nature, physical or human, can be taken for granted, but the traditions and the institutions and even the symbol systems are consistencies won and defended through constant struggle to steer and to domesticate change. Every individual's actions manifest a pattern of growth and decline, every society develops and degenerates (sometimes with many processes simultaneously showing aspects that are in decline while others are improving), and vocabularies and grammars evolve constantly. Yet patterns are maintained without which communication would be impossible, habits are formed, and institutional roles defined and kept—for a while and to a certain degree—stable. Every action, after all, is itself a change, and even when it is repetitive and occurs within some consistent larger setting that controls its effect, it nevertheless has an impact.

Process could not be perceived if it were not change according to pattern, newness within a frame of stability that includes a consistency in the perceiver who gathers up data from many moments and acts, and sees the consistency. That is why the social world is not a total chaos: individual actions are directed into courses of action, and these courses of action are integrated into concerts of action by groups, which we can understand, symbolize, and anticipate at all levels. It is the work of institutions, which pass on the traditions regulating life, to acculturate individuals into socially acceptable courses and concerts of action that become habitual and to harmonize roles within concerts of action.

Many processes are easy for a reasonably informed person to recognize. My students and I were able to identify without great labor about a hundred large-scale processes of planetary or regional significance. As a heuristic aid in discovering and classifying them, we employed the ekistics functions grid of the distinguished planner and architect, Constantinos Doxiadis.[1] All of the world and regional processes we identified are

1. See Constantinos Doxiadis, *Ekistics: An Introduction to the Science of Human Settlement* (London: Hutchinson, 1968). Doxiadis coined the term *ekistics* to signify the network of socioeconomic-political relationships operative in any human

extremely complex, some being vast concatenations of involved (but distinguishable) subprocesses, such as industrialization. We were able, however, in every single case to identify without difficulty criteria for measuring the vector, rapidity, and intensity of change. A good measure of the extent to which a world system has already emerged is the fact that the University of Toronto library could provide statistical data pertaining to about eighty of these processes, much of it from United Nations agency and World Bank sources.

A couple of examples will perhaps suggest what I mean by such measurable criteria for determining the vector of processes, either for augmentation or diminution. A criterion for increasing crime would be the number of major criminal acts per year; statistics are available for all regions of the world, largely by nation. Consider the much larger process of industrialization. There are any number of criteria which can be used to measure the rate of industrialization, but a handy one is the use of electricity per capita. Gross national product per capita would also seem to be a good criterion, though adjustments have to be made for certain resource-rich countries that are not highly industrialized. A comparison of Saudi Arabia's gross national product per capita with its electricity use makes this point clear.

That some rather spiritual matters touching the human soul could be measured and represented by numerical criteria came as a bit of a surprise to me. But when one recalls that in dealing with processes, one is observing large-scale, on-going changes which result from millions of individual decisions and actions, the observable impact takes the form of consistent patterns of events which modify entire milieux, inscribing themselves into the underlying strata of being, which at some level are measurable.

Institutions

Recognition and understanding of these processes is a necessary, but not a sufficient, step toward controlling them, to whatever extent we

---

settlement of whatever size, from a single household to the ecumenopolis, the emerging planetary-scale human settlement. He then classified activities carried out in human society as responses to the obvious needs of human nature for nourishment, shelter, education, political order, and so on. He showed how these types of activities relate to each other and to the various scales of human settlement.

may be able to. This is actually a task that falls largely to institutions. The institutions are not just instruments for the transmission of traditions for their own sake; they are also for attaining what leverage we can over some of the large-scale processes relevant to our desires. The institutions seek through collective action to shape these processes in accordance with the visions of their traditions. Institutions are moved not by raw natural desire, but by natural desire that has been influenced to some extent by traditional visions. Identification of the strategically placed institutions is vital if one wishes to affect processes that, if left uncontrolled, menace regional or world systems (war, economic collapse, civil chaos). Enhanced knowledge of the relevant processes is also necessary for anyone concerned with the health and success of any given institution. The tensions arising from the drag of tradition, the anticipation of tradition-inspired vision, the innovative elements, and the dynamic forces of changing process make up the stuff, the political-economic-spiritual reality, of human existence molded by institutions.

Systems of Signs and Symbols

Signs and symbols, which include not only ordinary and scientific languages but the treasures of artistic and liturgical symbols, are the means of expressing the traditions and their institutions. Through this medium action is mobilized. Expressions of ethnic cultures, for example, are centers of emotional investment on the part of whole peoples and thus trigger important processes and events. Such cultures, which represent themselves through symbols, have a "flavor" that reflects the experience sedimented within them, subtly influencing the action guided through their medium.

Human beings live in their symbols, relate to one another through them, invest them with their being, and are in turn molded by them, all to an extent that can scarcely be exaggerated.[2] Semioticians do manage to exaggerate, at times making it seem that nothing else of significance exists except symbol. But the truth that our approach to everything is guided by the symbolic structures that have formed us culturally means

2. A profound description of the ontologic nature and all-pervasive role of the human word in our lives can be found in Hans Urs von Balthasar, *Wahrheit der Welt*, the first volume of *Theologik* (Einsiedeln: Johannesverlag, 1985), 175–200.

that appropriation of traditions and critique of correctly read language are inseparable.

Events

Events are happenings that establish and change the course of the processes and may be (1) particular constellations of intersecting processes, (2) significant decisions by those holding the levers of power, or (3) mobilizing symbolic breakthroughs. Events are not subject to universalization and hence cannot be dealt with by science, but they nevertheless become part of the intelligibility of a given line of development. They can be studied after the fact by locating them along the lines of the various relevant and intersecting processes. Looking back through a tradition, the moments of crisis—of decision—often stand out clearly. One sense of history emerges as the confluence of processes and pivotal decisions are studied in an attempt to understand the significance of changes in the tradition.

Traditions

Traditions involve all of these elements. A tradition is founded in a vision about reality as a whole or some part of it, and thus by implication at least, about how to deal with certain processes. A tradition grows out of founding events; its epochs are marked by crises—literally when a cut has to be made that changes the accustomed direction of a process or processes. Every tradition to some degree institutionalizes itself to assure the continuation of its vision of how certain processes should be sustained or altered in the pursuit of envisioned goals or ideals. To do this, the institution develops a symbol system that elaborates the founding vision as a way of passing it along, adapting it as needed without losing the heart of the tradition.

If we look back over the interaction of the five elements, do we discover in their dynamics a strong bias towards conservatism? First, consider the nature of the energies constantly flowing into the system, the energies of nature mediated primarily by human nature. This is not raw force, but natural needs of a definite sort, determined at the base by the given structures of the ecology and by the biophysiological makeup of man. Man is in turn formed by habit resulting from acculturation that is

guided by institutions according to established traditions and that is
expressed by every form of symbol. These symbols have been painstak-
ingly built up over time through the preservation and consolidation of
creative actions. All of this achieves an order which society as a whole is
loath to see disturbed. Creativity, breakthroughs, and new insight inevitably disturb it, however, requiring that traditional institutional arrangements be modified.

Even a casual glance at the difference between the ways in which
breakthroughs are accepted in a tradition of science and in a political order
or a tradition of revelation shows that this change occurs in a variety of
ways. Different kinds of institutions and symbols systems show markedly
different degrees and kinds of resistance to change. They must be studied
concretely, tradition by tradition, and facile generalization must be avoided.
The differences render the task of integrating traditional visions into a
single, ecumenic wisdom most difficult. At first, one might be tempted
to say, optimistically, something like this: if we think of the traditions,
especially the explicit traditions, as generators and transmitters of the
symbols in which the experience of mankind is given flesh and if we see
their institutions mobilizing human action in keeping with this wisdom,
then it becomes clear that, since mankind shares one nature and a single
planetary field of action, integration into an ecumenic wisdom becomes a
central human endeavor in our time.

But it is one thing to try to follow the unfolding of one great tradition, and it is quite another to attempt an understanding of how the
many great traditions interact in the present planetary setting and, still
more difficult, how the truth claims they incarnate and transmit may be
translated into a common set of symbols referring to one universe of
Being. A sinking feeling at the thought of trying to understand the
world situation is unavoidable. The "world modelers" have produced
little more than hopelessly abstract world econometric models. Even
Johann Millendorfer's interesting Laxenberg model with its vaunted
100,000 connections is the merest skeleton. As yet little has been done to
integrate most of the processes my students rather easily identified and
even quantified. The Laxenberg model makes no reference either to the
traditions or their great institutions.

Still, why is this critical? One way of looking at it is to compare
political science with political philosophy. A failure to consider traditions
(not all of which are concerned with relations and loci of power) does not
make futile the scientific study of power loci and relations (political

science), even in the form of a model. But questions of "why" and "how best" cannot be answered without the broader base offered by traditions of different types. Put another way, how can Plato's *Republic* be definitively labeled "political science"—or even "political philosophy"? If we are in and of an emerging world system, the resulting complexity of growing relations between its formerly separate parts demands that we refrain from excluding whole parts of that system. As we look for lines of order in the midst of this fluid reality, traditions appear a hopeful focus, a place to begin. They transmit man's noblest and most ambitious visions. They maintain an essential intelligibility, sometimes for millennia, into which is gathered the effects of a series of events that inspire the coherent action of many coordinated institutions.

7.

The Relevant
Explicit Traditions

Super-Institutions of Highly Influential Traditions

Traditions of association and of revelation are most readily visible in the institutions that incarnate them. More than their procedure manuals, constitutions, and canonical documents, it is the consistent action of people playing their roles in the institutions that makes us aware of the existence of these traditions. Philosophic-scientific traditions, on the other hand, are centered to a greater extent in their texts, though the universities, research institutes, ashrams, monasteries, and so on that they spawn are significant players on the world scene, not as vast hierarchical institutions commanding the actions of millions, for the institutions are usually small, but through their cumulative influence. Museums and symphony orchestras are not as important as the works they display, but without them the artistic traditions would suffer and some would disappear altogether.

I have elected to start this survey of the world system with a reflection on the great institutions, while remaining aware that the traditions behind them are the ultimate goal of my appropriation and that certain traditions of idea manage to animate key people without incarnating themselves in the most visible institutional ways. Philosophic thought and scientific attitudes are good examples.

If we start by asking ourselves which institutions now appear to make the largest impact on the planetary situation, we can then reflect on the traditions that are making their presence felt pragmatically in the world through the human action guided by those institutions. Then we can ask, for instance, how the traditions passed on by those institutions become symbolized. How do those symbols work on the masses they form? How is the vision of their goals held up, and how are millions effectively acculturated into them and galvanized to action that is guided to forge civilizations? This method will accord us a more concrete approach to the interaction of elements in the world system. By surveying the greatest contemporary institutions, we will gain an initial understanding of the dynamics of these immense, long-lasting structures and prepare the way for an eventual appropriation of traditions.

The two most immediate and visible institutions at this moment—despite their fading significance in recent years—are the so-called superpowers, followed by the governments of the other powerful industrialized nation-states, such as Japan, Germany, Britain, and France. The government of China, by virtue of the immensity of its population and its huge and strategic land mass, is also important, as are the governments of India, Pakistan, and the islands of Indonesia—countries which, though poor, are so populous they retain strategic importance. We can check this intuition of what may prove important by considering which of the many human functions analyzed by Doxiadis and catalogued on his ekistics grid are significantly influenced by these political powers, and with what intensity, actually or potentially (particularly if open warfare were to erupt between them).

But sheer size is not all there is to determining strategic importance. In the case of the two superpowers, the vastness of their populations and land masses is supplemented by military forces backed by an industrial power devoted to it. Japan, with a small geographic expanse, a population less than half that of the United States, and lesser military power is a strategic giant because of its industrial-economic power. Tiny Israel, with a population about the same as the metropolitan Toronto area, has a strategic importance grotesquely out of proportion to its size because of its location and its centrality to the clash of traditions in an area that engages the vital interests of many great powers. One result is that Israel possesses the fourth largest air force in the world.

How has so much of the power and order of the entire world been concentrated in such few institutions as the governments of the great powers, and how have the allegiances of billions been formed and mobilized by offshoots of two basic secular visions, Marxist and post-Enlightenment liberalism? Such a disproportionate situation seems to be telling us something essential about the very nature of man and his affairs, about the tendency of high-technology modernism to spread indefinitely, even seeking to leap beyond the planet. Is this megalomania unsound, gnostically driven, or does it flow from something in the nature of man, rather like Teilhard de Chardin's vision of the noosphere as a development of evolution?

Before beginning with the most obviously ideological of the two disproportionate giants, the vast and increasingly shaky empire dominated by the Union of Soviet Socialist Republics, it is worthwhile to point out a reality hovering over all the great powers, indeed all nations. A noosphere phenomenon itself, it constitutes an essential part of the context in which all governments operate: nations, regardless of their traditional patrimony or the ruling ideology, are now having to come to terms with high technology. This is the most radical leap since the outburst accompanying the discovery of "civilization" in Egypt and Mesopotamia during the third millennium B.C. As a result, in all societies there is a collision between national and international technological traditions and tension between the demands of old faiths, new ideologies, and the economic-social-political-technical realities of the present world economy. A new world of symbols is spun all about us, communicated almost instantly by the industrialized mass media to every modern society—but nowhere is it well digested. New institutional arrangements are everywhere putting unprecedented demands of adaptation on huge masses of people, touching everyone and occurring faster than even our remarkably flexible and expanding management systems can handle.

That is why when one seeks to understand what is happening to a country like the Soviet Union nothing is more important than an assessment of how it is coping with the processes of industrialization and urbanization, the high-technology transformation of the workplace, of daily living, of military forces, and of agriculture. If it is to guard its independent character and not be swallowed up by more dynamic systems, a country's ability to keep up with or exceed its rivals in transforming and generating new possibility and power is central in determining the need for its traditions and institutions to undergo more massive change. (*Perestroika,* for instance, is a term that has become familiar several years after I first drafted this paragraph.)

The Union of Soviet Socialist Republics

The government of the Soviet Union once proudly presented itself as the vanguard socialist state—a revolutionary kind of institution—the orthodox transmitter of the scientific tradition of Marxist-Leninist analysis (its principal symbol system) and the builder of an order demanding completely new institutions and a re-education of the peoples. It attempted to explain and justify all its policies in terms of that set of doctrines, and it considered itself the "Third Rome," authorized to evolve the official teaching of this doctrine in the course of experience with changing times, and to be tutor to all other nations.[1]

The genuineness of this orthodoxy and the claimed spiritual hegemony was challenged, to be sure, especially by the second greatest socialist state, the People's Republic of China, but doctrinal zeal is difficult to distinguish from the simple push and shove of these two great powers. Soviet relations with certain Social Democratic parties were also complicated by conflicts of ideological faith. François Mitterand, the socialist president of France, has long been a vigilant opponent of Soviet power, probably more so than was Charles de Gaulle.

Perestroika burst on the scene because of a loss of faith on the part of a new generation of Soviet leaders, a crisis on the level of the philosophical tradition itself, brought on when these tough pragmatic leaders were finally forced to look at the results wrought by the "means of production and distribution" that had been adapted and evolved by the Leninist-Stalinist-Brezhnevian state. The economic failure began to sap the foundations of the great military machine that protects and projects Soviet power. But worse, the moral discouragement, the anomie in Soviet society and in some of the satellites became so overwhelming, no one could ignore it. It is now eight years since General Jarezelski, in a secret meeting, begged Cardinal Glemp for help in lifting the Polish working class out of its profound moral slump. Glemp replied, "Give us paper, give us freedom and we can help." Something of the same sense of despair occurred in the Soviet Union. It was reflected clearly in *Soviet News and Views,* the propaganda paper (now defunct) issued by the Soviet Embassy in Ottawa. It is frankly enunciated in Gorbachev's addresses to the Supreme Soviet and in his talks around the country to workers. The extent of the corruption is no longer covered up. The sense of being a worthy vanguard of anything is compromised. What has gone wrong? Blame is pushed further and further back, now reaching Lenin himself; perhaps even Marx will not remain untouched (I recently heard on television a deputy of the Supreme Soviet saying that Marxism itself should be questioned). The practical problems are so enormous, even the opportunists know there is something wrong philosophically. One does not have to be

1. The claim of being the "Third Rome," of course, is not new. Russian Orthodoxy similarly claimed the Patriarchate at Moscow to be the spiritual *tertium Romanum* upon the collapse of Constantinople in 1453.

an Eric Voegelin to see that understanding of the present situation is impossible without a diachronic analysis of the evolution of the interplay between vision and institution since the beginning of the Marxist gnostic endeavor.

Rarely in the history of great institutions have their leaders undergone such a loss of confidence. Pragmatically and strategically, this spiritual crisis is of capital importance in the world situation. Its causes lie deeper than problems with "central plan command economic organization." Moreover, questions of economic organization and political reform cannot be separated from issues of freedom and human rights. At least an entire anthropological faith is coming into question. For my part, I agree with Voegelin about the need for a return to the roots of the Western intellectual tradition to understand the clash of faiths in the Enlightenment that produced the great gnostic experiments of the twentieth century.

The institutional reality of the Soviet state encompasses the ethnic reality of many distinct peoples, all with proud linguistic and national traditions. These realities are recognized in the way the Soviet Union was structured as a federation of republics (fifteen, plus sixteen more "autonomous republics"). But the Russian domination of the Soviet Union manifests another old tradition, one that is not articulated as doctrine but is clearly lived out as implicit fact: that of Russian imperialism, which itself is rooted both in the normal tendency of well-consolidated powers to expand, and in the old Russian Orthodox idea of Moscow as "the Third Rome."

The seriousness of recent outbursts of ethnic turmoil prompts me to emphasize even further that the loss of confidence at the center of the legitimacy of the Muscovite hegemony in the name of the superior, international truth of Marxism-Leninism has led to a boiling up of grievances and a renewed push for independence. In the last chapter I stressed the extent to which we identify our being with the ethnic symbol systems in which we live. Given any weakening in more internationalist visions—Christianity, Islam, international socialism—the reigniting of ethnic and national ardors is inevitable. That is why I shall address below the question of appropriating this "national" reality.

Anyone seeking to assess the dynamic realities of what remains of the Soviet Union today must therefore bring together all of these factors: the tradition of Muscovite imperialism fed by the Third Rome mythology, the "burden" of spreading the new orthodoxy of Marxist-Leninism, the conflict with the Maoists heretics, the boiling cauldron of unhappy ethnic minorities, and the normal expansionism of a great power.

Modern social reality is becoming staggeringly complex. Not only have many societies grown to heretofore unimaginable sizes—the Soviet Union with its 280,000,000 people embracing so many distinct nations and many more peoples enfolded in its imperial outreach—but added to the complexities of managing any society of this scale come the innumerable vital traditions and subtraditions of scientific, technological, industrial, and commercial existence, which have a life of their own and in the centrally planned economies are straining to free themselves from bureaucratic domination.

I read recently that the estimated number of technical terms now existing in the English language is ten million. This represents the growth of hundreds of thousands of new centers of concentrated human activity, each more inventive and powerful than the richest and best-organized agricultural estates of the eighteenth century, each apparently contributing to this wealth of technical language. These centers of activity are powerful educators, forging and passing on wholly new technical traditions with institutions that require legions of new men and women with technical minds. Consider for a moment just the growth of microelectronics and with it information processing, which have exploded from almost nothing in 1950 to a vast network of traditions, from hardware and software design to manufacturing technique. One could fill a small library with the magazines and technical journals that have sprung up in an effort to hand on to experts and hobbyists the latest developments of the various subtraditions.

The Soviet Union, with its rigid system of economic planning and controls, fell disastrously behind the United States, Japan, and western Europe in the whole sphere of microelectronics and data processing. But see how difficult it is to get a proper perspective on such complex matters. In terms of what goals is this disastrous? If we are considering military strength, Russia loses somewhat, but by using central command to concentrate the best brains in support of a coherent defense strategy, by stealing the West's technology where needed, and by building slightly less up-to-date weapons in greater quantities, there is no sure military disaster for the Soviets. At the Bourget Air Show in 1989 it became apparent that the MIG-29, visibly based on the McDonnell Douglas F-18, is more maneuverable than its inspiration and has comparable avionics capabilities and weaponry. When, by skillful manipulation of

Western political forces, the Soviet Union can stop the deployment of weapons as favorable to Europe's defense as the Enhanced Radiation Weapon ("Neutron Bomb") and slow development of missile defense systems, one also sees that technological inventiveness is only part of the game. In the commercial field, where they do not intend to compete and can hold the vast public of their empire captive as purchasers of inferior goods, disaster was held at bay for decades. Lower productivity is of course a serious problem, and although it may in part be offset for a good while by the central command structure's ability to shift resources at points where they are thought strategically important, the economic news coming out of the Soviet Union since *Glasnost* suggests that time has run out on these shell games.

This is but a tiny sample of the complexity of the interaction of traditions, institutions, symbol systems (especially the many languages and the tension between Communism and the religions), and processes within a well-defined area commanded by a super-institution. Before further consideration of the intellectual challenges with which these realities confront us, let us consider for a moment the other colossus.

The United States of America

The other superpower does not incarnate a well-consolidated ideology like Marxism-Leninism. As Michael Novak has pointed out, the theory that gave birth to the democracies of the Enlightenment and influenced their political-economies is much less important than the practice that subsequently married free market economy, representative democracy, and a certain culture of fair play and enlightened self-interest to produce, mostly by improvisation, the social welfare (partly free market, partly state-regulated) democratic societies of the West.[2] From the start, the "openness" of the corresponding institutions, which both affected and were affected by the ideational traditions involved, has marked a considerable difference from Tsarist Russia, from which developed the Soviet Union.

Among many unusual elements that go into the makeup of the central institution, the government of the United States of America, is the Constitution, a unique symbol that transmits an institutional vision by

2. Michael Novak, *The Spirit of Democratic Capitalism* (New York: Simon and Schuster, 1982), 19–26.

drawing on experience in governing as well as more distant history, yet also including bursts of creative freedom. The Constitution, designed with checks and balances, provides to this day a strange kind of framework, subject to the most bizarre twists of interpretation as Supreme Court Justices try to get it to provide the guidance they want in a particular era. Then there is the relative rootlessness of the governed—the mass of people, with the exception of a handful of natives, being recent immigrants—a fact reflected in geographic and social mobility without parallel anywhere in history. Important, too, is the vastness of the continent, a characteristic the United States has in common with the Soviet Union. The riches and mobility made possible by rapid industrial development have combined to make of the American superpower a society able to assimilate foreign populations rapidly. Although assimilation is anything but perfect, the nation is not characterized by the imperial model of Russian hegemony on its dominated Georgians, Turks, Ukrainians, and others. The problem the United States has with the minority among black people who have not yet become "bourgeois," the native peoples, and some recent arrivals not only pales to insignificance compared to the ethnic complications of the other superpower, it is probably less explosive than the looming problem of the Muslim workers in France, Germany, and Italy.

But this openness and ability to assimilate has a price in terms of tradition: the resultant society seems increasingly lacking in focus. If there is a goal uniting this people, it would seem to be the desire to improve the individual's material situation in an atmosphere of freedom. Life, liberty, and the pursuit of happiness remain the common aim, though the operative notion of happiness tends to get flattened into a desire for material prosperity with too little attention to the full challenge of spiritual well-being.[3] (At least that is the impression one gets; unfortunately it is impossible to establish responsibly.)

At the same time, the nation is allowing a culture to be foisted off on it by "image merchants" holding a vague "liberal" agenda and no concern for the nation's Christian past, with the result that its proud history is

3. It need not be so. Lawrence R. Brown notes that the Preamble to the Declaration of Independence is understandable as the language of the Middle Ages: "We hold these articles of faith to be the revealed truth: all souls are created equal and they are endowed by God with certain inalienable rights, among which are immortality, free will and access to grace" (*The Might of the West* [Washington, D.C.: Binns, 1963], 528).

now producing something of an artificial mishmash, "the American Way of Life," packaged and merchandised around the world by elites in New York and Los Angeles with no roots in middle America and no appreciation of its traditional culture. Still more innovative than any other society, it seems increasingly reluctant to come to grips realistically with its problems. This goes so far as to compromise the nation's ability to turn technological innovations into lasting marketing success. The lack of focus favors a narrow pragmatism without a stomach for long-range planning. Another effect is that, capable as it is of dramatic initiatives such as deregulation, the nation as a whole is showing cultural tendencies to live chronically beyond its already great means.

This charge is economically easy to establish. Significantly, the other superpower has pushed the limits even more, given its stagnation. But the two countries handle the problem differently, the one using its great power to borrow madly from the whole world, the other, while it too allowed its former satellites to pile up unserviceable debts (especially Poland and Hungary, and Romania) at home, has handled the problem by keeping its people—but not the elite—in straitened circumstances while maintaining an iron military discipline over them. This policy is now bankrupt in the satellites, and with such recent events as Moscow's capitulation to the Ukrainian coal miners, it is obviously reaching its limit in the Soviet Union, which has recently borrowed as much as it can.

The lack of strong ideological focus, the openness of the system, the tradition of enterprise and self-betterment combine to make the United States the ideal setting for the flourishing of the scientific and technological traditions. There is, however, one fly in the ointment: weaknesses in the educational sector (not a "system," for again the decentralization leads to the most disparate variety of schools and universities). Some of the weaknesses have in the past been supplemented by freely buying the best products of other societies' educational systems—the "brain drain" to the U.S. remains fairly formidable and is an important tradition made possible by the openness of the society. At the same time, many processes which together spell trouble for social stability are symptoms of a certain hollowing out of the whole complex from within because of the inability of very large numbers of individuals to cope adequately with the demands put upon them and because the confusion and lack of focus of traditions has led to a slackening of personal discipline. Interestingly, these same symptoms of social anomie are to be found in spades in the leading socialist countries of Europe and in all the Western democracies.

The immense scale, the rapid change, the social complexity, and the lack of focus all lead to a crisis in governing such a society. The government is enormous and impossible to steer very well. Principal agencies are at war with one another. The lack of central discipline corresponds to a lack of foresight. Eight years of an administration dedicated to cutting down its size only saw the federal government grow.

Other Great Nation-States

Each of the great nation-states constitutes a formidable power. The ability of the governments of France, China, or Brazil to mobilize the energies of tens of millions of people (a billion in the case of China) makes of these institutions, with their hundreds of subordinated state institutions and regulated private ones, enormous players in the world system and unsurpassable levers over many regional and even world processes.

Each of these great institutions dominates a region, and weighs in heavily on the world scene. Grouped together in alliances, they can multiply their power, as we shall see in a moment. But within the considerable territory each commands, these national governments are singularly powerful tutorial influences over the lives of individuals, and they control, directly or indirectly, a large portion of the total disposable human energies. That is what makes control of the symbols and processes we call "politics" such deadly serious business.

The governments put proud national traditions to their own service, using them not only to mobilize action for the sake of the common good, but to enhance the position and prestige of those who represent that "common good" in government. Just as government agents will do what they can to make tax monies appear the largesse of government— rather than involuntary contributions of the citizenry—so, too, they will tend to blend the mystique of national traditions with the aura of powerful office and then have both redound to their personal credit. Of course, the cult of personality reaches extremes in the totalitarian states, but with the help of the media it is a process that seems almost unavoidable under all forms of government. Popular fascination with key personalities and their views, the traditions they incarnate, is not entirely pointless.

A Note on Appropriating National Traditions

If national traditions put to powerful use by governments are such important factors in our situation, is it not important that we appropriate them? What would appropriation of a national culture require? I believe there is not only a need for a much more formal, methodic appropriation of our national traditions than we normally undertake, but also that such appropriation should enjoy a high priority in the strategy for the pursuit of truth. National pride is a powerful force in the affairs of men. Moreover, one finds oneself constantly drawn into controversies that require fragmentary appropriations of part of the national traditions. But, for reasons I shall explain as we proceed, I would not begin my appropriation there.

What is it to be part of a nation and what would it mean to come to grips with, for instance, America? Many implicit traditions are bound up in that reality, all needing explication if they are to be confronted as truth claims. Much that makes up *ethnos* is implicit, lived, so successfully acculturated we barely are aware of it. But there is also explicit tradition mixed in with nation. We should start by getting clear what we mean when we talk of America. It is, first of all, a phenomenon of my own consciousness, but also a notion I share in some way with many other people. For some of these, the experience for which the symbol America stands is probably so divergent from my own that the concept is used by us analogously, though there is a core of univocity in our mutual reference to an agreed-upon expanse of geography and a political entity cemented by the institutions of government. So this much is certain: America means a particular piece of real estate and the government that exercises considerable control over the people who reside within its boundaries.

The United States of America is not under relentless military attack by neighbors who refuse to accept the common notion of its geographic expanse. The common understanding of what constitutes its borders is just that, an agreed understanding. Israel, for instance, and Kashmir, to name two of many less-happy lands, do not enjoy the benefits of such a consensus. America is here the beneficiary of a widespread tradition.

Its governmental institution also carries on a tradition, one that stipulates how the governing is to function and that is expressed in a written constitution supplemented by a considerable unwritten code of government. The Constitution is a "canonical" document for government, and the Declaration of Independence and probably the Gettysburg Address, curiously enough, have assumed a similar status as texts to which all refer when defining what the country stands for—the stated ideal that governments should strive to realize. The Monroe Doctrine may also fall into this category. *The Federalist Papers* play a unique role in giving further access to the founding vision of the United States of America by showing it as the embodiment of an ideal of how free men should live and govern themselves through, as Lincoln later would put it, "a government of the people, by the people and for the people."

Once he gains some grip on the founding fathers' vision this republic was to incarnate, the appropriator must then study the development of that ideal as the country grew and passed through wrenching crises. Classical commentaries are of course available, De Toqueville's *Democracy in America* being as valuable for understanding the concretization of the vision in its first half century as the *De civitate Dei* is valuable for understanding the crisis of Christianity in the last years of the Empire. The Civil War, the great industrial and western expansion, the coming of age as a world power in World War I, the test of the Great Depression, the response of the New Deal, the emergence into the global scene as a superpower by World War II, the trials of the nuclear age, the Korean conflict and the opening of the Cold War, the vast expansion of the Sixties, the Vietnam trauma, Watergate, hyperinflation, stagflation, runaway deficits, the falling share in the world market—all these crises must be taken into account. If one is to grasp the essence of America today, he must evaluate the impact of these events on the evolving awareness of the ideal held by various segments of the population.

The absence of an official ideology, the diffuseness of any sense of nationhood and national ideals, and the fact that the nation is really driven more by an institution (government) than by an explicit vision held up by a "holy scripture" makes of this, as of most democracies, very much a pragmatic affair. This means that the appropriator must search for the sense of the tradition in the unfolding of sociological and political processes as they happen, rather than in grand declarations of eternal visions alone. Without such perspective on its history, from the beginning of the republic to recent events of historic impact, the appropriator cannot discern the vector and significance of these complex, ongoing processes. This is not true in the case of ideological nations such as "People's Republics," "Islamic Republics," or a state like Tanzania guided by Julius Nyerere's ideology of African socialism, though final critical appropriation of those lived traditions requires, as with any other, confronting the cohesive stated ideal with the hard realities with which it stands forever in tension.

Despite my efforts to underscore what there is of explicit ideal and visible governmental institution, American ethnicity remains largely implicit and very pluralistic and diffuse. When I reflect on my own sense of being American, I am not sure what derives from the influences of family, social class, and region, and what is perhaps shared by most Americans. Even among those attitudes which are widespread throughout the country, it is not easy to determine which are characteristically American and which belong to a more general mind-set dominated by notions of modern technological efficiency.

I can, however, make some good guesses and ask some worthwhile questions about this *mixtum-gatherum* of habits and attitudes. For instance, I suppose most Americans have grown up accustomed to finding quick and simple answers to their needs, so they do not like unnecessary complications. For example, most American transit systems have a single fare, and when the American encounters a European fare system that is based on paying by distance and social category and that may require eight inputs on a ticket machine, he is appalled (just as he is when he observes French construction workers fumbling around). Likewise, Americans are used to making acquaintances easily, but they are less likely to make lifelong commitments to friendship, as do many Europeans—or at least they did when they were less mobile. Many of these ethnic characteristics do not imply great truths, but only represent differences growing out of particular experiences that signify nothing more transcendent. Others may reveal the foundations of a group's natural faith, however poorly thought out.

Even these few observations, offered by way of illustration, suffice to reinforce the points I have been advancing. Ethnicity is so implicit and so diffuse that it makes a poor starting point for methodic appropriation. After twenty-five years of thinking about tradition, I am no closer to putting some defensible, logical order into the appropriation of implicit traditions beyond my initial decision to start with the most fundamental explicit truth claims that form the visible core of one's ruling ideal and then, with that structure of belief exposed to view, to discern the aura of orchestrating implicitness, the subtle attitudes and habits involved in putting beliefs into practice and that in turn quietly mold those beliefs. That is why I chose not to begin my methodic appropriation with my Americanism but with a much more explicit tradition central in my life.

(Not everyone enjoys that opportunity, because not everyone participates, through their natural faith, in a tradition as explicit as Catholicism.)

On the other hand, as we have noted, ethnicity and nationalism are such powerful emotive forces in the world that we cannot ignore them, either in seeking to deal pragmatically with the local, regional, or planetary situation in political terms, or when we come to the moment of personal critique. For the latter, allow me to cite a crude example: I know some Ukrainian-Canadian Catholics about whom I would wonder what takes priority, their allegiance to Christ and the Church or their attachment to advancing the cause of keeping alive Ukrainian national fervor in Canada. If ever such persons become interested, not just in emoting, but in reflectively, critically searching for the truth, they will have to ask themselves for an accounting. But in my own case, ethnicity does not form the strongest and most guiding allegiance. I am not even much of an "ethnic Catholic." It would be a mistake, however, to assume an answer to the question of just how much Catholicism internationalizes one. Casual observation of "ghetto" North American Irish Catholicisms and peasant Québécois Catholicism suggests that one can be steeped in a kind of Catholicism and remain just as ethnic as the Ukrainians I described a moment ago. The potential for Catholicism to raise one's sights beyond the immediate ethnic horizon is certainly there. But that is getting ahead of the story. The reader understands better, now, I hope, why I would deal with all these issues of implicit ethnicity only after clarifying the more accessible field.

Military and Trading Alliances and the Force of Nationalism

Observing efforts to forge larger institutions that combine some of the sovereignty of the member states to achieve what the statesmen perceive to be a common transnational good reinforces what I have just been saying about the strength of old ethnic traditions and the cohesion of governments of the national states as longstanding institutions. How jealously the nations guard their prerogatives, even when the need for more expansive cooperation is a life-and-death matter, as it is in NATO. After thirty years, for instance, the level of cooperation in weapons development and procurement, though improving slowly, is still pathetic.

Since the writing of most of this book, the enthusiastic movement toward a warming of national relations has swept Europe. The attitude is changing, paradoxically, just at the moment that disarray in the East appears to many Europeans to have eased the military threat. Wiser heads recognize the potential for mischief if *Perestroika* renewal falters, as many think it will, and the Beijing reaction sets in, with the Red Army still fully intact. The changes, for example, in East Germany during November 1989 are particularly interesting when one reads that the former ruler, Erich Honecker, was prepared to unleash a "Beijing June" upon his citizens, but was successfully opposed by the commander of the Red Army contingent stationed there. Now that the Soviet Union itself is in some disarray, the Red Army's first task may well turn out to be a Jaruzelski-style takeover from Gorbachev, sparked in part, one might guess, by the appalling tent cities that are the only accommodation available for troops and their dependents returning from their former East-European postings. In any event, it is foolish to assume that the Red Army will never return westward past the Soviet border.

To what extent this inertia comes from ethnic distrust and to what extent from the reluctance of those who hold power in governmental institutions to give up any of it to umbrella organizations is hard to say. At the same time, territoriality, the need to affirm a sense of "our group" in opposition to "them," plays the dominant role in the care and feeding of nationalism.

Planetary-Scale Political and Economic Organizations

Much misunderstood and much maligned, the United Nations and its member organizations are key players in the emerging world system. A dense network of international agreements governing the study and often the regulation of many processes on a planetary scale has rapidly arisen: the Food and Agricultural Organization, the World Health Organization, the International Civil Aviation Organization, the International Labour Organisation, the World Meteorological Society, the International Atomic Energy Association, the Postal Union—the list, which goes on and on, is vast in scope, dense in its effects, and all very recent in the history of the planet.

To the list of such institutions we might add the International Monetary Fund, the International Bank for Reconstruction and Development (World Bank), the General Agreement on Trade and Tariffs, and the

Organization for Economic Cooperation and Development. These institutions are developing traditions of their own, visions of the world and accumulated know-how within the spheres of activity assigned to them. They are forming a subclass of international technocratic bureaucrats with a planetary vision of human affairs. Just how far these institutions, agents for the alteration of mentalities, penetrate in a given country is difficult to measure.

Most of these developments are "institution driven": the emerging traditions are more a fabrication of the new institutions than vice versa. By contrast, scientific, philosophic, and religious institutions are usually modified to serve the tradition as its vision evolves. In the international sphere, unfolding processes are manipulated by well-ensconced institutions. When a growing need is perceived, institutional arrangements are improvised; a vision of what is going on is developed retrospectively, often after a certain *ethos*—an attitude and a sense of ways of doing things—has been in practice, the subsequent formalization then guiding further perceptions of what is needed. Much of the emerging world system is thus being constructed pragmatically.

International Corporations

The infamous multinational corporations have developed in very much the same way—in pursuit of perceived opportunity, international institutions were pragmatically fashioned. Since the institution usually has a focused and practical goal, its growth demands a minimum of long-range vision and a maximum of accumulated know-how. There are exceptions, companies where the coefficient of vision is greater than usual, and they often become the great corporations. For example, the visionary leaders of Texas Instruments corporation grasped early on the implications of the microelectronic revolution they were instrumental in starting. A whole plan of research, development, production, and marketing was unfolded, with a twenty-year time frame. Patrick Haggerty, the general manager, and Eric Johnsson, the founder, gave much thought to the kind of mentality and culture that would be required to sustain such a rapid evolution and carefully considered the development of new forms of industrial institutions to produce that culture. They even designed a new kind of industrial building with a half-floor in which it would be easy to change utility lines, a factory that is still proving flexible thirty years after it was built in Dallas. (I was startled in conversations with both Johnsson and Haggerty by the degree of explicit, philosophical awareness lying behind what they were doing.) IBM, too, has been characterized by a sustained effort to achieve long-range planning, requiring an unusual degree of corporate self-awareness and an articulated vision of the emerging technological world. A good example of how such vision can reshape industrial institutions is to be found in Alfred Sloan's memoir of his experience at General Motors, in which Haggerty saw a model for his own planning.[4]

These corporations have had to fight to institutionalize devices for renewing and maintaining the commitment to their vision as they settled into bureaucratic ways of carrying out their everyday business. Texas Instruments went so far as to establish a planning group with a scope of twenty-five years, to which it invited the retired heads of the Banque de France, Daimler-Benz, the New York Stock Exchange, and Nippon Telephone and Telegraph. IBM struggles mightily against the cumbersome bureaucracy this giant institution has developed. Having developed a culture suitable for a time of rapid growth and almost complete market domination, IBM is finding it hard to adapt to a situation in which it must cut away deadwood and generally prove itself more nimble. Yet its cash flow is so enormous compared to any other manufacturer that it can, like the Soviet Union, achieve extraordinary results when it wants to throw huge resources at a problem.

Many intellectuals are too busy waving their fists at the supposed imperialism of transnational corporations (either because they prefer a socialist internationalism, they uncritically sustain a nationalist fervor, or they merely react in understandable fear to any concentration of power that is relatively uncontrolled by society) to study this world-scale civilizational overlay dispassionately. It transcends the geographical and conceptual boundaries of the various national cultures and puts down roots into them while pulling increasing numbers of people up into the new structures and acculturating them into the new international technological civilization. (Bata International, with shoe factories and stores in ninety countries, takes pride in sending Asiatics to oversee Latin American operations, and Latin Americans to Africa, for just this purpose.)

So rapid and dazzling are these developments that they can blind us to the depths of tradition lurking beneath the shiny surface. I know a recently retired Boeing 747 pilot for Air France, for instance, who trained

4. Alfred P. Sloan, *My Years with General Motors* (New York: Doubleday, 1963).

in the *Armée de l'Air* (partly at U.S. Air Force bases) and spent most of his adult life all over the world. A thoroughly modern aviator, as at home in what he calls "*mon bureau*," the flight deck of the massive Boeing, as he is in his Bastide near Aix-en-Provence, he remains, nevertheless, as thoroughly French in his instinctive reactions and attitudes as a Burgundian vintner. Habitually criticizing French failures to modernize while complimenting American know-how, he has little idea just how irredeemably French he remains. The very sharpness of his criticisms of all things French is very French. It would never cross his mind to live anywhere else, however. His family, immediate and extended, interrelate in all the typical French ways, to the point that even his new German son-in-law is being drawn into the French family machine.

Our various acculturations almost seem to occupy different levels in the brain, where they have little interpenetration, a phenomenon similar to the ability of the aged to remember what happened in their youth but not what happened yesterday. We compartmentalize our activity in the different institutional roles we play. We have all known people whose whole persona changes the moment they walk out of the office, and all preachers rightly rage against the restriction of religious attitudes to Sunday morning.

As good scientists, we must be very cautious in drawing conclusions about the extent and depth that an internationalizing, technological mind-set penetrates in a given society and about the depths of secularization. In some cultures, adoption of industrial ways can occur with lightning speed—witness the Korean transformation—while others seem to resist important features of it for generations, perhaps forever. How Japanese does a thoroughly modernized Japan remain? Is Hong Kong more westernized at the core than Japan? How does one reliably measure these things?

International Churches

Shortly, we shall consider the great religious traditions as treasures of wisdom and insight. But their pragmatic importance deserves mention in the present context, for through their institutions they are large, dynamic actors on the world scene.

Neither Islam nor Hinduism, or for that matter the great Hindu offshoot of Buddhism, is organized in the tight-knit, institutionalized way of some of the Christian churches. This diffuses their influence, but one should not be deceived by that—locally it can remain quite formidable. In some regions, Islam, especially Shiite traditions, can be tightly organized and have an enormous impact on society. Christianity, on the other hand, seems better equipped to cope with the emerging world system on a global scale. This is not surprising, since Christian traditions had much to do with the evolution of this civilization. This is because Christianity is the missionary religion *par excellence.* Of course, Islam, too, is missionary, but it was from its conception a sociopolitical force, conquering and molding vanquished societies, and it has had great difficulty finding a mode of separating church and state. Islamic nations figure heavily in the regional scene, but there is no international Islamic Church with a global perspective. The regional penetrations in Africa and Europe have stimulated the beginning of strategic thinking in centers of Arab wealth in the Persian Gulf region and in the cultural center, Al Ahzar. An orchestrated campaign to destroy Christianity in Africa (two hundred churches have been burned in the last decade) and construct Mosques and Islamic cultural centers throughout Europe, paid for by Arab oil money, is beginning to show signs of renewed international thinking. It will be important to observe Islam's ability to survive secularizing pressures in those open European and North American countries where Muslims are a small minority.

The fact that Christianity grew up in opposition to the state power of the mighty Roman Empire has conditioned the Church mentality and structure in a totally different manner, instilling considerable independence, especially in the West. The Catholic Church is the oldest and largest such institution, the church with the greatest presence across the globe. The Papacy is emerging as principal moral spokesman on a world scale. But how is the Church actually affecting the world much? It is still advancing as missionary in far-flung areas, especially in the middle of Africa, Korea, and Indonesia. But it has also been suffering from the inroads of extreme secularization in its old homelands, seriously in North America and parts of Latin America, and catastrophically in parts of Catholic Europe. Yet even in the worst-hit areas, it shows an ability to invent new institutional forms—secular institutes, charismatic communities, *Opus Dei, Focalari, Communione et Liberazione, Communidades Ecclesial de Baje,* the Eternal World Television Network. In Latin America, the Philippines, and parts of Africa, it is carving out new roles for itself, political, social, and economic as much as strictly devotional. Its political impact in Poland, Chile, the Philippines, and South Korea has proven decisive. In some of the most compromised situations—Holland, the United States, Brazil—Rome has been slowly, prudently reasserting itself, seeking to maintain orthodoxy without provoking outright schism.

It is difficult to assess the pragmatic importance of the various churches for the entire planet. Stalin's question, "How many divisions has the Pope?" is difficult to answer, even on a national scale. National states project their political presence through military power, foreign trade arrangements, investments, and aid programs. Churches enjoy none of this kind of material power, though they can influence members' attitudes and they are active in society through their charitable work. One can get an idea of the power of a corporation by examining assets, market share, research and development expenditures, and cash flow. If one studied Mass attendance and vocation figures for France, to take an example, one would see only catastrophe ahead for the Catholic Church. What would not show up in statistics is the transformative effect of the new leadership under the Archbishop of Paris, Jean Cardinal Lustiger, and several new bishops, nor would the intensity of fervor and the creative intelligence in certain renewal movements be evident.[5] Subjects of religion, taboo in intellectual circles fifteen years ago, have become in many instances the focus of interest, as Communism's troubles have sent many back for a more critical look at Marxism itself and as the narrowness of positivism has been relentlessly attacked by phenomenology and by thinkers like Voegelin. Whether such a trend will in due course translate itself into larger movements of popular religious devotion remains to be seen, and what effect increased devotion would have on the impact of the Church community within the broader society is hard to fathom.

The World Council of Churches, too, shows interest in political influence and attempts to change the world. This can become highly effective when its moral prestige is thrown behind movements fostered by one of the great worldly powers, such as the peace movement. But even prag-

5. The decline in vocations to the priesthood has reversed, and since the start of the present Pontificate, they have increased considerably all over the world, except in Oceania. Whereas the Jesuits in France, who many would say have lost their focus, currently have one novice, Cardinal Lustiger's archdiocese has a healthy flow of new vocations. One new religious order, in many ways like the "old" Jesuits, has one thousand seminarians and as yet only two hundred ordained priests.

matically, it is not on the obvious, overtly political level that the churches and other religious agencies work their effect. Religion influences life-styles in the subtlest ways, through spiritual impact. These changes can work their leavening long before it becomes possible for the observer of society to grasp the seriousness of the transformation.

When we turn later to religious traditions, not as sources of pragmatic influence on the world situation but as transmitters of treasures of in-sight, we will raise the question of their perennial truth; that truth is already on the pragmatic level the key to their ultimate transformative power. It can work long after the institutions founded to pass them on have lost their direct pragmatic influence over everyday history. Consider how much the Roman Republic influenced the American and French revolutions through the medium of texts (and monuments), that is, as a spiritual influence, more than a millennium after its demise. Such consid-erations, difficult to ascertain, remind us of the need to be cautious: man is not just a material agent; what happens deep in the soul, quietly, even hidden at first, can come to mold the whole of history.

Urban, High-Technology Society

Scientific-Technological Traditions

In considering the great powers, we mentioned the traditions that motivate these institutions and that they pass on. But we have yet to consider them as traditions in their own right, transcending this or that governmental or industrial or banking institution.

Heidegger, searching hard for a word to express the essence of the mod-ern world, a term rolling mind-set and effective structures into one, re-ferred to the encompassing interpretive horizons characteristic of the high-technology epoch along with the world they engendered as the *Ge-stell*, or "framework." By this he tried to point to the emerging world sys-tem (which I refer to as "urban, high-technology society") and in particu-lar its tendency to establish a way of living and thinking that closes off ties to the past. (I am not as relentlessly opposed to this emergent world as Hei-degger was, in part because of my expectation that authenticity is possible to us and hence that the "framework" is not so rigid as he supposed.)

Those steeped in these traditions and formed to their ways of inter-preting the world label all who are not so versed (still a majority of mankind) as "underdeveloped." Because an "efficient" society is indeed adept at producing prodigious wealth, its new missionary thrust reaches out to liberate the unfortunate masses from their poverty and bring them to the promised land of industrialized, urbanized society. From this endeavor has grown an entire development industry with international institutions and corporations, including many development "missionaries" willing to live in the bush.

Acculturation into the traditions transmitted by these institutions is long and highly organized. In medical school, for example, the capital investment by society is enormous—a quarter million dollars for some specialists. It is not just technical information and methods and habits that are being passed on, but a way of being-in-the-world, a set of horizons of interpretation that make possible doctor-patient, doctor-doctor, and doctor-government relationships. Research, instead of being a gentleman's inquiry into the laws of nature within the pattern of a well-balanced existence, becomes a driving pursuit of marketable knowledge, the stuff careers are built on, and it is the workaholics, the ruthlessly ambitious "self-made man" and "liberated woman" who set the pace and the tone, while obsessive loners often provide the inspired wherewithal.

What the resulting society, for all its technological and economic wonders, has not produced is a widely understood, coherent, all-englobing theory of itself as a democratic, entrepreneurial, social-welfare, open society, nothing to correspond to the sweeping socialist ideologies which reign supreme in the lands under Marxist domination. That is not the fault of the United States or Europe, but reveals something about the pragmatic development of this entire culture. One result is that Western technological societies maintained a defensive stance against the Soviet bloc in political and military terms, until the contrasting rhythms of development overwhelmed the Communists.

It is always dangerous, of course, to be on the defensive. Paradoxically, the society of high technology was from the start overwhelmingly on the cultural offensive. But this has not been part of an explicit strategy and therefore has not led to an overall plan of advance such as the Soviets possessed. Western societies do not seem to know how to draw the maximum political advantage from their superiority. The situation reminds one of Athens against Sparta or the crude Romans: despite their inventiveness, the Athenians ended as servants. The big difference is that Athens and Sparta were on roughly the same scale in brute power, territory, and technological sophistication, whereas the Western alliance, with its 600 million people, western European and North American land masses, and vastly superior wealth, while a loose affiliation, is two or three times more powerful than the Soviet bloc and much wealthier.

The Marxist-Leninist Tradition

Until recently, Marxist-Leninist theory has given the Soviet bloc solid, not to say suffocating, coherence. Although the weakness at the core has now caused that unity to collapse, for decades this theory has helped arm the coalition with a long-range, self-conscious strategy, steadily directed from Moscow. Iron discipline was maintained in the populace, using a military model of control. For example, while a million illegal immigrants a year pour uncontrolled into the United States, even today no one can get into or out of the Soviet Union without permission.

Given the poor economic and stagnating social record of the central command countries inspired by the Marxist-Leninist tradition, how can its ideology still attract interest as a serious approach to mankind's problems? An answer must be given on two levels. First, pragmatically, the ideological tradition is kept relevant and alive by the powerful institutions that have a vested interest in maintaining it—whatever Marxist governments and Communist parties remain. It is rather like a religious studies department whose professors have lost their Christian faith but do not want to resign, so they use Christianity and largely subvert it in the process. I cannot comment on the degree of sincere belief in Marxist analysis within the Chinese *Nomenklatura,* but I can testify from personal experience that the cynicism within Russia was very high indeed. Since *Glasnost* has allowed revelation of the extent of the practical disaster, the loss of faith reveals the depths of earlier cynicism. Be that as it may, the ideology remains a convenient tool for giving the society a conceptual unity and a strategic coherence, it provides a civil theology without which it risks coming apart. Whatever the vision this inspires, it is carried into practice by the unitary nature of the central command structure which places all economic, political, and cultural control in the same highly leveraged hands at the top of one vast hierarchy. Coherence brings stagnation and peculiar contradictions because central planning lacks the tight feedback loops needed in such complex organizations and hence becomes hopelessly remote from the working level, where most operating decisions are made by the individual agents who have do the work and buy the goods. Tight police control persists, however.

But Marxism and Marxism-Leninism should be considered as well on the entirely different theoretical level. What Marx achieved was a synthesis, Hegelian in ambition—and to a degree in inspiration, although entire dimensions of Hegel are ignored by Marx—a synthesis of socialist economic theory (many of his economic ideas, if not indeed most, are derivative), utopian political dream, and materialist anthropology incorporating a kind of social Darwinism in the idea of class struggle, all surcharged with a dose of Feuerbachian atheism, Nietzschean before its time with an overtone of superman liberationism. As eclectic as it may be, this vast "materialist dialectic" synthesis remains the only sweeping, well-worked-out conceptual effort to provide a framework for pulling together insights into the new industrial society.

Although this ideology has been relentlessly criticized both as an overall system of explanation and in much of its detailed analyses, the many people of ideological temperament who crave a well-worked-out thought structure into which they can fit their experience still find it attractive because no one has succeeded in replacing it with an equally coherent and sweeping overview of man's situation in this planetary epoch. For those who reject a transcendent Absolute but nevertheless desire to possess an overarching view of man's situation, the secularized redemptive eschatology of Marxism still provides, *faute de mieux,* a religious substitute of some attractiveness. Its relentless materialism validates the exercise of the will-to-power, its class warfare structure offers justification to frustrated men of resentment, its utopian goals offer hope to those who desire a better world. The fact that it produces its own "church," the Party (often now a "Social Democratic Party"), organized for struggle against a clearly defined devil, gives it a practical attractiveness at the same time. This quality helps it survive any manner of intellectual critique. Marxism still functions as an effective faith.

Capitalism and the Open Society

The Marxist term *capitalism* marks an effort to reduce the complex reality of "open society" in the industrial era to the abuse of capital, the amassing of the great material source of power, the acquisition of the "alienated" fruits of hard-working men's labor to be used to hold them in place. As a starting point for the analysis of entrepreneurial, social-welfare, mixed democratic society, with its proud traditions of rule of law, respect for human rights, and openness of communication, such a concept is obviously not just inadequate, it is a deliberate distortion. It would be like labeling Christianity as Papism, and proceeding to analyze the history of the Church as though papal power were the central reality.

It is in fact significant that there is no widely accepted word for this powerful factor of open democratic society. This suggests both that it amounts to a very complex, diffuse set of phenomena and, as I have been saying all along, that it is not ideology-driven. Suppose we were to follow Karl Popper and call our kind of society simply "open society."[6] This emphasizes a different central characteristic, its pluralism of institutional structures and traditions, its tolerance of differing viewpoints, and its dynamism. Open society rests, as Michael Novak has shown so well, on three pillars: politically, it demands democracy; economically, it requires an entrepreneurial market system modified by a social welfare "safety net" (a need discovered in practice, though when and how much a given society can afford without strangling the wealth-generating machine that pays for it is still hotly debated); finally, it needs a culture in which rule of law is respected and a sense of teamwork and fair play predominates. Selfish and unbridled opportunism can bring the system to ruin. "Enlightened self-interest" has to be understood in a truly enlightened way and acculturated into the agents who make such a fluid and complex society function.

As this kind of society is still poorly understood, successful transmission of the many traditions out of which it is woven may happen tradition by tradition, but a strategy seeing to the overall well-being of such societies is difficult to conceive and pursue. Parents, educators, and statesmen must have some idea of how such a society works if they are to assure that all the disciplines and knowledge required are transmitted to the next generation and if they are to impede certain current processes from compromising its future. Consider a danger we highlighted in our capsule survey of the United States as a superpower: poor general education of ill-disciplined children by undereducated, bureaucratized teachers could lead the society to teach such narrow specialization at the higher levels that the society would soon find itself short of good strategic thinkers and overall managers and statesmen able to cope with a planetary situation

6. Karl Popper, *The Open Society and Its Enemies* (Princeton: Princeton University Press, 1950).

and assure a satisfyingly human application of the great power the society's technology mobilizes.

It is not that large-scale problems are not considered in open societies. On the contrary, the social sciences are poring over them and think tanks galore are active. Yet global understanding remains weak, quantitatively and qualitatively. Even key notions familiar to an elite, such as market, profit, and self-interest, are not accurately and adequately grasped by masses of the populous and are mischievously deformed by ideologues. Ecological issues are badly understood, which leaves public opinion vulnerable to manipulation by forces with a narrow agenda. Witness the five-billion-dollar nuclear generating station of Long Island Lighting sitting idle. No society can afford blunders of this magnitude.

In a strategy for the pursuit of truth, what place should we accord to study of this phenomenon of the open society? Since it is not consolidated in a single, coherent, explicit tradition, its history cannot be appropriated in the methodical (but still demanding) way one might appropriate the Catholic or Marxist traditions. Even if one could decide upon the essential truth claims and deficiencies of the American tradition so far as it is explicit, critically coming to terms with them and with that society's political stands and social practices, it would be far from achieving an appropriation of the traditions of open society. Open society is a loose weave of implicit and explicit traditions and institutions on many levels, precipitated institutionally through many governments and incarnated according to the varying styles of many ethnic traditions. The democracy and capitalism practiced in Japan is not the same as that evolved in the Netherlands. Each nation has found its own solutions and woven its own ethnic version. One could, and should, raise many questions both about the adequacy of these different solutions to the local situation and their fidelity to the ideal as the intellectual world is coming to understand it.

The difficulties in understanding the traditions of open societies must not be allowed to discourage us because these societies are too vital to contemporary man, both practically and theoretically. They are immensely rich repositories of practical wisdom and hard-earned experience. I remember the leaders of *Solidarnosc* in Gdansk telling me, in the years just after the military crackdown in 1981, how they were studying *The Federalist Papers* and the works of John Locke and John Stuart Mill in an effort to understand better how democracy works, so the next time they would be ready for power.

Although we cannot avoid to some extent running along behind the rapidly unfolding processes, we must improve our ability to control complex institutions, at least sufficiently to allow society to maintain itself before the threat of internal disintegration and external domination by those with another system that is coherent but suffocating. Only through an intelligent effort to rise above mere pragmatic muddling-through will that be possible. Developing methods of critical appropriation through adequate understanding of the history and the theoretical underpinnings of the system are a necessary part of achieving this.

My concern with the traditions and institutions bundled loosely together to form the armature of open societies is first of all pragmatic: I believe we need to understand what is going on, and those whose natural faiths include a commitment to democratic society surely want to protect and enhance that openness. But there is also a concern regarding implications for theoretical truth, the larger wisdom. That, too, is rooted in my natural faith, for I believe, for all the perils besetting modern democracies, open society is truer to man and to Being than any other basic way of organizing human society. In any event, is this not an area into which the seeker of wisdom is obliged to inquire?

As we shift our attention now to the appropriation of traditions for their theoretical truth, we should notice that critical appropriation of the practical reality of open societies moves quite naturally toward the theoretical. It is vain to attempt an understanding of the institutions of free society without rendering as explicit as possible the anthropological assumptions underlying the motivation that led to their founding and that continue to fuel efforts to improve them, just as we must come to understand what is different (and certainly anti-Christian) in the underlying Marxist materialist anthropology.

Now that the United States of America has celebrated the two-hundredth anniversary of the Constitution, thinkers are more than ever wrestling with the question of just how Jewish and Christian is the view of man that founds and justifies such a polity. The underlying theoretical issues are coming to the fore, and none too soon, as Western society runs a serious risk of dissolution before the onslaught of the most extreme pluralism any society in history has ever experienced. Moreover, there is reason to worry about what will become of democratic capitalism in those societies, like Japan, with little Christian understanding of man in their background. Upon the course of the present theoretical debate (witness Allan Bloom's *The Closing of the American Mind* topping the bestseller list) may depend the survival of open society. Being closer to the truth is no guarantee of existence.

For my part, I shall not attempt to enter the debate until I have secured the philosophic ground. Only when I have critically appropriated that mainstream tradition reaching from the Hebrew prophets and the Greek philosophers through the fathers and doctors of the Church will I be prepared to defend what I understand of the nature of man. How can a Christian take a philosophic stand regarding man before examining seriously, for instance, the question of nature and grace, nature and supernature, as the tradition has debated it? Suppose the followers of Henri de Lubac and Hans Urs von Balthasar are right, when, returning to the Church fathers, they insist that with the redemption grace permeates and lifts up nature? If one is to refuse such an interpretation, as the de Lubacian David Schindler accuses Richard John Neuhaus and Michael Novak of doing in a recent controversy over "The Catholic Moment," one should do so knowing the tradition and hence understanding at least something of what is at issue.[7] I can sympathize with Neuhaus and Novak when they intimate that if the Christian conception of man cannot be successfully maintained in a secularized version, then entrepreneurial democracy and open society are doomed. But one cannot responsibly dismiss Schindler, claiming to speak in the name of the most authentic current in the tradition, by declaring emotionally, "But that would be intolerable!"

Traditions as Treasures of Wisdom

Bodies of Knowledge and Know-How

To this point in our survey of the world situation, emphasis has been on the practical impact of certain massive institutions and the traditions which lie behind them. Now we shall change our perspective and instead of considering the pragmatic importance of the traditions, we shall con-

7. See David Schindler, "Once Again: George Weigel on Catholic and American Culture," *Communio* 5 (Spring 1988): 92–120; and "Catholic Public Theology and Post-Modernity: On Richard John Neuhaus' *The Catholic Moment*," *The Thomist* 53 (January 1989): 107–43. This debate was carried out variously in the pages of *Thirty Days, Crisis, Communio,* and private correspondence from the fall of 1988 into the fall of 1989 and was the subject of two *Communio* conferences.

sider the larger truth question: their contributions to wisdom. The issue now moves beyond how we manage such forces operative in the world to what we can learn from the traditions, what is stored up in their symbols, what may be of lasting value in mankind's institutional creations and above all in its search for theoretical understanding. Behind this new focus lies the deeper issue of strategy, not just how to manage the emerging world system so that we may survive, but how to manage our personal research. The real question of the present section, then, is: How may we establish a set of priorities for our personal work of appropriation?

Here again we shall focus on traditions that have inspired institutions and cultures whose influence is evident. There may be wise traditions we unfortunately ignore because for some reason their impact on the affairs of men has been minor. But let me invoke again what I have called an assumption in favor of Being: if some tradition were in fact passing on some formidable revelation of Being, the very fact that it contained an illuminating breakthrough would make it tend to persist and propagate. In due course, it would presumably become difficult to ignore.

The major contributions to theoretical understanding have been made by philosophy, the sciences, and religion. Art, literature, and political innovation have all contributed to theoretical insight, but much of what has been understood about the efforts of the poet, the painter, the architect, and the statesman has been taken up into theoretical reflection and come to us through philosophies, theologies, and the natural and social sciences. Like acts of love, the personal impact of beauty and the poetic on the individual is powerful, potentially of fundamental and lasting influence, but often never explicated and hence difficult of access for reflective, methodical, scientific inquiry and scarcely able to provide the basic frame for such inquiry. Von Balthasar—to take a lesson from the thinker in our time with the most ambitious vision (his trilogy composed of *Herrlichkeit, Theodramatik,* and *Theologik* stretches over seventeen volumes and constitutes the summit of his eighty books and five hundred articles)—did not start with his aesthetic, *Herrlichkeit* and *Theodramatik,* but ended his research there after securing the theoretical framework through more formalizable ontological inquiry now found in the *Theologik.* The great explicit statements of the arts—the musical scores, the novels, the paintings, the monuments—may have implications for Being that are inadequately reflected in philosophy, but they remain accessible to all individuals, who may go back to them at any time, helped and hindered by their formal philosophical reflection.

Returning then to what I perceive to be the most influential traditions operative in the world system, let us consider the great scientific, philosophic, and theologic traditions from the standpoint of their contribution to theory. First, we will consider the sciences, not this time for their immense technological impact, but in their role as sources of truth. Here we encounter a sociological paradox rife with significance: to speak of the sciences as *sources of truth* surprises my rather anti-technology students, who appear unaware of the extent to which our entire society grows out of occidental ways of thinking. They do not realize to what extent scientific traditions of thought have, since Plato and Aristotle, molded our ways of being-in-the-world (as Heidegger would say), which are not those of other peoples. Indeed, they are surprised to learn that the same word, *science,* properly applies to what Plato and Einstein do. Arnold Toynbee designates this "the Western Technological Civilization," and considers the secularism which accompanies it to be essential to it.[8] His view of the essence of occidental civilization is radically oversimplified. But we have readily agreed that there has indeed emerged from old roots some such civilization and that it is invading the entire world.

My students, like Toynbee, resist questioning the truth of these ways of interpreting the world that have originated from science. I often find that even after a year-long "Introduction to Philosophy" in which I defend the claim that there are occidental ways of thinking and that these ways of interpreting the world extensively condition our way of Being because they mold our approach to truth, the students still take as natural, necessary, and common to all mankind (and so above critical reexamination) what are in fact truth claims about Being that come out of a widely shared, occidental, natural faith and are very much in need of radical critical evaluation.

Our philosophies and our sciences are not merely pragmatic ways of dealing with things, but vast storehouses of insight and experience, aspects of which are starting to have a serious impact on the mentality of much of mankind. In a future volume I shall consider the roots of these sciences in revelation as well as in philosophy and their complex relationship with the Jewish and Christian religions. Perhaps the most economical way to make the point here that these treasures of wisdom we

8. Arnold Toynbee, *An Historian's Approach to Religion,* (London: Oxford University Press, 1956), 150.

call the sciences are, after all, sets of truth claims affecting globally how we look at things and not just a passing parade of models with spin-offs in effervescent technological innovation is to contrast for a moment what Voegelin calls the cosmological way of thinking of the ancients (as well as many contemporary tribal people) to modern man's mental landscape. At this juncture, I shall oversimplify and caricature both termini of the development to help bring out the enormity of the impact of science.

Cosmological man lived (some tribesmen still do) in a small, closed, static universe, one in which things simply are what they are—changing little, they are taken as exemplars of eternal archetypes. In the eyes of cosmological man, there may have been some change in the world, a degeneration from a golden age, but it does not affect the "whatnesses" of things. A spark of spirituality associates man with the gods, who themselves are generated from the chaos conquered and ordered by the founding God. Man's Promethean efforts to change the world are arrogant threats to the eternal order and are punishable by death. Chthonic powers are always boiling just below the crystalline eternal order of things, reflected in the ever-repeated cycles of nature. They may be placated if one knows the magic incantations, and they are held at bay by good order resting on sound law.

When one contrasts with such a cosmological view the contemporary, science-influenced understanding of man and his cosmic setting, he is struck by this fact: certain aspects of the present overview curiously fit Judaeo-Christian revelation better than they do the cosmological view. The astrophysical theory that an incomprehensibly vast cosmos has been hurled into space-time from an explosive point of initial energy goes much better with a revelation of creation by an Infinite Source than it does with the closed cosmos of most of the other traditional religions. That man has been formed of the very "slime of the earth" with the spirit breathed into it by the same Infinite Source to crown His creation and that he is being educated for participation in godhead are easier to reconcile with an enlightened understanding of evolution which sees the complexifying and interiorizing creative active working up from the lowest stuff of creation, than are visions of man as slaves of gods in a fixed universe.

This is, as I said, a vast subject. The physicist-theologian Stanley Jaki's contention that the Judaeo-Christian sense of the inherent intelligibility of a divinely willed world gave impetus to the search for sense has to be assessed.[9] The point is that central to the challenge of appropriating the contemporary situation of mankind must be an enhanced awareness and critique of the scientific way of viewing the world, understood with sufficient historical depth—that is, from its beginnings in Greek philosophy and with its transformations, first by the fathers of the Church, then by the doctors in the Middle Ages, the mathematic-mechanical physicists, and again, to some extent under the influence of Kierkegaardian existentialism (so claims Niels Bohr) in recent times. Its relationship with the technological mentality is likewise important, as there exists there a cross-fertilization with profound ontological implications.

The reflections of Ellul, Toynbee, Heidegger, Marcel, and others on the nature of the technological mentality and the organization of technological society have made a brave beginning in this latter regard. Unfortunately, these critics have been generally so negative about certain dehumanizing aspects of technology that they often fail to communicate much appreciation for the insights achieved by science and their positive impact on our wisdom. The contrast of "Western Technological Civilization's" way of Being with those inspired by the great religious traditions is indeed startling. One of the advantages of serious appropriative study of the religious traditions is the contrast they afford with what has emerged in the West. The challenge is to bring together in a single wisdom the enduring truth of both kinds of tradition.

Great Religious Traditions

Man's million years or so of existence, the very short period we call *historia* (the first records of experience in writing date from just before 3000 B.C.), has seen the rise of the great religions. Most of them are not even three millennia old, the three and a half millennia or so of Mosaic Judaism and Judaeo-Christianity being the oldest continuous tradition. Nor are there many such traditions. Less than a half dozen "higher religions" have developed and persisted: the Abrahamic family; the Hindic family with its Buddhist offshoot; the Confucian (with some elements of Taoist thought absorbed); and the Zoroastrian, which hangs on through a few remnant societies such as the Parsees in India and which is the only one of the great religions almost to have disappeared, through

9. See, among other works of Stanley Jaki, *The Road of Science and the Ways to God: The Gifford Lectures* (Chicago: University of Chicago Press, 1978).

conquest by Islam.[10] All the others remain important forces in the world, the Abrahamic being pragmatically the greatest, the Hindic and Buddhist and Confucian being more limited geographically and in their present attractiveness to converts as ways of living. Each of these traditions, with its many subtraditions, is inexhaustibly rich, and each makes claims on all of us as an expression of truth that deserves to be taken into consideration in leading our lives, in worshiping God, and in fashioning society.

I had my reasons for beginning my own work of methodic appropriation with the Catholic tradition, reasons argued both in terms of strategic importance in the world system, antiquity and richness of the truth claims put forward, and personal impact on my own life. Because these will be spelled out in a subsequent volume, they will not be elaborated here. It was in the spirit of pursuing ecumenical wisdom that I began the experiment of appropriating the most influential of the shoots from the tree of Jesse, Catholic Christianity. I intended to combine a reasonable level of sound scholarship with a practical sense of the need to avoid bogging down in enticing side issues to get to the heart of the matter and then move on to other traditions.

Fifteen enjoyable years and three book-length manuscripts later I have a more realistic view of the enormity of the task of coming to grips with just one of these traditions. Readers will have to judge for themselves whether the progress I believe I have made in bringing out the essence of the tradition helps towards the goal of ecumenic wisdom. It certainly has enhanced my awareness and love for my own tradition, and I believe it goes a way toward making the claims of this tradition more understandable, more "translatable" for people approaching it from natural faiths basically informed by other traditions.

One thing has become clear to me as a result of this work: the way toward an encounter between the exponents of the great traditions requires extensive epistemological preparation. The nature of the truth question and the challenges it poses is now clearer to me for having undertaken this work, as well as the research towards my later appropria-

10. Much of the former domain of Talmudic Jewry in Mesopotamia and of Nestorian and Monophysite Christianity from the Levant to China conceded itself into Islam after the devastation of the Mongol attacks, which still have that part of the world in the grip of wasteland. Latin Orthodox Christianity in Africa, as well, generally faded into Islam.

tion of another of these great traditions, Islam. The necessary relation between the pursuit of authenticity and the goal of progressing toward an ecumenic wisdom while becoming more critically aware of the epistemological and ontological implications of one's view of things has impressed itself upon me.

8.

A Single Wisdom
from Various Traditions

Are Experiences Translatable?

I have been implicitly arguing against the naiveté, not to say destructiveness, in the present planetary situation, of a skeptical live-and-let-live pluralism in which the various traditions would be supposed to reside comfortably isolated in their separate worlds. But, though it sounds nice to call for an ecumenic wisdom, we must not in turn be naive: such a project demands nothing less than moving toward a unity of discourse, in function of an adequate project of reason. Such a project assumes the ultimate translatability of all experiences, based on faith in the unity of Being and the commonality of human nature. Rendering this project and the unity of Being and of human nature credible is the task of another book. But allow me at least to explain here the problem of translatability.

In those cases where a certain objectivism applies, when there exists outside consciousness some thing or situation to which persons of different perspective can have basically perceptual access, then the problem of translation is not too serious: one can direct the other's attention to the aspects of things accessible to both in experience. "Cut off only the dead branches of that linden" translates perfectly into French as *Coupez seulement les branches mortes de ce tilleul* because what is referred to—a tree of a well-known type, the act of cutting, and the notion of a branch—are all based on common experience of easily accessible and isolable things. But this should not seduce us into believing it is easy to integrate, for instance, experience of art and scientific knowledge of nature into a single wisdom. C. P. Snow's "two cultures" phenomenon poses real difficulties.[1] Yet we need to understand how poetic experience

---

1. C. P. Snow, *The Two Cultures and the Scientific Revolution* (New York: Cambridge University Press, 1959).

and scientific experience are both situated within the life of man and to what aspects of Being they refer.

But another kind of problem arises when one person attempts to transmit to another a radically different experience from any he has had, of things to which he has no direct access. This happens often in the transmission of history and even in relating different psychological experiences. It is also the challenge posed with a vengeance by the traditions of revelation.

Let us consider these traditions of revelation because they are, as we have seen, important to the study of tradition and for understanding the life of man. The Bible speaks of faith in things unseen. The interior life is in so many ways an uncharted and murky depth. What is the suitable form of discourse for talking about these matters of revelation? Under what conditions can the believer talk meaningfully with the nonbeliever about matters of faith, given that the person outside the tradition does not share in his religious experiences and so possibly has nothing to pour into the space opened by the believer's symbols?

Discussion between religious believers from different traditions has its own problems, but they are less severe than between religious and non-religious persons, since a base of similar experiences is available to all religious parties. That is why, I suppose, the most formally structured dialogue is going on between various branches of Christianity, and to a lesser degree, between Muslims and Christians and between Jews and Christians (in Israel it is even going on, quietly, between Jews and Muslims). Some religious groups have sought to make progress by sharing experiences together. In Madras, Hindus and Catholics have been seeking for over twenty years to share certain experiences by living them together, developing dance and even a Catholic mass with Hindi forms. Still, their translation for one another of experiences requires passage by way of philosophical discourse if they aim at universality of assent. But are their faith experiences universalizable? If so, how?

At the heart of the issue is the question of the possibility of communicating experiences to another who has not had them. *Experience* is central because what the symbols of religion represent are not mere descriptions of things nor mere assertions of principles derived from things—though these, too, figure importantly in religious discourse—but lived interpersonal relationships. The nature of this experience constitutes a central issue to be explored.

Maximum Differentiation of Experience

Eric Voegelin advanced as a claim he considered scientifically defensible that the philosophical and Christian consciousness, growing out of the event of Greek philosophy and out of the Christ event, represents the maximum differentiation of experience through the revelation of the *Logos* in history.[2] By this he means that through theological reflection on the Christ event, capturing the insights of Greek philosophy and culminating in a summit in the theological syntheses of St. Augustine and St. Thomas, it was given to mankind to achieve the fullest, most thoroughly articulated, and most balanced understanding of how men relate to God, to nature, and to one another.

Now there is a demanding truth claim! To anyone who has not wrestled with the *De Trinitate* and *De civitate Dei,* or looked through the immense vision of the *De Veritate* or the *Summa Theologiae,* the claim may seem, on the face of it, preposterous. Yet the highly respected political scientist, Voegelin, has not been laughed out of the academy for making it. Rather, he has added fuel to a renaissance in studies of the tradition. But how can such a claim be examined critically? Voegelin himself warned of attempting to develop methods in a vacuum. That is why I have set out to learn how to approach a great tradition critically, and because I am sympathetic to the claim of its maximum differentiation and can see its central molding effect on our own civilization and through it on the emerging world system, as well as its impact on me, I seek to learn by doing, by appropriating the Catholic tradition. I am now working through the essential symbolic and institutional systems of this tradition, looking at the symbol-institution-setting interaction, seeking to comprehend this most-differentiated experience, hoping to discern from the perspective of my own natural faith its lasting contribution to an ecumenic wisdom and to see what it could mean to claim it has achieved maximum differentiation.

Of course, the reader of this volume is not expected simply to bow down uncritically before Voegelin's intriguing but awesome claim. It would be understatement to say it is controversial. I bring it up here both

2. Eric Voegelin, *The New Science of Politics* (Chicago: University of Chicago Press, 1952), 79. Voegelin's defense of this idea stretches from the 1952 Chicago lectures in *The New Science of Politics* through the five volumes of *Order and History* (Baton Rouge: Louisiana State University Press, 1956–1985).

to show the dimensions of the challenge confronting those who take the search for ecumenic wisdom seriously and to confess that I myself take it seriously.

Voegelin makes a corollary claim that is equally grave: he contends that modern "gnostic civilization" represents a regression from this maximum of differentiation achieved in the Middle Ages. He claims we have lost the sense of the openness of the soul.[3] Because men could not live with the uncertainty of faith, they sought to substitute for divine revelation about man's situation systems of thought through which they could feel secure in a dominating vision of Being. Starting with the eschatological speculations of Joachim de Flore at the end of the twelfth century, this kind of construction became progressively secularized and resulted in the great voluntaristic and necessitarian systems of Hegel, Marx, and the fascists.

Voegelin warns in a letter to the sociologist, Alfred Schütz, that the sense of Christian claims must be recuperated. To do this scientifically, they must be approached historically; they are to be understood in the context of the time in which they exploded onto the scene, in order to get the measure of the challenge they pose to contemporary thought.

What the men of the eighteenth-century Enlightenment held against Christian dogmatics (enlightened thinkers are repeating it today), namely that theological statements—unlike statements concerning sense perception—are meaningless because they cannot be verified, is the very starting point of Christian theology. On this point Thomas would agree with every Enlightener. Dogmatics is a symbolic web which explicates and differentiates the extraordinarily complicated religious experiences; furthermore, the order of these symbols is a descriptive system, not a rational system capable of being deduced from axioms. (We must note the insistence of Thomas that Incarnation, Trinity and other doctrines are rationally impenetrable, i.e. rationally meaningless.) Here, it seems to me, lies the greatest value of Christian theology as a store of religious experiences amassed over more than a thousand years, which has been thoroughly analyzed and differentiated by Church fathers and Scholastics in an extraordinary cooperative enterprise. To set up against this treasure hoard (without having exhaustive knowledge of it) philosophical speculations of a monotheistic, pantheistic, dualistic, or any other kind of speculations [Christianity, for Voegelin, is none of these—it is trinitarian] which inevitably rest

3. Voegelin, *The New Science of Politics*, 164. This theme constitutes the subject of research in his five-volume *Order and History*, a work I consider essential for anyone struggling to understand the dimensions of the truth question.

on individual thinkers' very limited experiences, seems to me, I am bound to say, brash mischief-making, even if the mischief is committed by thinkers such as Bruno or Hegel or William James.[4]

Voegelin is using the term *rational* here in the arbitrarily narrow sense given that term by the enlightened of the eighteenth and the positivists of the nineteenth centuries. I assume he also intends *verify* in that narrow sense. While what he calls this concatenation of rationally impenetrable symbols cannot be known within the confines of an arbitrarily limited eighteenth-century rationalism, if knowledge is understood to embrace the whole person, heart and mind, theory and practice, then the term impenetrable falls away. Hans Urs von Balthasar spends much of the first volume of *Herrlichkeit* examining the ways in which the Christ event is experienced and verified, with an ample empirical element in what he calls this "aesthetic experience."[5]

If Voegelin is right in claiming that the maximum of differentiation—that is, both the full scope of man's relations to man, to nature and to God, with openness to revelation and the most adequate categorical scheme for dealing with all these dimensions of reality—has been achieved at the summit of this tradition, then this tradition is not just a stumbling block, but it is also, paradoxically, the inevitable rallying point for ecumenic dialogue.

Before such an imperialistic claim is dismissed out of hand, the student of history should recall that it is from the Christian tradition that the major impetus for ecumenic unity has originated. This is no accident—maximum differentiation brings with it enhanced self-awareness. That is why the evolution of the Christian tradition in modern times, despite the gnostic contraction, has generated the project of authenticity, which discovers its root in the project of (properly understood) rationality.

The complex dialectic of this development—from Thomas and Bonaventure and Joachim de Flore, through Renaissance skepticism, the fracturing of Christendom in the Protestant revolt, and Descartes' search for absolute certainty; through Hobbes and Hume and Kant, with the discovery of the transcendental unity of consciousness; through the great gnostic deformation of Christian vision by Hegel and Marx's perversion

4. Eric Voegelin, *The Philosophy of Order,* ed. P. Opitz and G. Sebba (Stuttgart: Klett and Cotta, 1981), 456.

5. "Aesthetic experience" is the theme and subtitle of the first part of Balthasar's *Herrlichkeit* (Einsiedeln, Switzerland: Johannes Press, 1961–1964).

of that; to Nietzsche's apotheosis of the will-to-power and Heidegger's effort to recover authenticity in the midst of the ultimate gnostic debacle—is a convoluted and essential tale, incomprehensible without Christianity. The reader should recall where we began in the first two chapters of this book. There it was pointed out that the measure of the rational must be taken from the standpoint of the maximum differentiation, that broadest illumination and fullest spelling-out of reality achieved by the tradition in its greatest syntheses.

The point here is that reason must not be so construed as to exclude any realm of genuine experience, intelligence must seek ways of relating all realms of experience to one another, and reason, understood as the philosophic faculty seeking universality of vision, must develop instruments of thought able to accommodate, analyze, and synthesize every sort of experience. For this to be possible, one must begin the development of categories at the point of maximal differentiation of consciousness, to make sure nothing is arbitrarily closed out.

The Pursuit of Truth as a Communal Enterprise

As Voegelin points out, the tradition's elaboration on the core symbols of revelation is an extraordinary cooperative enterprise; the pursuit of truth has always been a community undertaking. We cannot therefore criticize or appropriate the truth of a tradition, nor relate it with that of other traditions, without considering how the community that keeps the tradition alive actually functions. The appropriator has to seek to enter into its collective horizons of interpretation, situating himself at the point(s) of breakthrough (what Voegelin means when he warns Alfred Schütz that the symbols have to be understood in the context of their "explosion onto the scene") and following critically the evolving development of the symbols. Leaps of individual creative genius should not be underestimated. But if the Church has an Augustine in its midst, it is because of a Monica and an Ambrose. There would be no Thomas without Albert, no Albert without the Dominicans and the medieval disciples of Aristotle—including the great Arabic and Jewish translators and commentators. Albert, Thomas, and Bonaventure would be unthinkable without the institutional setting of the Sorbonne, and the University of Paris would not have been what it was without the cathedral schools of the twelfth century. More fundamentally, the religious experience of them all was mediated by the entire witnessing Church, hierarchical and popular.

This obvious fact fuels the Christian conviction that the genuineness of personal religious experience is to be tested only within the bosom of the Church, in the setting of the refined results, the entire interweaving of the community's millennial experience. It is why people pursuing the spiritual life turn to a spiritual director, entrusting themselves to a person experienced and knowledgeable in matters of the soul, who will act as a guardian of orthodoxy and guide the soul toward deepening experience of the core realities.

Spiritual experience of the transcendent entering into the human time-space within the sensorium of the soul is not something subject to communal experimental verification, like the discovery of a new virus. Yet such experiences are subject to a kind of test by communal wisdom. There is a long-accumulated experience of such matters, transmitted by masters of the spiritual life. The ways such discipline is maintained in various Christian traditions compared with certain Muslim (especially Sufi) and Jewish traditions, and contrasted with the thought control of fanatic sects, would yield important insight into the dynamics of spiritual life (and even have pragmatic importance for those concerned with the phenomena of fundamentalism, with Scientologists and Moonies, and with terrorists).

Long-lived spiritual communities have had to learn the hard way about the pathology of false prophecy. The masters know how rigorous is genuine spiritual cultivation and what discipline is required to open up the space wherein the graces of a special participation in the divine life can be accommodated. Speaking now only of the Christian spiritual traditions, it is interesting to note that the greatest of them always back up their deontic authority with the official authority of the Church at large. That is not the case in some non-Christian traditions, though in some traditions within Islam there is a kind of public acknowledgment of the authority of the greatest masters—in the case of the Ayatollahs in Iran, for instance. Paradoxically, the more institutionalized and dogmatic nature of the process within Catholicism probably has something to do with its masters of the spiritual life having much less involvement with the political life of the community than do, for instance, their Shiite counterparts in Iran.

Against the background of that long experience of community in the spirit, it can be appreciated why many Christians persist in the belief that ecumenic dialogue must be conducted in full union with the Church and under the prudent guidance of the Christ-ordained, hierarchical, pastoral leadership. Adherents of other traditions entering into such dialogue should also take care to represent their communities as truly as possible (which involves authority differing in form and exercise by tradition) if they are to present honestly and fully the accumulated wisdom of their traditions. That their institutions may not be as highly articulated as the Catholic church, the teaching authority perhaps not as explicit, takes nothing away from the validity of this contention. In ecumenic dialogue it is the voice of a tradition, and with it a perennial wisdom, that should speak, not just the untested opinion of an individual.

Yet it is the lonely individual—this conscience—which must judge in the final critical moment of appropriation. My only point here is that whether he is appropriating for himself or representing the tradition in ecumenic dialogue, it is the truth of the tradition, lived out and lovingly fostered and protected by the entire real community that is at issue; it is that socially loved and lived truth which he has to judge, not something he makes up for himself.

The symbols used, the language spoken, are in every case those of a living community with a long tradition. This realization makes all the more urgent the question with which we began: Are such symbols translatable? While I am convinced of the possibility of translatability, I will show in future work that it is no easy task. Translatability is at the core of communication, and what is more difficult than communications between human beings?

 **III.**

Tradition and Authenticity

9.

The Ultimate Structures and the Problem of Ideology

The present planetary situation is no different in this respect than the past: proponents of conflicting traditions often collide on the battlefield. Despite the hatred, the incomprehension, and the pathology manifest in these conflicts, ecumenic appreciation of the great traditions as cultural treasure houses of true experience is alive in some circles. It was a driving force behind the Oecumenical Second Vatican Council and in the World Council of Churches, for example. This is not surprising, given that Christian belief in creation and the brotherhood of man has contributed singularly to the development of the present ecumenic situation and that it is invading other traditions on the wings of economic development. Some, such as Buddhism, are by their nature well disposed to such openness.

However clear the historical demonstration of the role of the Christian doctrine that God is love in bringing about the present ecumenic strands in the world situation, secularists obviously are afraid claims of revelation will just fuel more intractable and violent dogmatisms, and for Muslims or Hindus to be sympathetic to the claim that the vast medieval Christian theological syntheses should be studied as centerpieces to the search for ecumenic wisdom might well require a miracle. Indeed, the enormity of claims by Christianity makes of that tradition particularly, as Saint Paul put it, a "stumbling block" (*skandalon* was his exact word).[1] Until the rich details of that vision are spread out, as I seek to do in a later volume, no one can reasonably be expected to believe that a theological tradition can so direct post-Enlightenment rational inquiry in such a full and balanced a manner as to make possible the recovery of the maximum sense from our experience in a way that respects the sensitivities of all other traditions.

1. 1 Corinthians 1:24.

187

It is one thing for the nonbeliever to have to swallow the claim that we cannot understand the present planetary situation adequately without a respectful confrontation with Islam or Hinduism or Marxism or Christianity in all its varieties. It is quite another to ask him to accept that the great medieval syntheses of Augustine and Thomas be looked upon as summits of differentiation giving the sole adequate measure for criticizing the Gnostic contraction of symbols—the modern closing of the soul to entire dimensions of reality, especially to transcendence toward the divine and the depths of the interior life.

Yet this much is fact, as I have stressed: the tradition out of which the sense of development has itself developed, the tradition of critical inquiry which, beginning in the thirteenth century, gave birth to mathematical physics and from which psychology has sprung, is just that occidental Greco-patristic-medieval symbol system. Even if one contends that modernity and the Enlightenment turned in some ways against aspects of the tradition, study of the tradition is necessary to knowing how and why the shift occurred, how continuity was maintained, and even how Christianity learned from the Enlightenment.

Why then are so many academicians so shy? Why was Voegelin able to blast the academy justifiably in 1952 in *The New Science of Politics* for its "pathological" and "gnostic" narrowness? Why do the professors, as good scientists, fail to investigate the core of the tradition, our own roots, thoroughly, dispassionately, critically, fairly? I venture to suppose that most readers will have the impression that one does not have to become a Muslim to appropriate Islam, though instinctively one realizes that he needs a much more sympathetic understanding of Muslim beliefs than the average occidental possesses. But I will bet most people fear that one will never go far towards sympathetically understanding the maximal differentiation of symbols in Christianity without risk of becoming a believer, or that only a believer can be sufficiently interested in the tradition to appropriate its truth claims. It is as though getting too close causes contamination.

So we return to the great naiveté underlying the sweet project of pursuing ecumenic wisdom. The pursuers of wisdom do not exist as cool, appreciative, analytic, thinking machines. We are all insecure and have psychological blocks hampering our ability to see, sometimes even our wanting to see. "*Voir et faire voir,* this is the goal of the present work," are the memorable first words of Teilhard de Chardin's *The Phenomenon of Man. Voir et faire voir,* "see and make seen," that is the goal of the pursuit of wisdom.

Why is it so hard to see? Why do we fail to see so much that surrounds us? Why is communication so difficult? Unless the present project for seeking ecumenic wisdom lays the foundation for a realistic and true anthropology that can help us see why we so often fail to see and what the sincere person might do about this, we shall have really seen nothing. That is the real question of redemption. The problem in approaching Christianity is that we all recognize that our own occidental tradition is steeped in it. If one is a believer, he remains defensive of attacks on the Christian understanding of man; if he is not, he is going to be cautious and suspicious despite himself, wanting to keep his distance. For most occidentals, Christianity is still a danger. At least that would be true, if I am correct, of all but the most totally secularized. Islam, on the other hand, poses no emotional threat to most of us.

But is it necessarily so that one is taking a risk in getting too close to sympathetic understanding of Christian symbols? As my own problem was just the opposite, it is hard for me to judge. I have had no difficulty studying Islam with great sympathy and respect. On the other hand, I must admit that I have found it difficult in struggling for some detachment from my own Christianity, and I do not claim that I have altogether succeeded, despite the heroic help of two atheist assistants most eager to make me see my own blindness. This experience enhances my sympathy for the nonbeliever when he feels resistant and reinforces the desire to illumine our existential engagement in Being in a way that respects the depths of our passionate engagements.

How does one convince the academy to take Christianity seriously and to treat it fairly when so many, since the time of Voltaire, Diderot, and Hume, hate what they think of as Christian? In a strange way the academy is itself a stumbling block on the path to wisdom. I have no good answer to this dilemma. But I did not invent it. Christianity hangs over the scene as at least part of the center of the history of Being with which we must come to terms if the search for truth is to be honest, however difficult one or another appropriator may find it to approach. Our recognition of the ideal of scientific detachment need be accompanied by no naiveté about the psychopathological blocks to attaining this virtue central to authenticity. Culturally formed need and desire and psychic blocks can steer or mislead the will, which should be the foundation of the search for truth. But there is no neat solution for us all to become suddenly less blocked.

It is not difficult to describe the kind of attitude necessary if progress toward ecumenic wisdom by way of finding what I call ultimate structures is to go forward. Nor is it impossible to sketch out those ultimate structures of experience and thus to see in a preliminary way the dimensions of the needed ecumenic wisdom. In doing this here by way of conclusion I hope to make clearer the central role of the most differentiated treasure house of symbols, thus completing the justification for my taking it as subject of my first methodic appropriation. I start my conclusion by sketching out the attitude or comportment that has to underlie such a quest because it can serve as an ideal for the education of future generations, contributing to our chances, as a society, of achieving a healthy development.

Development will go on in any event. We are required to act every day. Each of us has an attitude (*Verhalten*) toward the reality that surrounds us. There is an objective, ongoing need to develop an appropriate overall attitude to guide our acting-searching. But we have seen the ambiguity of this notion of situation, of the surrounding reality that reaches, according to focus, from the daily preoccupations of our little local setting out to the limits of ecological concern in the cosmic one. We have suggested the inevitability of addressing the question of its ultimate dimensions. What are the ultimate structures which we know we do not adequately *com-prehend*?

A humble, realistic, searching, resolutely nonideological comportment, grounded in the will to truth and characterized by a love for a sense of balance that will accord every thing and every person its rightful place, is the only attitude that can move us toward the healthiest development. This balance will be protected only by a correct understanding of how these dimensions, the ultimate structures, basically relate. Ignoring any one of them leads, as Voegelin would put it, to an arbitrary closing of the field of experience and hence to ideological mischief, a lopsided personal and social development.

Toward a Nonideological Attitude

The needed ecumenic attitude does not imply a mindless acquiescence to the skepticism that hides under the positive sounding term *pluralism*. It does demand, however, that we *allow the other to be*, first by welcoming him into our space despite the fact that he threatens the security of our laboriously built mental and institutional constructions, not merely tolerating his existence, but working for conditions that will assure his well-being while respecting that of the ecological system, the other nations, and the world social and economic system.

Ignoring the inner Being of the Other is not allowing him *to be.* Love—for that is what is at issue here—demands more than simply not destroying the other ontically. Being aware of the ecosystem is not enough: we have to cherish it. Environmental neglect causes the deaths of entire species through mindlessness, and may end up compromising our very existence on this planet. The socioeconomic system is the context in which the tranquility of order and the hope of material prosperity is pursued. It is our collective action within that system that impacts the ecosystem. The socioeconomic system is our mutual responsibility, however discouragingly complex and vast it may have become. Isolation does not allow human spirits to flourish. Tolerance in the form of benign neglect is not the road to wisdom.

Genuine openness to transcendence—true spirituality—should produce in the soul receptivity to all being. This is what Voegelin means by maximal differentiation. The *analogia entis* should make it possible for the categorical scheme of thinking to articulate so widely that it is able to accommodate every aspect of God, man, and nature that experience can reveal to us. Christians call this state of soul *charis,* "love." Christianity, rightly lived, should be the ecumenic tradition par excellence. When we observe the failures of Christians to be open, we see that there is more to achieving the attitude of love than merely conceiving of it and preaching about it. ("Not everyone who cries 'Lord! Lord!' will enter the kingdom of heaven. . . . Be not hearers of the word only but doers.")

It is vital to explain that in elaborating my sense of the appropriate attitude and the corresponding context, I am working from a *Seinsgeschichtlich* (historical becoming of Being) perspective. Anyone familiar with contemporary phenomenology will grasp what I mean. What I mean by a *Seinsgeschichtlich* perspective is this. All reality presences in consciousness, and hence is reality interpreted; interpretation is from a point of view, conditioned by the horizons of one's understanding, in which epochal horizons a long history of understanding the world is incarnated. Critical reflection must strive for awareness of the sense conditioned by those horizons. That critical seeing requires, as Heidegger says, taking a step back behind the history of the development of those horizons, back behind the whole becoming of the tradition of interpretation, of Being's illuminations and obscurings of itself, to the presuppositions of all interpreting within a tradition, and—to the extent all horizons are conditioned by human nature—to the basic structures of all interpreting (the *Eksistentialien* of *Sein und Zeit.*)

The present study, with its concern for translatability and its hopes for the project of ecumenic wisdom, has stressed what von Balthasar terms "the discipline of the object." The overall project of which this volume is a part will muster the experiential evidence for this faith in the self-presenting of the object as guide and anchor for the deployment of interpretative horizons. Adequate attention to the objective component within experience can protect the thinker from the temptation to what I shall call *Seinsgeschichtlich* reductionism, a form of idealism from which not all Heideggerians escape. It might also be called the history of ideas relativism syndrome. For example, the Copernican revolution is not only a change of direction within the history of ideas, but the discovery of a truth and correction of an error: the earth really does rotate about the sun, though in daily experience it rises and sets above a (to the observer) stable earth. I shall argue that such respect for the objectivity of what is actually given in experience goes hand in hand with and demands the attitude of love. There I shall also explore reasons that love is easy to talk about but difficult to achieve in practice.

Starting from Our Interpretative Horizons

Awareness that the horizons of interpretation develop historically has been accompanied since Hegel and Comte by the uncritical supposition that the sense of such a development is somehow progressive. The horizons of each succeeding epoch were presumed, somewhat as in the natural sciences, to take up those of earlier eras into a more adequate synthesis; the earlier truths are, as Hegel says, *aufgehoben* ("overcome" or "synthesized"). Such "Enlightenment" progressivism, fed by experience of the evident progress of science and technology, falsifies the much more ambiguous and complex relationships existing between the horizons of the distinguishable epochs within occidental experience.

Heidegger has the merit of showing the error of progressivism. Insisting that the horizons of each epoch, having a distinctive point of view, conceal Being as well as revealing it, Heidegger effectively derails the Hegelian project, which proceeds as though Being's task were to produce the "Kingdom of God on earth" by working dialectically with mankind to achieve an ever improved state of affairs. To allow partially to shine forth is at the same time partially to conceal, a certain forgetting of what may have been seen more adequately in certain respects in an earlier epoch. Among other things, such a truth arms us to respect every epoch and to be prepared to search in it for what it has to offer to perennial wisdom. At the same time, it warns us against accepting the formulations of any epoch, including our own, as though requiring no critical correction, particularly through remembering what was earlier seen (*anamnesis*).

When, against the backdrop of the whole history of the suite of epochal openings (*die Seinsgeschichte*) recorded in the symbols that express mankind's experiences, we seek to discern the character of our own era, what do we discover? This is a vital question, for it is within the light of this time and much shaped by it, including its institutional arrangements, that our own thought and search for an ecumenic wisdom goes forward. For one thing, we must attempt to uncover and evaluate the presuppositions that permitted contemporary scientific thought. But here is where Heidegger has failed to be generous. Somehow the sense of the glory and the cosmic sweep of contemporary science is diminished if it is seen only through the limitations of its own technological offspring. The Einstein-Bohr-Heisenberg-Bohm way of conceiving of the order of the universe in its becoming gives the occasion for radical ontological questioning.

Then we must ask what contemporary experience grounds the opening towards the transcendent, especially the kind of transcendence I shall term the Christologic (to be discussed momentarily). It is arbitrary to reduce present-day experience to awareness of technological organization; it includes a tension, everywhere evident, between a life of modern high technology and various forms of the continued life of the spirit. To treat the technological aspects of society as developed ones and societies and sub-societies within high-technology nations as underdeveloped is to adopt uncritically Enlightenment progressivism. Heidegger's efforts to marginalize spiritual life do not do justice to the breadth, depth, and variety of the reality and hence fail to illumine the nature of the tension between the scientific mentality and the interior life of the spirit opened toward transcendence, which can be felt in the souls of individuals and observed in the struggles within society (blatantly, for instance, in the abortion issue).[2]

2. See Heidegger's statement, "Here and there exist little communities of love" ("Nietzsche," in *Holzwege* [Frankfurt: Klostermann, 1950], 234).

Avoiding an Idealistic Reductionism

While the horizons of interpretation both focus attention and strongly influence how whatever presences is taken up into larger structures held in consciousness and is thus interpreted, neither the focus brought by the perceiver nor his subsequent interpretation determines totally what actually presences. This is a fundamental realistic point for which I shall argue extensively in later work. Science is indeed a daughter of philosophy. But it is also, as Heidegger would say, a *Geschick* (from *schicken,* to send)—a gift of Being, a gift of the mysterious source of all breakthroughs that lies beyond, and not an inevitable development. Heidegger underplays one aspect of this particular gift. As Stanley Jaki has shown, science does not merely grow out of Greek philosophy; it originates in its modern form as mathematical physics in a thirteenth-century milieu in which faith in the ultimate intelligibility of the world is rooted in the belief in creation.[3] This point will prove important in what follows.

So theology is likewise one of the mothers of modern science. It, too, is *Geschichtlich;* the form God assumes in our representations will of course be influenced by the horizons of interpretation of the time. However, neither the impact of the transcendent on human lives nor the objectivity of the genuine discoveries of science are exclusively functions of the horizons of interpretation.

The experience of transcendence—the Christologic, in the Christian tradition's case—by the saints and prophets, even the common experience and thought of the Church, does not depend exclusively on the particular ontological horizons of an epoch; the way they are capitalized on, institutionalized, and interpreted will of course be essentially conditioned by the epochal horizons of interpretation. Certain kinds of revelations, certain institutionalized relationships within already established settings, are conceivable only in particular eras. For example, the relations between the pharaoh's chief architect and the slaves who built the temple at Karnak were totally different from those possible between the production engineer at IBM and his workers, who hold over his head the threat of unionizing. But other kinds of relationship, rooted basically in the core of human nature, happen typically in every era. This perennial "given-ness"

---

3. See Stanley Jaki, *Science and Creation: From Eternal Cycles to an Oscillating Universe* (New York: Science History Publications, 1974); and *The Road of Science and the Ways to God: The Gifford Lectures* (Chicago: University of Chicago Press, 1978).

of human nature, its basic stability throughout the course of human history, is but one kind of ontic given-ness which enters into the dialectic of Being and beings to which we now should turn. What is the contribution of the self-presencing ontic?

The Dialectic of Being and Beings

With the advance of history, horizons of interpretation have to be expanded radically because of breakthroughs. I am not forgetting what I just said against a simplistic Enlightenment faith in progress when I acknowledge that certain breakthroughs achieve definitive expansions of interpretative horizons within a tradition. The breakthrough on Sinai to consciousness of history is an event there is no going back on, short of a cataclysmic destruction of the carriers of the tradition. Likewise, the Copernican revolution and the breakthrough to a sense of the development of the cosmos and of evolution are irreversible. Such breakthroughs render invalid certain earlier views, but do not overturn *all* thinking that went on in earlier epochs.

Although breakthroughs are events in consciousness and result in "decentering and recentering the horizons," to use Merleau-Ponty's phrase, they have a strong ontic component. To begin with, they are concrete events, involving particular persons and individual acts, and thus may be situated, which most often is not irrelevant to their significance. They are often centered on the discovery of a new kind of real thing, or a new objective aspect of things. Finally, the new vision they permit founds traditions. Even the Sinai breakthrough and the Greek discovery of the soul, which do not focus on things, were *events,* involving historically situated individuals and affecting interpersonal relationships.

A dialectical relationship exists between the ontic and the ontologic. Previously established horizons make possible the presencing of certain entities in certain ways. But this presencing is not merely an effect of the ontological situation: it is primarily the self-giving of entities (*die Seienden, ta eonta* in Greek, hence "ontic") possessing internal structures of their own; these things are always able to impose new elements upon consciousness, which, unless psychologically blocked, will open up to accommodate their offering, beyond what had been called for by the previous horizons, the anticipation, or the space-opening focus. This is a central ontological point that, if missed, will inevitably result in a slide into either idealism or skepticism. I will attempt to walk the tightrope between them.

Consider an example. Before the advent of the internal combustion engine, petroleum played a minor role in man's life. With the discovery (breakthrough) that a fuel could be extracted from crude oil and exploded in reciprocating engines, interest began to rise, not only in finding reliable and cheap supplies of crude oil (an altogether new concept), but in exploring what could be extracted from it. Petrochemistry and petroleum engineering, as well as seismic exploration, drilling technique, and transport and marketing techniques, grew up together, a whole world, complete with its own concepts, language, institutions, and now traditions—the petroleum clusters of industries. The concepts, language, traditions, and inculturated institutional roles exist in the many subjects who participate in the world of oil. But crude oil actually does exist in nature, as do refineries, pipelines, and reciprocating petrol engines. If oil were to run out, the industrial complex immediately dependent on it would collapse, and with it certain ways of viewing the world and an entire vocabulary of symbols.

Subjectivists so emphasize the deployment of certain interpretive projects as allowing certain kinds of particular things *to be* in the first place that they undermine credibility for objectivity, reducing the *noemata*, the things known, to mere products of consciousness. It is indisputably true that only my attending, for instance, to this tree in the garden permits it to stand in consciousness. Further, what is perceived is seen in profile and within the limits of what my senses are able to receive. We now know that human senses capture only a small portion of the radiations present in a given environment. Those radiations that are taken in are received, as Saint Thomas would say, "in the mode of the knower." Furthermore, I interpret the sensations received in the light of my experience, which informs the whole, accounting for my ability to *re-cognize* these sensations as the presence of an apple tree and not an evergreen bush.

All the more striking, then, that scientists, having come up with imaginative notions of altogether new kinds of entities, invent instruments which will provide meter readings demonstrating whether such things, after all, actually exist. When the "interpretative" side of the equation has been admitted, it remains true that the real electron microscope and what it presents in the way of structured data make demands, telling the scientist not only what he was expecting and what he can readily interpret (and what is almost unintelligible to the uninitiated), but also conveying matters he was not expecting and which oblige him, if he is honest, to alter his theory somewhat.

What we receive through the senses is indeed received in the mode of the knower, but it is received as data, as givens, partial and to be interpreted to be sure, but nonetheless stable and open to exploration. The knower, if he is in love with truth, must submit to the discipline imposed by the object. Since what he is presented with is presented as structured—that is, as wholes with intelligible internal relations between the parts and external interrelationships between the relatively freestanding wholes (the "substances") themselves—what data provide us is not only information about ourselves and the limits of our modes of perception, but also information about the things themselves so far as our modes of perception give us access to them. One sure sign that they do give access to the things themselves, limited but real, is that we have been able to learn that there is more to things than is readily accessible to unaided sensation. This is the point of our fashioning instruments that extend the range of our perception—all on the basis of the reliable and steady indications that are readily accessible to the senses.

Development of the horizons of interpretation at the invitation of the data permits more things to presence, which invites further expansion of horizons, which in turn opens a further space for exploration—in this way the "ontic-ontologic" dialectic moves forward. In the development of experimental science, such a dialectic of interpretative horizons and data is usually progressive, as we observed earlier. Where the object is less empirically given, hence less experimentally verifiable, the discipline demanded is less rigorous and more interactive, and the element of patient, devoted love comes even more to the fore. This is most clearly the case when other willful centers of initiative are involved. Recuperation of forgotten differentiations is, as we said, less progressive than anamnetic—a remembrance of things past. The correct relating of the properly experimental-progressive element and the anamnetic interpersonal one is crucial.

We are resistant to a change in familiar, traditional horizons. Abrupt "paradigm shifts," as Thomas Kuhn calls them, only occur when evidence impossible to accommodate through the old model piles up and forces sudden change. One must not lose sight in such paradigm shifts of the continual and massive role of the ontic givens.

Putting It All Together

All this may be summed up in the phrase "objective interpretation," by which I mean that the world is interpreted as being really in itself all the qualities we predicate of it—it really is dynamic, expanding, many billion years old, and so on—and that it is all this quite independently of the thought process that has laboriously come only lately to discover these realities. In the light of this hard-won objective knowledge, we judge the sense of the development of science: we now know the ancients (the great Heraclitus of Ephesus alone avoiding this error) were wrong in interpreting the world as relatively small and static. The knowledge that permits us to make this judgment is based on elaborate inference from complex data (the red shift in the light spectrum from the galaxies, for instance, interpreted as light from a source speeding away from the observer) and hence is subject to correction, some of it perhaps radical, in the light of new data. But it is certain enough for us to dispose confidently of the ancient view.

The experimental method has thus resulted in discoveries that in Heideggerian terms have stretched our "Being horizons," permitting the discovery of objective ontic dimensions which burst the time and space bounds of traditional occidental cosmological thinking. This has invited thinkers to be open to new gifts of Being in the form of a radically new way of conceiving of the universe. The certainty of the scientists' knowledge of these things varies. Of some suns, planets, galaxies, and comets, there can be no doubt, but certain particles, certain forms of radiation, and certain relationships may later prove to have been inadequately formulated elements of imaginative models, useful to handle particular data within the standard theory at a stage in its development, but which in the light of later discoveries are judged inadequate, misleading, or just plain wrong. They and the model to which they belong are meant objectively, and indeed they are objective, though they may prove partly erroneous.

The discovery of new data drives development in science. It may have trouble changing our views, but it is the primary motive when such change occurs. The evolution of ontological horizons of interpretation, at least in the experimental sciences, is ontically driven. It is the data which today demand that the thought of Being be extended to embrace the ontogenetic and the prehistoric, a vast opening of horizons indeed.

But has the ontic had this effect in other spheres? Earlier, thought had to open its horizons toward the transcendent, to accommodate whatever happened on Sinai, through the prophets, and in Jesus Christ (the Chris-tologic again). I would argue that these are all ontic events triggering breakthroughs, requiring paradigm shifts. Whether these events happen only in the sensorium of the soul, as some say, or include visible phe-nomena in time and space, their nature should be investigated when the tradition is appropriated. Interpretations of what happened in each in-stance and of the meaning coursing through these events as history may clash. But something's having happened is not open to doubt, and the truth of any interpretation depends on a willingness to receive in each case all the evidence that has been transmitted about what happened.

From this it would appear to follow that thought should come to grips with the significance of every event that has influenced the Being of any of the great traditions. That is true, and a reminder to us that we must remain open to all Being. But it ignores at the same time our need for focus if we are to search. The progress in science did not just happen—the thinkers were looking for something.

In beginning our search naturally from within our own occidental tradition, we see why it is central. First, it is our own, and for better or worse it has molded our own interpretative standpoint. Only through appropriation can we take the needed step back. Second, we have seen it also makes the most encompassing claims, in relation to which all other ontological claims—so it pretends—should be situated. It has the audac-ity to hold itself up as the never-to-be-surpassed keystone of an overarch-ing ecumenic wisdom.

Our own tradition requires some sort of awareness, then, of all the articulations achieved in the occidental tradition, inevitably including high Christian theology, in which the tradition's sense of the significance of all that happened is thought through and preserved. With this tradi-tion's sense of the infinity and providence of the source, of creation *ex nihilo*, of the *analogia entis*, of man's reality as *imago Dei*, and of the scope of the transcendent's prophetic relationship with human history, and with its will to catholicity of truth and to the achievement of universal broth-erhood, it claims to provide the most ample context of contexts known, one which it would indeed be difficult to imagine logically exceeding.

But unfortunately the breathtaking scope of a claim does not establish it as true. Nor is Christianity now or in its history immediately obvious as a center of great openness. Like the other missionary Abrahamic religion, Islam, Christianity has been, throughout much of its past, aggressive and insensitive to others' liberty, bringing with it European civilization, often imposed by force of arms. At a time, however, when the message of "scientific" socialism is itself imposed by arms on ungrateful populaces, and Arab and Iranian Islam, for instance, shows few signs of what we have previously considered as a liberal outlook, Christianity has accepted from the Enlightenment an appreciation of freedom of conscience that is paradoxically more genuinely Christian than some of the Church's own earlier behavior. The anti-Church establishment Enlighteners have helped the Church realize certain implications of its own understanding of man. The maximal differentiation is having its rightful impact at long last on social development. This new understanding and this new kind of praxis can now be incorporated into the attitude with which the Christian approaches dialogue with people of other traditions in the mutual search for truth. Highest differentiation need not be a cover for cultural imperialism.

On Maintaining a Space for Genuine Dialogue

The pursuit of truth, as a social enterprise, requires the maintenance of a space-time for inquiry, a set of practical institutional arrangements inculturated into people in the form of roles and correct attitudes, including a commitment to the pursuit of personal authenticity. These are the fruit of a certain sociopolitical-economic development which has not occurred everywhere. Indeed, it is the product of one tradition. Truth is not something that just happens, however large the irreplaceable element of the gift of Being may be. Truth also has to be actively sought; it emerges from institutionally guided action—research, sustained dialogue, contemplation (even the individual's acts of contemplation require support). The necessary institutions assuring a peaceful society, education, research, and contemplation are gifts from the past; the hard work which goes on within them results from gifts of vocation. But the present action must be deliberately carried out by the present agents.

The truth question, and the pursuit of an ecumenic wisdom, may be an occidental development, but it is not merely theoretical or parochial. The search for truth in the form of ecumenic wisdom and for institutional arrangements to reflect the sense of human solidarity is the central challenge confronting the human race, a quest bequeathed to us by Being and our "being-here" (*Da-sein*). Neither atheist socialism nor liberal humanism—the one with its model of central control, the other with its mixed entrepreneurial, social-welfare-state, democratic model—shows, unfortunately, the slightest inclination to live and let live. The one preaches coexistence, the other, pluralism and the rights of man. The governments inspired by the first are in reality tyrannical, those of the other seductive with a passionate tendency, despite sincere concern for rights, to suck the whole world into its maelstrom of workaholic hedonism and adventures of inventivity. Neither has much place for God: the first is officially atheistic, pathologically persecuting religions; the second undermines them without even trying, through its busy-ness and *dis-traction.*

Genuine respectful tolerance, including a willingness to permit entirely different rhythms of existence from those of the industrial frenzy, should not be confused with the tactical maneuvers of coexistence. If one is convinced that the open society is best, and that a regime of genuine dialogue is the only viable solution for mankind in a planetary situation, one must paradoxically be prepared to struggle to maintain, and enlarge, a space for dialogue.

Everything we have seen in this study shows this will not be easy. Openness easily degenerates into a wishy-washy acceptance of pluralism, which breeds a soft relativism: the love of truth dies. Secular materialism degenerates into wars for markets and prestige. Totalitarianism methodically destroys all public openness. Secularism breeds a pathological distaste for the spiritual life. With all this, there may paradoxically be more searching discussion going on *sub rosa* in totalitarian countries than in many open societies, which have become superficial and disoriented. There is no way to prove it one way or the other, but one is free to wonder whether there is more searching for truth going on right now in Stockholm or in Moscow.

A Civic Theology for a Planetary Age?

No social struggle of the dimensions needed for the genuine ecumenic search for truth has ever been effectively maintained without a common faith. But how on earth can one envision a civic theology for a planetary age? I believe (and I am here going farther than any position even Eric Voegelin has defended) that a civic theology for the planetary epoch can be forged. It would have to marry a way of thinking (gathering up the sense from the development of the horizons of interpretation—a *seinsgeschichtliches Denken*—but respectful of the objectivity of science) with a belief in the need and possibility of joining the family of man into some kind of loving union, much as that envisioned by Christians who understand the Christocentric role of the Church as such a gathering into brotherhood, which they believe possible only under "the fatherhood of God." This union of the scientific-philosophic tradition of thought with the essence of traditions of revelation would be a first step toward an open society that is yet unified, without the split between "science" and "faith" that has characterized our civilization since the end of the Middle Ages. Such an ideal, rooted in the sense that all human life is sacred and the struggles for truth of all traditions are graced, would have immediate practical consequences by motivating the most open and respectful dialogue between traditions, coupled with every honorable and just effort to maintain civic and international tranquility so that it may proceed.

A liberal hashish illusion? It would seem so at a time when Muslim brothers have been massacring and even gassing one another across the Shatt-al-Arab waterway and in Kuwait City, and while sectarian hatred in Northern Ireland keeps the headlines flaming—the list of horrors could be made long. And when individuals in pluralistic society find it ever harder to engage anyone in serious discussion, the stating of such an ideal seems to ignore both the iron grip exerted on minds by both tradition in the bad sense (recall Chapter 5) and pathological forces.

Yet there is a model of civic representation that some of the soberest and most profound thinkers have vaunted as best institutionalizing the space needed for such dialogue. Jacques Maritain, John Courtney Murray, Eric Voegelin, Irving Kristol, Michael Novak, George Weigel, Richard John Neuhaus—none of whom could possibly be accused of fuzzy-minded liberalism—and many others would contend that only representative democracy, despite the danger inherent in it of degeneration into demagogy, adequately meets the contemporary requirement (belatedly but significantly, with the papacy's first unequivocal praise, Pope John Paul II can now be added to this list). Novak, Berger, Schall, and others further insist that only an entrepreneurial socioeconomic system adequately protects the necessary political openness, provided the state remains vigilant against monopolies, enforces laws protecting workers and the environment, and provides a social welfare safety net to relieve unnecessary suffering on the part of those unable to compete.

But the fact remains that most of the world enjoys no such conditions, and the lack of personal and institutional discipline continues the trend to relativism in open societies. Realistically, what ecumenic dialogue there is (and it is important, ranging from negotiations such as those of the General Agreement on Tariffs and Trade and European Economic Community to interfaith theological discussions of the most earnest kind) will go on mostly within the space of civic freedom opened by the democracies, a space into which representatives of traditions that have not developed democratic institutions are more and more drawn for discussion. These exchanges often result in a raising of consciousness about rights, procedures, and tolerance within other societies (the Helsinki Accord had that effect). The spirit of true democratic respect is spreading.

Arnold Toynbee, the historian of civilizations, while acknowledging that Christianity has a unique contribution to make to the ecumenic dialogue, emphasizes the need for all world traditions to be tapped if we are to overcome the spiritual emptiness that has been spread along with the West's secularized technological civilization to the entire world. It would be worth quoting his hopeful vision:

> The non-Western converts to the Western Civilization bring with them hope as well as fear; for they come trailing some still undiscarded clouds of glory from their own religious heritages, which they have abandoned a shorter time ago than the West has abandoned its Christian religious heritage. These undiscarded elements in the religious heritages of the non-Western majority of Mankind have now been brought, by the process of Westernization, into the world's common stock of spiritual treasure; and perhaps they may work together with the surviving remnant of Western Christianity to reintroduce the discarded religious elements into a Western Civilization of all Mankind, for better or for worse.[4]

The ideal is a difficult one. But what other road can mankind follow? Let us sum up some methodological pointers gained in this study which may be of help in pursuing it.

First, those at the center of such dialogue should attempt the kind of written appropriation of the traditions that have formed them, such as I am doing with the Catholic tradition. One must secure his own freedom. Only when critical distance has been achieved and one begins to enter more freely into the way of his tradition can the living source which gives it life reappropriate him as an adequate ecumenic witness to that life. The expression of this self-discovery is liberating to others because it helps to

4. Arnold Toynbee, *An Historian's Approach to Religion* (London: Oxford University Press, 1956), 154.

make one authentically present to them. It not only gives others the opportunity to criticize one's biases, it draws the biases out for themselves and for oneself. The effort forces both to articulate much that would otherwise remain on the margins of consciousness, even in the best ecumenic discussions, and to return reflectively to basic experiences from which their concepts derive.

Second, in attempting to translate the truth claims of others to integrate with one's own wisdom, one must develop hermeneutic sensitivity to the way the symbols function. How do we manage to break out of our private worlds into a common situation of shared feelings about things? Because our thoughts and perceptions transcend interiority, moving outward to the opening in which the things themselves, as well as their relations and settings, can reveal aspects of themselves, thus becoming reference points for our discourse and anchors for our thought and action, we must be more attentive to how precisely the symbols of various languages and cultures achieve this. We must learn an aesthetic appreciation of them that will unlock their true meaning for us and thereby reveal their ability to evoke Being.

Given the need for such rapprochement of traditions, which seems obvious to common sense, why is there resistance to this sense of objectivity central to a project of common searching for a shared wisdom? The source is moral. Objectivity is resisted because it entails our being beholden. We do not wish to acknowledge our dependence on others, to respect them, to be grateful. We do not trust our freedom to others; we reject guides to the proper use of our own freedom, labeling oppressive much that is often simply real but uncomfortably demanding.

The future wise development of mankind, while encouraging man's inventiveness and an outpouring of human energy, must discern and respect real limits. The point is not to define limits to growth, as though one could discern now the outlines of what mankind can achieve technologically. Certainly there are no limits to spiritual growth. What is needed, however, is to recognize the fruitful limits presented by the existence of others—other persons, other cultures, other kinds of entities, from the most inventive-cultural, to the most given-natural—and to search for the place in the larger order of things which most allows them to realize their potential. That is what theists mean by "in God's plan."

One develops as a self through ever more critically appreciative situating of that self in relationship to the possibilities that are handed to us by the traditions and are available in nature and in the pragmatic realities of the immediate situation. Appropriation of the most loving of those possibilities, the personal ones, finds us growing out beyond our old limits as we are taken up into the glory of ultimate Being itself. Wise development is development respectful of the true structures of nature and culture, it strives to preserve (*wahren*) possibility won after hard struggles, and it is ever sensitive and grateful to the transcendent source of all breakthroughs.

Toward a Method of Appropriating

Too often, in writing this introductory work, I have had to defer detailed treatment of a particular question to later volumes. I have thought this course prudent because one of our great mistakes has been, and continues to be, a willingness to reductionism, to shrinking the scope of issues down to simplified answers, which are then untrue to the complexity of the circumstances originally under discussion. I would not want to leave the impression that there are ten-second answers to millennia-old questions, or simple clichés that encapsulate everything one needs to know to master our complex, and complexifying, world system.

Although I will present in subsequent volumes an extended example of how one appropriates tradition, I include here this all-too-brief propaedeutic to the central work authenticity demands of us. Appropriation goes on spontaneously throughout the life of anyone who happens to be in a tradition the least bit reflective. Everyone begins life more appropriated by his traditions than appropriating. Criticism of the truth claims of a tradition is a mature act arising only in certain circumstances of openness and pluralism which, causing a crisis, also give us the noetic and psychological space—if the crisis is not too traumatic—in which to carry out critical reflection leading to appropriation.

Most such acts of critical reexamination arise spontaneously and take place piecemeal. Nevertheless, whenever I respond to an invitation to raise the truth question and I consciously come to a judgment of aspects of my situation, I then reverse the previous relationship (there is a sort of *con-versio*.) Instead of being mindlessly gripped by certain acculturated convictions, I now more consciously fit new phenomena into the scheme of my natural faith, my ongoing general assessment of how it stands with Being, and so come to judge its truth explicitly.

Our natural faiths are not all of a piece. We are compartmentalized and inconsistent in thought and behavior. Maturation demands, among other qualities, growth in integrity, which is not only consistency between what we say we believe and what we in fact do (the diminution of hypocrisy), but consistency between the various departments of our lives— a task with an important theoretical component—as well as the achievement of the openness to all reality that genuineness demands and that will assure coherent and generous action. Underlying the splintering of the world on the part of people who are victims of its *dis-traction* into little worlds, there runs nonetheless an all-coloring basic judgment (usually more implicit than spelled out, buried in less conscious layers of one's natural faith) about Being. It is on this level that we are basically either upbeat about things, thinking life is going somewhere and that there is meaning to existence, even when we fail to notice that many of our actions cancel each other out; or just the opposite, that we are nihilistic, convinced there is no meaning beyond the wringing of advantages out of little pleasures which happen to come to us along the way, or seeking great highs by going on ruthless power trips.

If acts of appropriation occur spontaneously and within narrow horizons as minor crises in life confront us with at least regional questions of truth, what is the need for developing a method of appropriating entire traditions in the widest possible context, towards which the research in the present study is directed? Without method we cannot hope to get a responsible hold on the traditions, institutions, and world processes which flow through us. That is fine in theory, but back in the real world, caught up with running life's errands, we have little time and inadequate professional preparation for such a task. What is the lonely, limited individual to do?

My basic methodological hypothesis is that an educated person can, with the help of the best works of synthesis in various fields, read into a tradition sufficiently to discern the central truth issues it raises. In subsequent volumes I shall show, by doing it, what this involves when one focuses on the central truth claims and hence seeks only the essence of the tradition. The kinds of questions which need facing are becoming sufficiently clear to me to share them in a preliminary way, as a conclusion to the present volume.

Two Different Challenges:
Encompassing and Appropriating

Two related but distinct kinds of problem confront the person who aspires to a methodic comprehension of the situation and to appropriative critical confrontation of the truth conveyed by traditions. The first task involves accurate description of the contemporary interaction of institutions, symbol systems, and world processes, with attention to the way in which the fruits of the past are made present through this network of interactions. This is motivated by the pragmatic goal of understanding better the tensions in the situation between competing and confronting courses of action. In doing this we seek to build a mental model of the world system, a representation of the dynamics of the interaction of the various elements manifesting themselves in the actual planetary situation. Every literate adult in developed society does this, whether haphazardly or in the more studious, methodic manner of the expert, who himself remains a haphazard builder of a world model outside his fields of expertise.

Building up such a view of the current world situation is not the same as appropriating a tradition. It is essentially descriptive and necessarily rather disorderly. We seek to bring light to a confused and complex situation by sorting out, relating, and weighing the pragmatic impact of the main organized actors with the most leverage on the situation. At this stage one is not concerned with the enduring truth of what the institutions purport in broadcasting their stands, but with their pragmatic reality, their actual and potential impact on events, their aid and interference with what we in our situation want. (I have avoided the word *political* expressly, as the issues transcend the political, even the ekistic dimensions, of human settlement, and the transcendent dimension is involved as well.)

But even the most cursory examination of the world situation shows there is no hope of understanding it with any adequacy without an encounter with the truth claims advanced by the traditions. That is the essential fallacy of many strategic summaries, and on the popular level of following the news through *Time, Der Speigel, The Economist,* and so on. The significance of the traditions' truth claims is a central part of the explanation of their force to move people, so it is also a *pragmatic reality.* Description of the situation opens up a second task, then: ultimate truth questions are raised by the actual situation and demand appropriation of traditions as an essential part of understanding what exactly is being claimed, what the experience behind this is, as preparation for responding to their challenge.

That response demands incorporating the insights of distinctive traditions in a single ecumenic wisdom. In Part 2 of the present volume, I offered a few thoughts about the daunting challenge of judging truth claims cross-traditionally. The problem of translatability will be elaborated more fully in other volumes. So I shall close this volume with some general methodological indications, valid generally for study of the most extensive and richest explicit traditions, which because of the sweep of their truth claims provide particularly daunting challenges.

Appropriating Vast Explicit Traditions

Focus is everything. Unless one approaches history with a question providing focus, he will wander (perhaps happily, but not seriously) in the marvelous halls of the great museum of life. The project of authenticity, with its existential decision, arms us with this focusing question about the tradition to be appropriated: what are its central, still relevant (that is, existence-directing) truth claims?

The core of an explicit tradition is constituted by its formulated truth claims. Judgment of their validity, in the light of practice as well as the development of theory, is another, later matter, which follows after we have gotten clear about what is actually being claimed. The first question to pose regarding an explicit tradition, then, is who is authorized, according to the tradition's own self-understanding, to speak for it? What is the legitimate source of the tradition's explicit claims?

Some explicit traditions are more tightly institutionalized than others. The Catholic tradition provides an extreme case: it is so articulated through its institution that one can say without hesitation who speaks for the Church, because the Church itself has made this explicitly clear. It is the College of Bishops presided over by the Bishop of Rome, who himself is empowered to speak in the name of the entire Body of Christ. In many institution-driven traditions, it is not hard to discover who, constitutionally, speaks for the tradition. In IBM, with its relatively old and strongly explicated company culture, it is the prerogative of higher management and ultimately the board of directors to interpret the tradition and to change it; in the case of the United States of America, it is

Congress, through law, and the Administration, through bureaucratic regulation, both subject to overseeing as to constitutionality by the Supreme Court.

Where part of the tradition is the passing on of an authority structure, the texts emitted by those appointed to the express task of official interpretation become an inevitable focal point of all debate about the meaning of the tradition by those serious about living it. No one concerned with the truth of Communism should ignore Mr. Gorbachev's rethinking of the Marxist-Leninist tradition. He is remaking the tradition itself. The total significance of the tradition being appropriated lies, neither in its "Scriptures" (for example, IBM's corporate policy manuals and approved corporate histories, colloquially thought of as the "Big Blue Book"), nor in later formulations of its vision of the world, nor in its deviations in practice from what has been expressly built into the symbols, but in the tension between all of these.

In searching for the essential truth claims, one seeks to understand them as expressions of an organic whole vision, and to see them as they have evolved continuously from the founding vision. The driving force of the fundamental project contained in the founding vision is a central unifying force.

The Historical Depth behind Present Affirmations

The next task is to put some depth behind the surface understanding of the institutionally formulated ideal vision. One needs to see how the tradition came to hold such things, how its understanding evolved and why, and what experiences have motivated its development. In appropriating the Catholic tradition, I found a study of its crises (in the literal sense of moments of essential decision) down through the centuries vital for such an understanding. The key to the formulation of dogma is the challenge issued to the tradition as it is being lived out on the part of groups whose understanding was believed erroneous by the Church. Heresy is the crucible in which dogmatic formulations were forged. In every tradition, there is competition for space-time within the ensuing institution, no matter how "spiritual" the tradition. To continue as a living tradition, even Platonism needs attention in the academy.

Only as I began to grasp what lay behind the tradition's present self-understanding and its interpretations of ancient canonical texts and creeds did I see the meaning of the conflicts which are now buffeting it. Some, it turns out, are contemporary forms of very old controversies, virtually inherent in ambiguities in the founding vision itself, or at least alternative ways of construing the founding vision or of conceiving an institution capable of bearing it. A good example of that is the congregationalist versus the episcopal (or hierarchical) model of the Church. In every instance, it was a help to recover the position of the opposition, the minority that lost the old battle and were then considered heretics by the main-line tradition.[5] Not only do their positions give perspective on the orthodox stand, but they provide the only relevant test of the cogency of the orthodox positions. These minority viewpoints offer space for disengaging oneself for a moment from one's own commitments to test their sense.

When one has come to understand in some depth the meaning of the tradition's truth claims as presently passed on and interpreted, including the reasons for alternative interpretations of the essential vision, then, in the final step of appropriation, one must take a stand. The appropriator has already to some extent loaded the deck through his earlier decisions about what truly counts as essential to the tradition. He cannot make such decisions along the way without some critical interpretation of the meaning of the truth claims. But now, in the overtly critical moment, he should seek to be as clear as possible about his reasons for taking the stand that he does, for marginalizing certain competing interpretations and hence for determining why he construes the orthodox position as he does. Understanding these claims in the broad context of one's natural faith, he seeks to integrate these truths into his overall wisdom.

All this is easily said. Obviously, however, the ontology and epistemology inherent in one's natural faith is playing a crucial (and largely uncriticized and unreflective) role from the start of the appropriation.

---

5. It is critically important not to limit this idea of "heresies" and "heretics" to traditions of revelation. In 1969 IBM's primary mainframe computer systems designer, Gene Amdahl, was refused permission to work on a faster version of the then current IBM product. Amdahl, convinced that it was wrong to withhold the newer product from the market, resigned from IBM and founded its main competitor, Amdahl Corporation. For the next ten years, IBM forbade its employees to use the name of Amdahl (man or company). As late as 1989, IBM was trying to come to grips with the impact of this "heresy" upon its corporate culture, especially since Amdahl Corporation continues to draw IBM personnel to its employ and IBM customers to its products.

Appropriation inevitably increases consciousness of one's own underlying philosophical-religious position. The very decision to look for the truth in a tradition makes sense only as a function of one's notion of the truth. What one is prepared to recognize and love as "the truth" is conditioned from the start of the appropriation by one's natural faith—conditioned, not determined, otherwise there would be no growth in wisdom as a result of the appropriation. (Thus, for instance, my own natural faith gives rise to the presumption in favor of Being.)

Throughout the present study, I have made no effort to hide the developmental concept of truth which motivates it. At the same time, I have hinted often that I believe such a dynamic concept of truth is fully consonant with the belief in lasting truths, even transcendental ones. Before undertaking the actual appropriation of a tradition that has massively formed my own natural faith, including an element of belief in transcendent truth, my next volume will explore the epistemological and ontological issues only brushed past in the present introductory work.

Appendix A

Glossary

Appropriation   The lifelong, critical, judgmental process through which one takes as full possession as he can of what is properly his, that is, of the relevant needs and possibilities of his situation.

Authenticity   The project of achieving the fullest possible self-understanding and self-control so as to be able to respond to the needs and possibilities of the situation.

Bad Tradition   The handing on of an illusion.

Being   Any particular set of interpretative horizons giving significance to phenomena as part of a particular world of meaning. In Gestaltist terms, Being is both revealed and obscured in the interplay of background (*fond*), understood as condition for the possibility of certain kinds of figures standing out, and those expressive figures through which alone we can glimpse the ground, but which by their assertiveness distract us from noticing the enveloping illumination of the Being that is revealed. Being (*Sein*) relates dialectically to being (*die Seienden*).

Breakthroughs   New revelations through fresh figures, the very event of which enriches the ground that makes them possible and that feeds off of the figures.

Democratic, Entrepreneurial, Social-welfare Economy   That loose mixture of implicit traditions, attitudes, and some articulated know-how constituting the influence of Western mixed civilization today. "Entrepreneurial democracy" for short.

213

Deviant Institution	One which comes to serve some other project than that for which it was founded.
Explicit Tradition	A tradition in which the institution that has been spawned as its custodian has, for whatever reason, taken the pains to state explicitly what the tradition wants handed on as a truth.
Faithful Institution	One which, in adapting the founding vision, respects its basic demands.
Genuine	In a general sense, that which is in keeping with actual reality. As *Echt,* the fruit of striving to keep oneself open to all of reality, as far as possible.
Genuine Being-Possibility	Either an insight (whether formal-apodeictic, or the comprehension of a structure in nature) that can at any time be repeated; or a divine command or prophecy; or a responsive founding act; or an artistic creative intuition as project, meant to be handed down.
Goodness	The combining of integrity with genuineness.
Good Tradition	One founded in genuine Being-possibility, handed on by faithful institutions.
History	The sum of inherited culture and accumulations of personal experience.
Ideal	A long-range goal for the realization of which conditions have to be created gradually over a span of time.
Illusion	A purported Being-possibility that is not a genuine insight, nor a true divine command or prophecy, nor the repetition of a responsive founding act. Illusion is a grasp of some aspect of reality that is forced to take the place of another, to which it tends to block access.

Implicit Tradition	What occurs as we learn, largely through imitation, a body language, a spoken and written language, and a set of roles in the various institutions that possess us more than we possess them.
Institution	Groups of people acting in concert through the playing of roles into which they have been acculturated by those charged with assuring the future of the vision of the tradition that the institution serves.
Integrity	A question of virtue, integrity results from living consistently according to one's best lights—that is, in keeping with the full range of reality insofar as one's situation permits him to know it.
Intentionality	Consciousness reaching out toward objects and goals ("tend toward" would be a viable translation of *intendere*).
Maturity	One's growth in responsibility.
Mythology	That fabric of beliefs woven of both genuine Being-possibilities and illusions. As these are inevitable, the term is not intended pejoratively.
Natural Faith	One's spontaneous, ongoing assessment of how it stands with the world, the result of the chemistry between temperament, experience, and what one has been taught to believe.
Nature	In general, the given structure of limits and capabilities. Human nature is that structure of limits and capabilities common to human beings.
Pragmatic Importance of a Tradition	How great an influence a given tradition is on the emerging world system, so that the prudent, reflective individual can gauge how much attention he should pay to it in order to have a clear understanding of what is happening in this world in which he and his society must try to survive and prosper.

Privileged Experience of Being   The founding experience of Being is privileged because only those who enjoy the initial breakthrough will ever experience, in its pristine quality, that horizon-opening. Whether it comes in the form of a flash of philosophical intuition, an unexpected theophany, the conception of a successful experimentation, or a pragmatic response to a growing need, pioneering moments are unique.

Responsibility   The enhanced control of one's development, both through better understanding of one's possibilities, and through the enhancement of one's virtue—that is, the good habits which permit, among other things, self-control.

Responsive (Genuine) Act   The willing into being of an organization in a way that respects the needs and founding possibilities of the situation.

Self   The aware center of initiative in the person. *Person, personality,* and *self* should not be confused.

Symbol Systems   Include not only scientific and ordinary languages, but also the treasures of artistic and liturgical symbols; they are the means of expressing and communicating traditions for a society and its institutions.

Theoretical Importance of a Tradition   A tradition's contribution to wisdom—the light thrown by its treasure of symbols upon Being—which in a given case conceivably could be great even though the world may choose to pay little attention, with the result that the tradition's contemporary worldly impact could be small or declining, but it would still be quite worth studying.

Traditions   Visions of part or all of reality, expressed in a treasure of symbols elaborated over time and passed down through institutions created for this purpose.

**World and
Regional
Processes**
Large-scale, ongoing changes of a social nature, important enough to call themselves to our attention.

World System
A network of interacting planetary-scale institutions behind which stand great traditions.

 # Appendix B

Combinations of Tradition, Institution, and Situation

Tradition	Institution	Response to Situation	Result
Good	Faithful	Genuine (*echt*)	Application of and to ideal
Good	Faithful	Ungenuine	Ideal improperly applied or exemplified
Good	Deviant	Genuine	Ideal may or may not be lived up to in individuals
Bad	Faithful	Genuine	Illusions will be followed
Bad	Deviant	Either genuine or ungenuine	Could be correcting the tradition or compounding the evil

Appendix C

Major Explicit Traditions
Influencing the World System

	Main Tradition	Major Subtradition
I. Traditions of Revelation ("Hard" form)	Christianity	Roman Catholicism
		Orthodox (Eastern Catholicism)
		Protestantism

Particular Tradition	Institution or Institutional Tradition
Latin Rite	Roman Catholic Church
Eastern Rites	Roman Catholic Church
Greek	Greek Orthodox Church
Russian	Russian Orthodox Church
Syriac	Armenian Orthodox Church, etc.
Anglicanism	Lambeth Conference
	Various national Anglican or Episcopalian churches
Lutheranism	Various national Lutheran synods
Methodism	National Methodist synods

Main Tradition	Major Subtradition
Islam	Sunna
	Shi'a
Judaism	Orthodox
	Conservative
	Reform

Particular Tradition	Institution or Institutional Tradition
Calvinism	Congregational, Baptist, etc. churches
The Sects	Society of Friends, Mormons, Mennonites, etc.
Evangelicals	Pentecostal churches, etc.
Various (four main) traditions of Sharia	Brotherhoods, loose groupings, etc.
Various Sufi traditions and brotherhoods	Brotherhoods, loose groupings, etc.
Zaidis	National groups
Ismailia	National groups
Other small sects	
Ashkenazim	Rabinnic Conference
	Chassidic sects
Sephardic	Rabbinic Conference
	Rabbinic Conference
	Rabbinic Conference

	Main Tradition	**Major Subtradition**
II. Traditions of Revelation (not "Hard" form)	Hindu	Vishnuite
		Sakla (Sivaites)
	Buddhism	Mahayana
		Tharavada (Hinayana)
	Confucian: Some influence remaining in Chinese formal organization.	
III. Political Idologies	Socialism	Leninism

Particular Tradition	Institution or Institutional Tradition
Many sects	Loose institutional structures
Many sects	Loose institutional structures
Tibetan	Hierarchy of the Dalai Lama
Zen, etc.	Monastic structure
Various national traditions	
Moscow-centered	USSR
	Balkan satellites
	Various national Communist parties
	Afghanistan
Moscow-dependent	Cuba
	Balkan satellites

Main Tradition	Major Subtradition

Maoism

Particular Tradition	Institution or Institutional Tradition
	Angola
	Vietnam
	Ethiopia
"Euro-communism"	Leninist parties independent of Moscow line
	Italy
	Iberian parties
Glasnost reformers	Poland
	Mongolia
	Hungary
"Revisionist"	China
Orthodox	Albania
"Titoist"	Yugoslavia
	Guinea
	Tanzania

Main Tradition	Major Subtradition
	Social Democracy
Capitalism	Democratic capitalism
	Authoritarian capitalism (with traces of feudalism)
Nationalist	Arab Nationalism
	African Nationalism
	National Liberation Movements
Radicalism and Fascism	

Particular Tradition	Institution or Institutional Tradition
	Various Social Democratic parties
	Sweden
	EEC countries
	United States
	Canada
	Japan
	Necessary international institutions (GATT, EEC, etc.)
	Dictatorial states allowing private capital (Chile, Brazil, etc.)
	Arab League
	Organization of African States
	Palestine Liberation Organization, etc.
	Red Brigade

	Main Tradition	Major Subtradition
IV. Philosophical and Scientific Traditions	Western Scientific Tradition	
V. Ethnic, National, and General Social Traditions		
	National-Linguistic	
	Pan-national ethnic groups	
	Tribal Traditions	
	Family Structures	

Particular Tradition	Institution or Institutional Tradition
	Baader-Meinhof gang
	Neo-Nazis, etc.
Traditions of various disciplines	Universities and schools
	Research institutes
	Scientific associations and their journals
	Fostered by national states and associations for the defence of a given language (Goethe Institute, etc.)
	La Francophonie
	Tribal organizations
	Nuclear and extended families

 Index

Appropriation: as critical process, 2; balance in, 3; dialectic of judgment, 22; starting point in traditions forming oneself, 25; orientation in an existential focus, 43; role of written form in validation, 44; choice of materials for, 46; problems of believers and nonbelievers in, 49; use of explicit traditions to access implicit traditions, 49; conditions of inquiry for explicit traditions, 64; problems with traditions of revelation, 86–87; problem of acculturation into use of specific symbols, 95; relation to security, 118–19; opening to possibility, 121; methodic and casual forms, 131–32; and national associative traditions, 152; method of, 205–6
—critical judgment in appropriation: gaining distance, 13; need to determine situation, 21; other cultures, 36; determining the essential, 44; avoiding idealistic reduction, 194
Art: truth claims in, 46, 69–72, 101–2; consideration of work as whole, 69–70; co-creativity in interpretation, 70; explicit statements in, 70; as horizon-opening, 71; representation and imaging, 71; sense of situation, 71; as vehicle for propositions, 73; relation to development in culture, 103
Associations: symbols of founding, 75; coercion within, 76; difference between tradition and institution, 76, 80; provision for future hypoc-

risy, 77; habitual living and Hegelian *Sitte,* 79; relation of legitimacy to public art, 81–82; as shaping civilization, 82; communities as co-founded in revelations, 104; institutions as elements of world system, 137; openness and flourishing of other kinds of traditions, 150
Authenticity: as creative self-development, 2; as starting point for development of, 3; necessity of attempting, 6; as ability to respond, 11; opposition to narcissism, 12; and genuineness, 13, 31, 112; and Enlightenment reason, 14; modern occidental nature of, 14, 30; as requirement for moving beyond sociological, 22; critical judgment in, 38; as comportment (*Verhalten*), 33; and critical judgment of associations, 79; distinguishing tradition from awareness of limits, 98–100; and faithfulness, 112; and goodness, 112; and traditionalism, 116; and focus on relevance in traditions, 208; and Heidegger on technological society, 162

Breakthrough: as genuinely new, 52; as recognition of the preexistent, 52; as privileged experience of Being, 53; and creation of symbols, 54; differences between revelation and other forms, 84; positive and negative forms, 89; role of error in event, 90; as closing of a figure, 94; role of co-creators in communica-

24; formation in traditions, 24; types of, 33; and responses to situation, 33; gaining critical distance from, 39; need to appropriate formative traditions first, 47; issues of religious belief in, 49; arbitration of faiths from various traditions, 106; judgment of good and bad traditions, 114; development of common elements for community, 132–33

Philosophy of History. *See* History: philosophy of

Processes: role of history in learning about, 19; significance and diachronic scale, 20; formation of large-scale structures by, 54; dynamic structures, 92; as generals, 92; elements in world system, 135; discovery through methods of ekistics, 136; differentiated from events, 139; domination by large associations, 151; and need to control complex institutions, 168

Reason, 15

Social order: structure of, 1; gaining insight into, 5; and integrity, 32; role-playing in, 32; relevant scale of traditions affecting, 52; interaction of implicit worlds of individuals, 54; embodiment in traditions of association, 76; need for civic theology, 77; collision between associational and revelatory religions, 77; inevitability of coercion, 78; communities of praxis formed in traditions of revelation, 84; types of religious community within, 107; endurance of, 126; processes as structural energy of, 136; lack of coherence in technological society,

163; Marxist-Leninist conformity, 164

Symbols: as a tradition's developmental history, 22; ideational forms enfolding the past, 69; relation to kinds of truths, 101; use by institutions, 131; in world system, 138; expansion under Western impact, 147; degradation into ideas, 177; need to communicate experience via, 177

—symbols in differentiation of experience: hierarchy of differentiation, 178–81; possibility of regressive development, 179; definition of maximal, 180

Traditionalism: unhealthy forms of, 42; and inauthenticity, 116; compared with elements of world system, 139–40

Traditions: role as transmitters of symbol, 5; implicit form and personal character, 20; as varied unit of study, 21; as storehouses of symbols, 22; planetary nature of Western civilization, 26; struggle for orthodoxy inherent in, 41; orthodox passing on of gains, 46; founding of, 52; origin in breakthroughs, 52; scales of, 52; founding symbolization, 52, 56; origins of, 53–54; determining conflicts between, 55; ending of, 56; separating implicit from explicit in canonical forms, 58; relevance of final form, 61; interplay of traditions in transmission of experience, 62; interpretative difficulties in multiple uses of same symbols, 65; need to deal with truth claims in terms of kind, 84; role of institutions in handing down orthodox experience, 89; differentiation of break-

ification as revealing stabilities, 74; failure of tradition types to form an adequate concept of, 75; in associations, 79; pedagogical role of institutions, 82; claims in terms of kind of tradition, 84; older truths inherent in new truths, 90; figures hiding grounds, 91; openness to context, 94; symbolic norms used in claims, 95; artistic, 101–2; role of core symbols as opening to ground, 105; kinds of claims and resultant communities, 107; plurality of kinds, 100–110; judging quality of evidence, 111; teaching dynamic nature of reality, 122–23; scientific/philosophic traditions as sources of, 171; method of searching for, 178; pursuit as a communal enterprise, 181; epistemology required for investigation, 195–97
—quest for truth: ideological constraints on, 2; acquiring critical distance, 4; as opening to Being, 12; and questions regarding cultures, 36; and translatability of experience, 37; dialectic of figure and ground, 40, 45; responses of closure, 48; and structure of tradition types, 51; impact of institutional participation, 53; relevance of multiple expressions in tradition, 62; juxtaposition of canon and practice, 63; preconditions of critical distance, 64; works of art as wholes, 70; message-bearing or imaging works of art, 70–71; situation-revealing works of art, 71; origin and conclusion in scientific/philosophic form, 73; dialectic of ideals and practice in associations, 82; dealing with claims of revelation, 83–88; entering a religious world-view, 84; inseparability of critique

in, 89; universality of application, 90; justification for truth claims by tradition type, 96; awareness of limits, 98–100; highly ideological systems, 165; examining open societies, 167; balancing the pragmatic and theoretical 169–70; creating a time-space for dialogue, 200; value of written appropriation, 203; encompassing and appropriating, 207
—relations of truth: hermeneutic problem and creation of worlds in breakthroughs, 52; kinds of claims made and tradition types, 66–67; dogma and practice in traditions of revelation, 87; error and deviation from genuineness, 111–12; qualitative and quantitative factors in development vectors, 137; centrality in tradition types, 142
—revelational truth: philosophic and "soft" traditions, 103; role of core symbols, 105; normative nature of revelatory breakthrough, 105

Western civilization: responsibilities arising from planetary nature, 34; critical traditions of inquiry, 42; situatedness of generalizing methods, 67; notions of criticism in, 67–68; emergence into world system, 133; impact of technology on world system, 144; growth of symbols, 147; relations in institutional superstructure, 155; reconstitution into technological society, 162; and formation of science, 171
World system: interaction of traditions, 133; as outgrowth of Western civilization, 133; influences of associations and institutions, 134; emergence of its own institutions and symbols, 134;